Charting the Core of the Inner Self

Now, more than ever, at the close of the psychological century, astrology and psychology have come of age together. Both disciplines are inter-supportive in appreciation for, diagnosis of, and consultation about human development. For over twenty-five years, Noel Tyl has brought psychological methodology into astrological symbolism and analysis. Now he crowns that effort with *The Creative Astrologer,* a master volume that places particular emphasis on creative and concise techniques of counseling.

In this book, Tyl presents what he has learned through a long career of experience, theorization, and experimentation; what he has absorbed from many thousands of professional consultations. Every analytical insight presented in this volume is real, from life, from experience.

The Creative Astrologer is a catalyst, a tool enabling astrologers to sharpen and focus their skills as they take astrology to a higher level of relevance and effectiveness in the new century.

About the Author

Noel Tyl is one of the foremost astrologers in the world. His twenty-three textbooks have led the teaching of astrologers for two generations. Tyl has written the professional manual for the field, the 1,000-page text *Synthesis & Counseling in Astrology* that has securely placed astrology in pace with the most sophisticated disciplines of humanistic studies extant today; and, as well, most recently, *Astrological Timing of Critical Illness,* which establishes a breakthrough position between astrology and medical diagnosis.

Tyl is a graduate of Harvard University in Social Relations (Psychology, Sociology, and Anthropology). He lectures constantly in sixteen countries, and maintains a client list of individuals and corporations throughout the world. His office and home are in the Phoenix, Arizona area in the United States.

In May 1998, Tyl was honored at the United Astrology Congress, the world convention for astrology, as the recipient of the Regulus Award for establishing and maintaining a professional image in the field. As well, he has been designated Director Principal of Milley-Dome/Johannesburg, a 62,000-square-foot ($10 million) domed complex now under development in South Africa as the Noel Tyl Learning Center for Astrology and New Age Exploration.

Tyl has just retired from his eleventh year as Presiding Office of AFAN (Association for Astrological Networking), astrology's world organization.

To Write to the Author

If you wish to contact the author or would like more information about this book, you may write to the author in care of Llewellyn Worldwide, and we will forward your request. Both the author and the publisher appreciate hearing from you and learning of your enjoyment of this book and how it has helped you. Llewellyn Worldwide cannot guarantee that every letter written to the author can be answered, but all will be forwarded. Please write to:

Noel Tyl
C/o Llewellyn Worldwide Ltd.
P.O. Box 64383, Dept. K740–4
St. Paul, MN 55164-0383, U.S.A.

Please enclose a self-addressed, stamped envelope for reply or $1.00 to cover costs.
If outside the U.S.A., enclose international postal reply coupon.

The Creative Astrologer

EFFECTIVE SINGLE SESSION COUNSELING

Noel Tyl

2000
Llewellyn Publications
St. Paul, Minnesota, U.S.A., 55164-0383

FIRST EDITION
First Printing, 2000

Cover design by Anne Marie Garrison
Cover art by Boris Starosta
Interior design and editing by Connie Hill

Library of Congress Cataloging-in-Publication Data
Tyl, Noel, 1936–
    The creative astrologer : effective single session counseling / Noel Tyl. —
1st ed.
      p. cm.
      Includes bibliographical references and index.
      ISBN 1-56718-740-4
      1. Astrology. 2. Counseling—Miscellanea.   I. Title.
    BF1729.C67 T83 2000
    133.5—dc21   99–045499
                                                                CIP

Llewellyn Publications
A Division of Llewellyn Worldwide, Ltd.
P.O. Box 64383, Dept. K740–4
St. Paul, Minnesota, 55164-0383, U.S.A.
www.llewellyn.com

Printed in the United States of America on recycled paper

Planets
do not make things happen.

People do.

The symbols of the planets
guide us
to understanding that process.

Recent Books by the Author

Prediction in Astrology (1991)

Synthesis and Counseling in Astrology—The Professional Manual (1994)

Astrology of the Famed (1996)

Predictions for a New Millennium (1997)

Astrological Timing of Critical Illness (1998)

Llewellyn's New World Astrology Series, edited by the Author

How to Use Vocational Astrology for Success in the Workplace

How to Personalize the Outer Planets: The Astrology of Uranus, Neptune and Pluto

How to Manage the Astrology of Crisis: Resolution Through Astrology

Exploring Consciousness in the Horoscope

Astrology's Special Measurements: How to Expand the Meaning of the Horoscope

Sexuality in the Horoscope

Communicating the Horoscope

Astrology Looks at History

Contents

Preface

IT WAS HARD TO STOP WRITING THIS BOOK BECAUSE IT OPENS up a new point of departure for astrology into a continually developing era of human studies. We could go on and on—and we will into the century ahead—about the drama of humanistic development, that which we can now see so dynamically through astrology.

This vision has not always been the case, though, and that is also what this book is about. Much of astrology stills hangs onto abject descriptions of formulized fate. In so many ways, and at so many levels, that way of using our gift is a dreadful waste of time.

This book presents what I have learned through a long career of experience, theorization, and experimentation; what I have absorbed from thousands and thousands of professional consultations; what I have harvested from the careers of hundreds of students in my Master's Degree Certification Correspondence Course; and what I have shared and tested in my teaching seminars throughout the Western World. Every analytical insight of the hundreds and hundreds presented in this volume is real, from life, from experience.

I am so grateful and respectful of clients whose cases illuminate this volume for their permission in presenting outlines of their development to benefit the learning process. The reader should know that these cases are not pulled from some special drawer of exciting lives; all of the private cases in this volume have been in consultation with me within the past year—most of them during the writing of these pages in January and February, 1999! The point is that every life has its drama, and all the drama presented here is normal fare.

Astrology needs formal education and exacting standards of learning and performance in analysis and in consultation. To that end, I submit this book as beginning and catalyst, and I hope that other studies like this will begin to fill the void, attract pedagogical respect, and encourage astrologers to meet together for study in Master Class format, to bring learning to life.

—Noel Tyl
Fountain Hills, Arizona
February 1999

Chapter 1

The State of Our Art

HISTORIANS DESCRIBE THE TWENTIETH CENTURY AS THE "Century of the World at War," the "Century of Crisis," the "Age of Extremes." It was in the twentieth century that warfare occurred on a world scale for the first time: World War I involved all the major powers of the world and, indeed, most of the states of Europe; World War II was similarly global among the major powers, with only the South American continent remaining nominally above the fray. Along with these two World Wars, wars in Asia totaled the highest number killed of the seventy-four international wars that occurred between 1816 and 1965.

Indeed, the horoscope for the twentieth century—drawn for that moment when the calendar turned at 00:00 hours on January 1, 1900[1] (see chart, page 2)—shows the prospect of international aggressions dramatically: Saturn = Sun/Pluto (Saturn square the midpoint of Sun-

---

1 Astrologers are alerted to a calendar bias in New Year horoscopes since the 00:00 hours time always places the Sun at the fourth cusp. Additionally, the Sun is *always* in Capricorn, and Mercury and/or Venus are usually in Sagittarius, Capricorn, or Aquarius. The New Year/Century chart will always be midnight for whatever area on the globe it is cast. It is the tension structures among the planets that can be telling in projection of the century ahead, as well as the tie-in of those structures with subsequent phenomenological charts like Mars-Saturn and Jupiter-Saturn conjunctions.

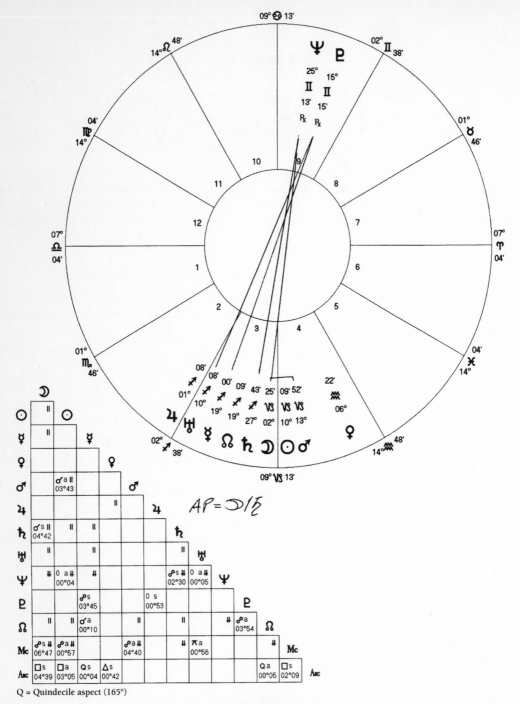

Q = Quindecile aspect (165°)

Figure 1
Twentieth Century
Jan. 1, 1900, 00:00 A.M. GMT
London, England, 000W10 51N30

Pluto, within 1' of exactness), "the illumination of power needs; the needs to control; new perspectives to be confirmed through struggle and ruthlessness"; seven conjunctions and five oppositions, all at a New Moon conjoined by Mars; and the Aries Point = Moon/Saturn (ambition, strategy, overkill on public display).

At the same time, in that century horoscope, we find Jupiter in Sagittarius peregrine, determined to dominate the horoscope: here was internationalism indeed, but *also*, here was higher learning. Uranus was also in Sagittarius, opposed by Pluto, suggesting an overturning of the status quo. Of course, this is a war-politics dimension, but it is also the creation of new perspectives (Pluto) for ego-recognition (Uranus), echoed by Venus peregrine *in Aquarius*. And there was Neptune opposed to the Moon and Sun suggesting "the awakening of special sensitivities, aesthetics, matters of the spirit, awareness of the subconscious (a twentieth-century word)."

This horoscope told us that this would also be a century of enlightenment(!), and I use the word "enlightenment" judiciously, since the climax of this century has been reached coincidentally with the entrance of Pluto into Sagittarius: when Pluto was in Sagittarius previously, in 1748–1762, it signaled the bloom of The Enlightenment (The Age of Reason). That Age was focused mainly in France as the movement began to reform the philosophical base of life through the teachings of classical times. Reason, rather than religion or superstition, was to become *the* tool of man within a strategic view of social betterment. It quickly spread eastward to Germany and westward to England and then, twenty years later, on to the young American colonies.

Our Pluto, now at the crest of a century of learning development, symbolically captures much more than the Information Age, the Communication Super-Highway, dramatically expanded world contact and sharing. It captures the Age of Psychology, the hundred years of psychology's existence as a discipline for academia and an arena for experimentation to appreciate the human condition.

At the turn of the last century, medical and experimental study of abnormal behaviors (early on, by Anton Mesmer, and later by Jean-Martin Carcot, in the main) were then enriched with philosophical and spiritual insights from William James (d. 1910). What was emerging through a maturation of the understanding of mesmerism (hypnosis) was the existence of "something else" behind awareness, the unconscious.

Then, as a trained neurologist, Sigmund Freud (d. 1939) departed from the laboratory and went far into the study of the mind within itself, pursuing "free association," the chains of thought that seemed to reveal important information about human development. He shaped a theory of the unconscious—unsavory forces attempting to break through into expression—which led to his *psychoanalytic* approach (repression, neurosis, complexes, defense mechanisms, the interpretation of dreams), and so much more. Freud's genius dramatically transformed awareness of the human condition the world over: the human being was born problematic and self-possessed (my term), and it fell to society to set the person right.

The Swiss scholar-physician Carl Gustav Jung (d. 1961) parted company with Freud over the latter's view of developmental energy as purely sexual in nature. Jung then pursued his own "analytical psychology," which incorporated the concepts of anthropology and parapsychology (the occult), as universal symbolism present in the collective unconscious.

Russian physiologist Ivan Pavlov (d. 1936) gave birth to behaviorism, linking response to stimulus in terms of "classical conditioning." This was further developed formidably by American John B. Watson (d. 1958). At the same time, Americans Edward L. Thorndike (d. 1949) and B. F. Skinner (d. 1990) linked rewards and punishment with the governing of behavior (operant conditioning) and developed strongly influential "learning approaches" to understand behavior.

Abraham Maslow (d. 1970) was the leader of America's humanistic school of psychology. He rejected Freud's psychoanalysis and the different schools of behaviorism. He saw the human as a creative being striving for self-actualization through the fulfillment of needs. For him—antithetical to Freud—the human being was born in fine balance, and it was *society* that threatened to corrupt the person's developmental process.

For the humanists, supported by the enormously enriched development of hypnosis and the practice of hypnotherapists, the unconscious was recognized as a positive source of energies. The unconscious was trying to arrange for the person to do what was best for himself.[2]

A host of other great psychologists have added strong and ranging branches to these mighty trees of learning. Now, at the end of the twentieth century, there are innumerable offshoots of these branches of study. Psychologists write more popular books and articles than academic papers. The "self-help" industry—some call it "pop(ular) psychology"—is enormously well-developed in sales and application throughout the world.

All of this affected our astrology by endowing and transforming it with keen psychological sensitivities.

---

2 Haley, 33.

Astrology's Humanistic Development

In 1936, with Freud's, Jung's, and Pavlov's giant psychological systems in full bloom—chiefly in Europe, not yet popularized in America—Theosophist Alice Bailey's French-born protégé Dane Rudhyar published in America *The Astrology of Personality—A Re-formulation of Astrological Concepts and Ideals, in Terms of Contemporary Psychology and Philosophy*. Historically, this text signaled the beginning of "humanistic astrology." The title alone encompasses mutual influence among psychology, philosophy, and astrology. Where England's brilliant theoretician, marketer, and writer Alan Leo, at the turn of the last century, simplified astrology in terms of practical technique, Rudhyar a half-century later challenged mind and spirit to new levels of conceptualization.

Rudhdyar's work was seen as humanistic *in reaction against* an astrology which, to that time, had been extremely event-orientated. Prediction had been the profit-orientated thrust of the astrology business for almost 200 years in England, the dominating force in early twentieth-century astrology in the Western world; the German school similarly, in the throes of the rise of Hitler, was chained to predictions of dire circumstances. The United States followed English texts and models of practice until after World War II.

Freud's ideas and work seemed to reflect the milieu in which he lived, i.e., prim-and-proper discipline working against sexuality, laced with the family upsets and social intrigues and aberrance that vented confined tensions. Similarly, the theosophical movement, claiming direct insight into the divine nature through a mystical system of religious philosophy, traveled from India to London to the United States, inspiring large enclaves of students, and providing the springboard for Rudhyar's work.

After World War II, the let's-get-back-on-the-track influences in society also affected astrology and pushed it to become practical and pragmatic. This development was led by the fresh work of American Grant Lewi and others who followed suit. In England, the work of C. E. O. Carter and John Addey (especially the latter, with his groundbreaking work with harmonics) began to show a new and earnest sensitivity to humanistic dimensions, the process of becoming, the ways to fulfillment in life.

In the 1960s, the Western world was seized with an idealized "up with the people" motivation and rationalization. Rudhyar's work and others echoing his themes attracted great attention and adherence, and the psychology-specific work in astrological technique and analysis began in earnest, especially in the United States and Switzerland.

These developments and maturation are our concerns in this book: establishing our legacy of development within this century in parallel with psychology, to appreciate the human being as fully as possible. While our astrology today is a macro-prod-uct of centuries of thought and development, it is, at the same time, a highly focused micro-system of individual psychological awareness and exploration. The humanistic call to illuminate the process of becoming defines the state of our art. Every astrologer is challenged to practice with the tools of astrology as creatively as possible, augment-ed by the findings and applications of analytical and social psychology.

Astrology in Pace with the Times

Everyone living in this time—as never before—is subjected to the threat, record, or reality of extremes: we see what wars do, we live through wars, we experience disloca-tion, loss, and deep trauma. Newspapers, books, radio, and above all, television estab-lish a global awareness inconceivable before this century. We not only know crisis, but our mentality has been fashioned *to expect crisis*.

We have more opportunity for and actual experience of education than ever before (therefore a break in education becomes a very important developmental deficit). We know about psychology, about experiments and findings that reveal our human nature. In the 1950s, with the explosion of Freudianism in America—through Euro-pean psychoanalysts exported by World War II—it actually became socially chic to be neurotic. We suddenly could buy books and read articles about dream therapy, partic-ipate in intimate discussions of sexual problems, participate thousands of times a day in behaviorist-controlled stimulus-response adventures called advertising, participate just as others were participating within ever more clearly demarcated sociometrically defined roles.

Then, with the proliferation of psychologically enlightened schools of therapy and an emergent air of competition to track one's brain waves, a backlash stigma attached itself to the seeking of "professional help"—why discuss problems with an analyst for so many visits, rake one's life through the mud, be dosed with exotic medicines, etc. Besides, which way of thinking was going to be helpful anyway?

With enormous population growth, the individual was getting lost, competitive pressures were ever rising, and the sense of individual crisis was pervasive. With prices for "help" rising, with insurance support infrequent, marketers and consumers alike gave birth to the *self*-help industry. Here was a way for the individual to pick the ther-apy—and the therapies adopted extremely acceptable names that made for great book titles and life promises—to lower the cost, and to maintain privacy.

In the midst of all of this in our lifetime, our astrology came of age. Its ideas and practice have had to reflect the milieu in which we live. It was important to know that the horoscopes we drew and studied of people living in our time were *not different* from horoscopes born in earlier times, at the end of the nineteenth century, the eighteenth century, or the seventeenth, etc. The horoscopes were not different, *but the realities being lived by the human beings were.*

The symbols we look at now in the horoscope refer to human developmental experience at levels and within networked connections that had never come to light before and had never had to be dealt with. The psychological century has not only given us more to know in order to understand ourselves but, as well, it has given us the permission, the license, and even the mandate to do so.

So our astrology has had to change. Specifically, *how we read the symbology of astrology has had to keep pace with the times.*

Astrology's Modern Technique

Allow me, please, to reiterate briefly—in order to illuminate some of the techniques used throughout this book—certain points of astrological observation that are developed and presented in great detail in my *Synthesis & Counseling in Astrology—The Professional Manual.*

A major premise in the modern view of astrological practice must be **to relate the horoscope to the human being**. This humanistic dictum may seem elementary and inconsequential, but consider the following: *if we stay reversed in this process*, i.e., relating instead *the person to the horoscope*, which is so commonly routined in astrological practice, we confine the person's life to what we know about astrology and the ways of life. This is a sobering thought, especially when we realize how much we *do not* know through astrology: we can not tell from a horoscope if it belongs to a person, an animal, a thing; a male or a female; race; genetic influence; religious affiliation; cultural inheritance; socially formed attitudes; fantasy content; accidents, and too much more.

When we relate the horoscope *to the person*, to the person's life as that person lives it, we are literally and explicitly *bringing the horoscope TO life, to a particular life reality*. The particular horoscope does become different from other horoscopes (even in the situation of twins!); the symbology adjusts itself through artful questioning by the astrologer; the individual's reality is revealed in terms and in dimensions shared by the person, the client. The astrology can then reflect the developmental issues in life, the extremes, the crises, the management of energies working toward fulfillment. This is an orientation *with* the facts of life—not *before* them or after *them*—and I submit that this is the way of the artist analyst in astrology.

Hemisphere Emphasis

The creative astrologer must include as much information about life as she or he can learn within analysis of astrology's guiding measurements. Hemisphere emphasis helps us in a flash: we can see and understand the orientation to defensiveness and self-protection (of the Ascendant) when the majority of planets are orientated to the East of the horoscope (and/or when planets to the West are conspicuously retrograde, calling attention contrapuntally to the East). The questions then, to guide the analysis, are: why is the defensiveness needed, how much energy has been routined in self-protection throughout development, what has this done to the comfort level with relationships, how long must this posture continue?

We can *see* and understand an alarm about "unfinished business" in the early home-life registered by planets orientated conspicuously to the North, below the horizon (and/or when planets above the horizon are retrograde, calling attention contrapuntally to the North). The questions then are: what about this unfinished business in the early homelife, what keeps it going in your life now, how has it affected your job development, your professional choices, your relationships, what can we do about it to put it to rest, to stop the drain-off of energy?

We can *see* and understand the orientation to "others," often in extreme giving away of the Self, when the strong majority of planets are orientated to the West of the horoscope (and/or when planets to the East are conspicuously retrograde, calling attention to the West contrapuntally). The questions are, what has happened to your own self-interests with so much caring for others, how do you understand your being pulled away like this, what are the self-worth concerns involved, when do you think a balance can be reached and what will it take for that to happen?

We can see and understand the orientation to being swept away by events, even to being victimized, when the strong majority of planets are orientated to the South, above the horizon (and/or with Northern counterpoint). The questions are: why does there seem to be no anchor here for development, what's missing in terms of grounding, how has this affected relationships?

This first impression of the horoscope is almost always crucially telling. I have been led to these observations in some 10,000 cases or more; I have begun as many conversations in depth and, much more often than not, brought the horoscope to congruence with individual reality. In this process, another maxim has been revealed: *this first impression based upon the general patterning of the planets within the horoscope hemispheres repeats itself over and over and over again throughout all other measurements.* A tonality is established for the life composition.

Aspects to Angles

And indeed, there are modifications, as the horoscope is brought more specifically into reflection of the client's reality. For example, squares between planets and angles are powerful punctuation within hemisphere emphasis. Think about this for a moment: a natal planet square to the Ascendant (and Descendant, remember) *will issue most often from the 4th or 10th House, suggesting high-tension parental involvement in identity development.* The discussion that can ensue is obvious (Neptune in the 4th square the Ascendant, general Eastern orientation, for example). Let's talk about what is suggested here, the confusion in the early homelife, the role that it plays in this sense of protecting yourself. Or (Mars-Pluto conjunction in Leo at the Midheaven square the Scorpio Ascendant, conspicuous Southern orientation), let's talk about this belligerence, this need and capacity to fight back in your world. What's it all about, why is it necessary, what are you getting out of it, how difficult is it to manage?

Hard aspects to the Midheaven (and IC, remember) will come from the Ascendant-Descendant area. This also links identity development with homelife tension, with a spillover effect into relationships. Questions following that line of observation will certainly bring the horoscope to life.

Saturn Retrograde Phenomenon

The conceptualization of Saturn retrograde, which I have presented for over twenty years, is very, very important. With Saturn retrograde, there is almost always the suggestion of a legacy of inferiority feelings taken on in the early homelife related to the father figure in the early home (usually the father), who was somehow taken out of the picture early on, or was there and passive, or was so tyrannical—any combination of these—so as never to have given the guidance of authoritative love.

This observation will almost always be reinforced by significator dynamics (the rulers of or planets within particular Houses and how they relate to other planets) among the Houses, i.e., the significator of the 10th and/or the 4th (the parental Houses) under high developmental tension (conjunction, square, opposition) with another planet or angle. And then, other Houses will immediately be brought into the mix: relationships, through the significator of the 7th (relating to or marrying one's parent substitute, over and over again?); the self-worth profile (the 2nd), the need to feel lov-able (the 11th); comfort with giving love (the 5th and the 8th); education interruption (significator of the 9th); mindset, kin (the 3rd); a blanketing of ego-presence (12th); and cooperation dynamics (6th). A scenario of development begins to emerge, which we will see developed in detail in the case studies in this book.

Within the historical development context of this introductory chapter, there is an important question to answer: Saturn is retrograde for long periods of time; many thousands of people are born then; do *all* of them face these difficult problems of family dynamics?

Unfortunately, the answer must be "Yes." But times do change. The Saturn retro-grade phenomenon reflects the family-values considerations in our time now. This symbol of Saturn in particular (because of its father archetype, etc.) has "reached out" to accommodate, assimilate, and reflect the very difficult developmental issues in our milieu, in our era. Perhaps it *will* change gradually in the next century when family dynamics are adjusted and require a changed outreach of the Saturn symbol.

Indeed, the phenomenon relates significantly to horoscope situations in past eras as well, but manifestations then were also different, needs were different, the social condition for the human being was different. Authority figures were perhaps more severe, or completely removed, but these conditions then were the norm, they were predictable, and family dynamics learned to cope; now, paternal figures behave dif-ferently with our social modifications of passive men, alcoholism, philandering, tyranny, and the home conditions are varied, introducing higher unpredictability (multiple marriages and father-figures, for example).

But the point emerges that, in our socio-developmental process now, we *need* the authority figure to show us love and guidance in order for our self-worth profile to be strong and well positioned for giving and receiving love, making relationships, and being professionally competitive. And that need that we have is different in its expres-sion when the Moon is in Cancer or Leo, in Pisces or in Sagittarius. *We learn to cope with all this in terms of our Moon and its occurrence by Sign and aspect.*

The astrologer must deal with these issues in order to reflect life most accurately with the client. It becomes a matter not of describing a state of affairs, but rather, *assessing the pervasiveness of the situation*, the degree of manifestation. It is not a nega-tive, nor a gloom and doom condition; it is *motivational*; it is an opportunity for improvement through understanding, and we will cover this in much more detail later in this book.

Here is an important psychoanalytic insight, which I have seen corroborated so many times in consultations: a critical, unhappy parent—let's say the father—projects his own weaknesses onto his children, finding fault with everything they do. Perhaps he wants the children to suffer as he suffers. The children of such a parent often have problems learning to like themselves because they are so angry, and it is so often the case that the children themselves adopt the parent's projective style and then put down others as well.

Exploring such an observation *invites objectivity by the client*, his/her being able to see the parent's problem within him/herself. Work can be done then to remove the client from the firing line of punishment or neglect.

Sometimes a client will say, "Well, that's the way it was all through my growing-up years, but now, we have sort of made peace, and things are—well, they're good, comparatively." Are they really? So much was molded in the "growing-up years." Has the pain been relocated into the adult relationship? Onto the job? Is your client imitating the early behaviors with his/her own children, repeating, extending the pattern?

Lunar Nodal Axis

My work with the Lunar Nodal axis has endured for two decades as well, repeatedly substantiated over and over again, thousands of times: any planet configured with the Nodal axis by conjunction or square suggests enormous maternal influence in terms of the planet or point configured. The questions are obvious: "Prince Charles, there is an indication here that we should discuss extreme maternal influence and its effect upon your development" (Moon in Taurus in the 10th, ruling the 12th, conjunct the Nodal axis).[3]

Needs

The planets are *need* symbols pressing for fulfillment. When I introduced Need Theory to astrology twenty-seven years ago, I wanted to invigorate the planetary symbols, to change them from being dull descriptors to being active symbol-forces for development. Planets do not make things happen; the needs we have, the needs that press for fulfillment, *these make things happen*.

Hard aspects to these need symbols parallel what develops and happens in life. Everything is led by the Sun's energy (by Sign)—its light shines everywhere—

---

3 Prince Charles: Born November 14, 1948 at 9:14 P.M., GMT in London.

synthesized with the Moon's symbolization of *the reigning need of the personality (by Sign)*, that which leads all. This will be repeatedly dramatized throughout this book.

Defense Mechanisms

We all need defensive behaviors in order to develop reasonably safely out of childhood into adulthood. The problem we see most often is that defense mechanisms become routined into *lasting behavior patterns*, still at work in the personality—indeed, often actually *defining* the personality in the main—when they are no longer functionally needed to such a great extent. Energy is drained from other causes; imbalances take place, and these undermine growth and fulfillment.

Idealism is a major defense mechanism. Whenever any one or two or three of the innermost planets—Mercury, Venus, or the Sun—are in conjunction with each other (even in contact through a midpoint picture), we can expect idealism to be extremely important in life development. When Neptune conjoins the Moon or when Neptune is oriental (last to rise before the Sun, in clockwise motion), idealism is similarly indicated. Idealism will buttress the personality against adversity, real or imagined. When an inner-planet conjunction is augmented through an aspect with Jupiter and/or Neptune, the idealism usually takes on a decided spiritual dimension.

Idealism portrays what is longed for, but the idealization process often creates a distortion. The distortion overemphasizes, justifies the projection, making it more powerful. When idealism is indeed so extremely focused (many clients will say, "Oh, yes! Idealism . . . big time!" or they will just stare at you as if "found out"), it is not tenable in reality and so it is often driven into fantasy, into private rumination. Idealism so easily gets in the way of reality, of finding fulfillment with the real, the natural, the accessible, especially in relationships. (Remember: being *un*realistic is almost always being idealistic.)

I said to a client with Mercury-Sun-Venus in triple conjunction in Scorpio in the 7th, trined by Uranus in the 4th, with the Moon in Cancer—after having heard her defend her parental situation with enormous eloquence until she had used up all the lovely words and the truth began to emerge—"Please tell me what you feel when I mention 'idealism' to you."

My client gave me an immediate reaction, in startled surprise: "Oh! I'm a romantic. I think my life should be what I read in books, what I see in every movie. It just should be like that, and when it isn't it's difficult for me." I suggested how this makes relationships difficult, since few can live up to the expectations. She agreed, and I added, "Unless, of course, *you idealize every relationship you're in.*" This stopped conversation cold for a moment, and we could then get down to business.

Grand Trines are classic defense mechanisms of self-sufficient behavior. The closed circuits of practical (Earth), emotional (Water), motivational (Fire), or social (Air) self-sufficiency usually include the Sun or the Moon, and in their self-containment work *against* relationships, that which the person so desperately wants but up to which she or he can not face. When the Grand Trine does *not* include the Sun or the Moon, the behavioral construct operates independently from the Sun-Moon blend profile of behavior and appears to be a separate realm of life-behavior (the ebullient day-personality who sulks and cries alone at night).

A female client has Saturn retrograde, ruling the 10th and quindecile the Sun (the common but dramatic 165-degree aspect of high developmental tension). This Saturn suggests the father phenomenon and immediately gives two corroborating parental measurements (ruling the 10th and contacting the Sun). Additionally in the horoscope, Venus-Neptune-Sun are in triple conjunction in Virgo suggesting cerebral idealization of enormous strength *to defend against the Saturn retrograde legacy of inferiority feelings.* Venus rules the self-worth 2nd House and itself is retrograde. (In Virgo, Venus suggests being able to traffic in emotions without necessarily feeling them). Finally, there is a clear Grand Trine in Water, including the Moon.

Read the paragraph over again; it is not complicated. We have the Saturn retrograde phenomenon; we have idealism that is cerebrally pronounced. The creative astrologer will instinctively know that *the two must be linked.* The idealism is defending the self-worth profile against those tediously demoralizing feelings brought forward some fifty years (in this case!) from the unfulfilled father relationship. Then, finally, all of this is routined in a closed circuit of emotional self-sufficiency as an ultimate protection. The woman is desperately alone, and her fantasy (the idealism) colors everything in her life, including her world of art.

The fact that Venus is retrograde (a second agenda) and rules the self-worth 2nd *and* the relationship 7th(!) completes our full awareness of this complex. The idealization this woman has created about relationships is something extraordinary; *everything* about her projections is designed to reflect back to shore up her self-worth profile.

Imagine *not* discussing this with the client! How incomplete the consultation would be.

An even simpler example: visualize Mercury-Sun-Moon conjunction in Aquarius (idealized humanitarian thrust) in the 2nd (the core of self-worth definition). This triple conjunction is opposed by Saturn-Pluto conjunction, both retrograde, Saturn ruling the 2nd and Pluto ruling the 11th, the need to feel loveable.

What could be clearer? The client's father had been passive in the early years, "dominated by my mother, who was very strict; I really needed extra attention from her and never got it." Here the idealism to save her self-worth concept is in the projection of being helpful to others, in the magnanimous Aquarian sense; *Mercury, within the triple conjunction, rules her 7th!*

Additionally, in this horoscope, Venus in Sagittarius, ruling the Midheaven, is opposed by Uranus retrograde in the 7th. She is indeed a professional humanitarian, a dramatic example of over-compensation. However, several days after our rich consultation, I got a phone message from this lady: "But please, can you tell me when I will meet my soul mate?" So enduringly pervasive is the idealism projected by Mercury, ruler of her 7th.

The point here is that even without the horoscope picture, you are able to understand *the linking of the psychodynamic behavioral principles* presented here. Congratulations. This is the way of the creative astrologer: following the guidelines of planetary pictures into the infrastructure of life development as we all know it, in the society we share, and then gaining corroboration from the client. In this way, the horoscope is brought to the client's reality, a scenario of development is revealed, and objective discussion can ensue.

As we shall see, *acceptance* of a situation, a pattern of behavior—even one preserved over fifty years—in a new light or in a clearer light is very similar to letting go of something (and is often accompanied by forgiveness). It is tantamount to living with a new reality. We see things in a fresh way. Recall when someone pointed out something to you in a picture puzzle or in a movie plot or in a piece of music—something you had not seen, heard, or felt on your own! Recall the sense of fresh assessment, re-evaluation, the letting go of tension. This is how the astrologer can help clients help themselves; we mirror life back to them in a new light.

Seeing the Scenario of Development

As we work with the translation of astrological measurements into psychological insight, we are discovering the connections between a person's inner needs and the outer environment: the needs press for fulfillment, and the environment—the early home, the educational system, relationships, the workplace, the community, culture and nation, the religion—receives those need expressions, those behaviors pressing for fulfillment, and rewards or denies them. These are the developmental tensions that lead us all to reach the sun.

With every case, the creative astrologer sees the drama anew. We must *anticipate* seeing the repetition of patterns of development, those that are acted out over and over and over again in our society, all around us. With this seeing, the horoscope comes to life as it relates to those patterns, to that process of becoming with which we are very, very familiar.

The earliest years are critical for personality formation. There is simply no doubt about it. A recent televised study shows a mother attending lovingly to her tiny child in a cradle. The baby coos and giggles in delight at the mother's loving noises and expressions. When the mother then turns away from the baby, turns her back on the child completely—just turning away, with no other alteration of mood—the child's expression suddenly shows bewilderment, loss, and, amazingly, discernable sadness; even fear.

The turning away or distortion of parental attention—one way or another, from absence or passivity to tyranny or sexual abuse—as it patterns itself to a norm, dramatically affects our self-worth awareness. The young organism then searches for ways to clarify identity, to feel good about her/himself. Earliest communication is modeled through parental and sibling reaction and models, and a mindset is formed, influenced strongly by self-worth imaging. Friends enter the arena to establish another source of personal reinforcement or rejection. The dynamics of giving and receiving love are organized, and relationship patterns follow those patterns. Patterns of defensive behavior, struggles with unfinished business, management of relationships, and waves of external events all assail the growing personality.

There *must* be difficulties in this process.[4] The difficulties teach us to live; they stimulate growth, pattern value judgments, and strengthen our decision-making process. Personality is the profile of how we have managed those difficulties, how we have patterned our processes of interaction with the environment.

Because we may not remember developmental difficulties does not mean we are free of them; so very often, I have seen what is tantamount to selective amnesia about large chunks of early homelife development. This is the way the organism sometimes protects its sensibilities; it is a coping mechanism.

The human being begins to form routines of evaluation, reaction, and behavior as soon as patterns of events are perceived; the more the stimulation is repeated, the

---

4 And those difficulties are explained and evaluated by the Grand Crosses of Houses: Tyl, *Synthesis & Counseling in Astrology*, 221–271.

more the routine of response *is needed for security*. Somehow, predictability of a situation makes it more manageable: we know what to expect, we know how we will handle the situation, how we will evaluate and react, no matter how bad it is. These patterns of tension and behavior suggest to the creative astrologer what has transpired in development.

It becomes extremely difficult to change the routined patterns of behavior. It is almost impossible actually to change personality. Everything about human nature works for homeostasis, a relatively stable state of equilibrium among different but interdependent elements. While we can not change personality as it develops in life, we *can* change how we manage it, and *that* is the therapeutic dimension that can be so rewarding in development, helping us to fulfill our needs more efficiently, with the circumspection we learn from experience and understanding.

This is the basic tenet of twentieth-century psychology, that if a person understands his or her thoughts and actions and the developmental sources from which they issue, then recovery is possible; there can be a redirection of emotions and energies for greater efficiency. This is an enduring maxim from Freud's postulations of *repression*, his core explanation of psychopathology. Understanding was the lifting of repression, and this was the essence of therapeutic cure.

If astrology breaks down in its applicability, I feel it is only because we do not see enough to bring it to life. We confine the person to the horoscope, to what we know about astrology, to what astrology teaches in its cryptic description of planetary symbology. We astrologers would be repressing that which is yearning to be individualistic.

Conversely, when astrology does bloom in applicability, it is because *we have enriched astrological symbolism with what we know about life*, with what we learn about an individual's personal reality. That occurs when we relate the horoscope to the life being lived. The confinement and repression begin to be lifted.

In analysis then, we make creative connections among patterns of measurements, among behavioral faculties working to fulfill clearly discernible needs. We make these connections among zones of experience as the inner environment meets the outer environment. A scenario of development—much like the lines of a dramatic play—emerges. And all of this is buoyed by the flow of time: from earliest development into the energetic bloom of developmental tension, on to the harvest of work and expression, and finally to the gradual somatic and systemic decline to the end of life.

The creative astrologer is vital to the astrological, analytic process. The planets are symbols only; they are awakened only by *our input, with our client's input; what we together* bring to the process of becoming. We must be alert to this focus upon *us*: tests have repeatedly proved that *"psychotherapeutic results are strikingly similar regardless of the theoretical framework followed by each therapist; that the personality of the therapist is more important than his adherence to a particular school of thought."*[5]

The therapists' credentials—Ph.D., M.D., or no advanced degree—and experience were *un*related to the effectiveness of therapy. The *type* of therapy and the length of therapy were *un*related to its effectiveness (with the possible exception of behavioral techniques and medical ministration).[6] Above all, in verbal therapy, *empathy* makes the difference, and for astrologers that empathy is guided by astrological measurements.

Our measurements provide many more keys to help unlock developments in the human condition. Since I have covered so many of them thoroughly in other works, there is no need to continue here. The ones that I *have* repeated here are important as helpful tune-ups for the dynamic approach to measurements that follows.

Our creativity as astrologers blooms best within the psychological maturation that, as we begin a new century, is indeed the state of our art.

---

5 A quote from the original experiment by George Mora, "Recent American Psychiatric Developments," *American Handbook of Psychiatry,* Basic Books, New York, 1960, page 32. The literature frequently reports repeated confirmations of this finding over the years and with different tests. See Kottler, 3, 51; Gendlin, Chapter 1; Frank and Frank, 173; Jourard, 139, citing Carl Rogers, 1958; Dawes, 52, 55, 75, for examples.

6 A Smith and Glass study (1977, *American Psychologist*); see Dawes, 52.

Chapter 2

Measurements and Emotional Content

WE SENTIENT BEINGS ARE EXTREMELY ALERT TO AND AWARE OF our development throughout our lifetime. Our minds interpret everything, absolutely everything, that happens to us. Feelings are born. These feelings define humanism, the thrust of psychology and modern astrology.

Just as Freud's inspired postulation of the ego, id, and super-ego and observation that their interaction applies to *all* areas of our experience,[7] so *all* our planetary symbols, working together, reflect the complicated process of becoming that is the human condition. Our Mercury shows how our mind needs to work best to be efficient in fulfilling our needs. Venus shows how we need best to apply emotions to social interaction. Mars shows what kind of energy we need to apply to get the job done the best way; Jupiter suggests the kind of reward we need in the process, and Saturn signals the essential interaction with controls necessary for our efficiency. Uranus, Neptune, and Pluto become modifiers of the

---

7 Freud postulated three personality components: the ego (Latin for "I"), that which emerges in development to handle transaction with the environment, locating situations to fulfill needs, specifically id-orientated needs (the Sun-Moon blend and the need structures of the planets as behavioral symbols); the superego (Latin for "above the I" or "Higher I," the restraints and cautions developed in the personality through identification with the parents, the conscience (Saturn); and the id (Latin for "it"), the primitive core in every person, the domain of basic drives that seek immediate gratification, predominantly sexual in orientation (contained in the spectrum of each planet's symbolism).

process: how intense, how creative (for better or for worse, of course), and how extreme. And all of this serves the projected focus of the Moon as symbol for our reigning need, illuminated and fueled by the Sun.

Feelings/Emotions

This process of becoming inspires emotions, the feelings that define our awareness. Working together, emotions and their feelings define who we are.

Feelings are born from interactions with the environment, with others and their constructs, as well as with our memories, personal dreams, and hopes. Feelings swirl about for significance, they engulf us, they form units that are just as transporting or destructive as winds that form tornadoes or currents of water that create determined streams and rebellious eddies.

We live in our emotions; how we *feel* about the past, present, and/or future tells us who we are. When we feel something—*because* we feel something—we feel that it is true. We easily turn feelings into facts: "I've been feeling worthless for so long, I really must be! Ha, Ha!"

Feelings motivate. "I feel anxious about this, I've got to do something!" Feelings accompany and actually dictate patterns of behavior; emotional content confirms who one is and builds predictability; the patterns are resistant to change because of the fear of transient insecurity: "It's the same old thing again, I married my mother! How many times do I have to repeat this pattern?" (While there is frustration, there is the routined feeling of security in the role being played out in development. No matter how awful it is. It is who one is.) Feelings can encourage externalized distortions in order to set things right inside. Feelings can be unbearable and invite the anesthetic of alcohol or drugs.

When we hide feelings, we gradually set ourselves apart from others and we become lonely. Unhappiness issues from those hidden feelings, which are always trying to come to the surface to be assuaged. Since we can not truly be ourselves when we are with others, expressing our *real* feelings, we *avoid relationships,* we shun intimacy. The creative astrologer will seek out the hidden feelings in a lonely, unhappy client, knowing that the longer those feelings are confined, the more distorted those feelings can become. A single event in past development, an old hurt, can isolate itself and fortify itself strongly with identifying feelings. This event can become a symbolic trigger for many other related concerns from long ago, gathering echoes in the progress of development, and living into the future.

Feelings start with self-awareness: I think, therefore I am, and since I'm thinking, *what* am I going to think about and how am I going to *color* those thoughts? The Ascendant is our point of being, our health center; it is where our life-energy system has come to Earth, but our *awareness* of development begins with movement into the 2nd House. The infant clarifies self by feeling bodily boundaries. We touch, we know; we are touched, we feel. We see contact made with us. The infant coos and giggles; the infant can as well show bewilderment, loss, sadness, or fear. The concomitants of self-worth begin to accumulate, conditioned by earliest interaction with the immediate family.

Psychologically, one of our major goals is to maintain and enhance our view of ourselves. As a primary source of motivation, the way in which we conceive of the self greatly influences *all* of our social cognitions. The self is the center of the universe.[8]

Normally, our judgments aggrandize our self-image: we improve our past and inflate our future. We do this because we need to! And the degree to which we do this—or do not—defines much of our self-worth profile, the condition of the 2nd and related Houses, the view we have of ourselves "down deep."

How we do this, *how* we build ourselves up, how we cope with occasional demoralization, with defeat, with frustration, how we manage emotions, express feelings, and relate to others doing the same in their life is the stuff of the analytical astrological discussion with the client.

Case Study: Marie

For this first case-study, "Marie" (page 23), please let me guide your analysis carefully.[9]

The hemisphere emphasis is clearly to the North, below the horizon, suggesting unfinished business in the early home that will be integrally important throughout Marie's development. We look for corroboration of this first impression, and we find it very easily through *Saturn retrograde* in the 9th House; and this *Saturn is squared by Neptune retrograde, ruler of the parental 10th*. In an instant, we are aware of the analytical core of the developmental process suggested in this horoscope.

We check the Ascendant and its ruler: *Mercury is retrograde*. When the ruler of the Ascendant is retrograde and/or under strong developmental tension, we can anticipate

---

8 These observations, derived from numerous social-psychological tests, are among hundreds presented by psychology professor Elliott Aronson in his brilliant compendium of experiments and narrative of analytical observation, *The Social Animal* (see bibliography).

9 Marie arrived for the consultation wearing a ring on the Saturn finger (third) of each hand. Years of experience have shown this to be a reliable indicator that the planet Saturn will be crucially important within the horoscope analysis. The planets are within; they emerge in many ways.

the need to talk about difficulties in identity development. Additionally, *Mercury is squared by Pluto*, and this is yet another corroboration of the early homelife tensions *since Mercury rules the 4th, the other arm of the parental axis (and squares the parental axis).*

The Sun-Moon blend here suggests "the blend of mental and nervous energy with deep emotional needs to be significant. If emotionally vulnerable, the mental energies can be swept away by the ideas and ideals of others, or one's heart can be tied to a cause."[10] We need to adapt the developing scenario to these probabilities.

We check the Nodal Axis and see that it is *squared by Neptune*, squared by Mars, and it *conjoins Saturn*. This is extremely important: the maternal influence (the Nodal axis) is dramatically suggested. Whenever Saturn-retrograde conjoins or squares the Nodal Axis, it is almost invariably the case that the mother rules the roost. Here for Marie, we have strong corroboration of an extreme home situation focused on the mother.

We are already able to start building *the anticipated scenario of development*: there is difficulty in identity formation working through early home tensions, undoubtedly focused upon the mother as dominantly influential, and also involving the father, probably in a passive way (due to the apparent dominance of the mother). We know that emotional needs to be significant were/are undoubtedly frustrated. We begin to look for a defense mechanism (perhaps *idealization*: a powerful, natural cover-up, diversion, and/or inspiration, normally attached to the place in life where grief is felt), and we can anticipate an involvement somehow with a cause (from the Sun-Moon blend). It all continues to hang together.

We check for the self-worth profile, the 2nd House, ruled by the Moon: here, the Moon is opposed by Mars (ruling the 11th, introducing anxiety, through the aspect, about being lovable) and conjoined with Neptune. We instantly see further confirmation of the developing scenario: the self-worth profile is strongly attacked through identification with, and probably aggression from, the mother. *Marie learns to feel unlovable.* We can also file away in our mind the possible creative connection between the Moon and Neptune: the mother's unhappiness with herself and alcoholism. (If this is so, will this be repeated in Marie's own adult life? As is so often the case; the repetition is a result of parent modeling.)

How does Marie learn to cope with the situation? Note that Mercury is automatically the final dispositor of the horoscope (since it is in its own sign) and it is retrograde.

---

10 All measurement meaning images presented throughout this book for the Sun-Moon blends, midpoint pictures, and
    Solar Arc contacts are verbatim quotes from listings in Tyl, *Synthesis & Counseling in Astrology*, page 82.

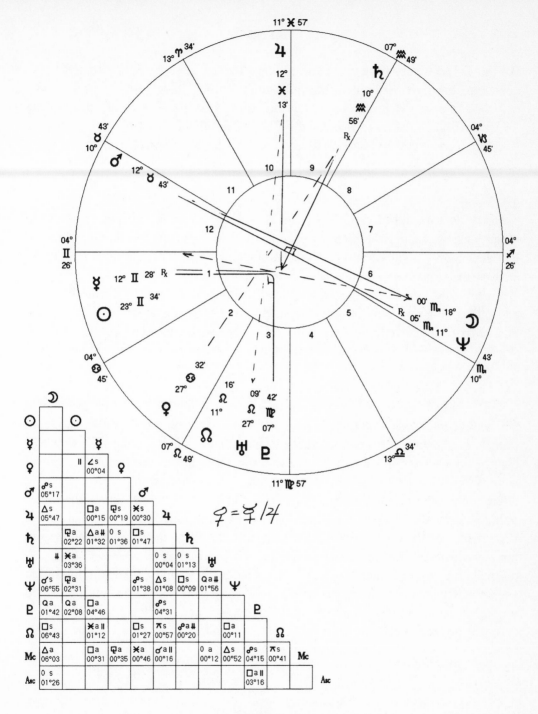

Figure 2
Marie

We can expect a very busy mind and perhaps two or more agendas pursued at the same time, one most assuredly being dedicated to coping, to defensive measures (note that there is also a Hemisphere orientation strongly to the East, centered upon the Ascendant). With the mind ready and willing to dominate the coping mechanisms, working to cover tensions over, to divert them, we can feel the welcome given to idealism. With the Moon conjoining Neptune and with the Moon quindecile to the Ascendant, we can expect a powerful obsessive tie between idealism and identity development.[11]

Lastly, we can note that Jupiter, ruler of the 7th, is highly elevated, trine to the Moon, exactly square to Mercury, opposed by Pluto, and quindecile with Uranus. Jupiter is highly involved within our scenario: *how are relationships involved with the accommodation or resolution of the developmental tensions?*

Marie easily corroborated and illuminated the parental situation: her mother "had a huge drinking problem" and was extremely cruel to the father "in order to control him." Marie also corroborated the self-worth anxiety: the mother had had a professional career in the arts that ended with Marie's birth; "my mother blamed her failure on my being born."

I then asked her, "And how has that hurt been salvaged by . . . somehow by idealism?"

Marie replied, "Absolutely. Enormously. I idealize everything. I even have a guru who helps protect me."[12] At this instant, listening very carefully, the creative astrologer hears "a guru who protects me," a strange turn of phrase, and makes a connection: this may be in reference to the father who was somehow not in the picture to protect young Marie. What is the care-taking (protection) dimension saying?

Our discussion explored her idealism, how it helped her, how it framed the values of her present relationship. And this coping mechanism had been sorely challenged: her parents had died within one day of each other (tr. Pluto conjunct the Moon) and her older mate recently had had a debilitating stroke (tr. Pluto conjunct the 7th).

The horoscope now came to life, to Marie's life easily, quickly: Marie disclosed that she was caretaker of an older man, a mate, who was severely ill. (Now we understand more.) He no longer wanted to live. The situation seemed hopeless, demanding professional around-the-clock care, which Marie could barely afford or personally

---

11 The quindecile aspect (pronounced in the Italian way, quin-deh-chee'-leh) measures 165 degrees; fifteen more or less than an opposition, registering obsession, enormous intensity, separation, upset. Please see Tyl, *Astrological Timing of Critical Illness*, for full development of the aspect, page 9.

12 Additionally, suggesting the idealism, there is Venus=Mercury/Jupiter.

maintain. The situation was getting in the way of Marie's career moves (in her mid-thirties), yet she could not place her man in a nursing home and improve her life. Why?

The creative astrologer is always on the alert to see developments from early home-life as models for present-life interactions with the environment. Might Marie's ministrations to her older mate be an echo, an echo bent on dissonance, of the high-focus relationship her mother had had with Marie's father?

I suggested to Marie that, throughout all this, she could very well be operating *against* the model set by her painful mother, she who had been so cruel to her husband. Marie's goodness to *her* mate was defining her goodness to herself. *It served her starved emotional needs to be significant, since she was supposedly the cause of her mother's failure in life.* Marie was involved with a cause. It was the ideal way for her to do things for herself on the emotional level.

Marie's feelings had been deeply pained throughout her entire life. We understand this further through Venus in Cancer—the relational need for love security (Venus ruling the 5th, love given)—in quindecile with Saturn retrograde, an extremely harsh aspect with obsessional need-overtones. Venus rules the 12th and does threaten to involve breakdown of Marie's health in manifestation of the extreme emotional hurt internalized throughout her body. Yet, she *had* been able to cope: she *was* talented in her work, *was* her own boss in the main, and had many avenues ahead for professional growth.

While she coped in the Moon-in-Scorpio fashion (see below) by controlling someone for self-significance, she was doing it with self-sacrifice and obsessive good intentions. How good did she need to feel to be secure enough to adopt another way, an additional way, to feel good about her relationship, i.e., put her mate into a medical care facility, and get on with her professional life? *Why should she fail professionally as her mother had?* These questions opened doors for frank discussion. Hidden emotions were being freed. The objective was to build up her work and career so that her self-worth would improve; personal reinforcement would develop as she relinquished the caring for her stroke-afflicted mate.

Marie had come to see me with transiting Pluto squaring natal Pluto the final time, normally a time of break-away from the way we have been doing things, the establishment of new perspectives, here specifically related to her work environment and growth (Pluto rules the 6th). Our discussion developed into her future from that point of understanding.

Coping Mechanisms

Psychiatrist David Viscott makes an intriguing observation: listening to oneself, on tape, for example, is uncomfortable *because we hear our own distortions.*"[13]

What public lecturer can deny that, in an effort to keep the narrative flow going and impressive, exaggerations creep in to augment the points being made? The text then changes slightly for the next presentation, when the same process occurs, and finally an entirely different balance can emerge from among the original facts.

What part of the intensity of a religious revival meeting is built on accumulated exaggerations to prove a point?

How often do we overstate a point in our past to make us more impressive for the future? How do we explain the divorce, the reasons for the raise, the loss of a job opportunity, a serious dispute, a bad review? How do these distortions become fact?

What are the concomitants of self-dramatization? What trouble do they get us into? What do they reveal about our self-image; our way of coping with fears and insecurities?

What does this word in our language *really* tell us? What does it really mean? Are we so used to over-exaggeration that we accept it routinely—yet, every now and then, we have to check and make sure we are really getting the truth?

Most problems that we have seem to come from *not wanting to see things as they are.* We want to avoid them. *We deny what should not be.* When we do come to grips with the truth about emotional situations, why do we refer to it as "the painful truth" or "the real truth" (as if there is an unreal truth), or "the hard facts"? In our way of speaking, why is truth called harsh and terrible?

Why does jury-selection expert in perception Jo-Ellan Dimitrius say, "Whenever the truth is threatening, we tend to reach for the blinders. . . . It is human nature to close our eyes—and minds—to things that are uncomfortable or disturbing?"[14]

I think it is because we rarely deal with the truth in emotional situations. We are accustomed to distortions. We believe how we feel. We feel *the way we need to feel in order to protect our self-worth, to preserve our self-image.* We justify, we rationalize, and we create an image of ourselves for ourselves, to protect us, to identify us to one degree or another, in one direction or another.

We distort by blaming: it is usually someone else's fault, isn't it? It's ALL someone else's fault! That someone else ALWAYS does this or that. All of this *displacement* and *overgeneralization* makes us feel strong, secure, and impregnable.

---

13 Viscott, 3–5.
14 Dimitrius, 13.

Yet, the self-image we manufacture is not always superb. Many people are terribly hard on themselves: the emotional content of their astrological measurements manifested in behavior weighs them down terribly. But even this is a means to get a special kind of indulgent attention: we set up excuses ahead of time, excuses for poor performance should it occur (like performers backstage nervously complaining before the performance that they aren't up to snuff); we prepare the sympathy that, if we need it, will coddle us back into security.

Some of us in certain situations *criticize ourselves before someone else does*, since we can not bear to hear it from that someone else. This self-criticism gives status away to another person and curiously attracts an indulgence from the one who is feared.

This emotional static occurs in the life of clients just as it does in the astrologer's life. The creative astrologer must be prepared to listen objectively *through the static* when it is presented in consultation.

For example, I wish I had learned years ago Dr. Chris Thurman's technique to shock a client out of the "I'm worthless" self-effacement type of emotionalism:

"I'm worthless," Angela said to me one day in our session together.

"Prove it!" I blurted out, much to her surprise.

"How far back do you want me to go?" she said caustically. "In high school, I lied to my best friend about going out with her boyfriend. I did that a lot. In college, I did drugs. And I not only kept lying about going out with my girlfriends' guys, but I slept with the guys. Then I flunked out of college. Then I got married to this guy I didn't love because he had money. . . . Shall I go on?"

"That sounds like ancient history," I said. "Besides, all you've given me so far is proof that you are capable of doing wrong things. I want proof that you're worthless. Does doing wrong things make people worthless?"

It is clear that, because Angela *felt* worthless, she therefore adopted the attitude that she *was* worthless.[15]

Again, emotions and their feelings so easily become facts, in distorted form much more than in truth. Emotions fuel our ways of coping with developmental tensions. The mind understands in one particular way and deploys the emotions accordingly.

This distortion serves a purpose: *it helps us to fulfill more of our reigning need*, which we see clearly indicated by the Moon in its Sign (fueled by the Sun in its Sign, i.e., the Sun-Moon blend). *We are aroused by tension*. We are supposed to announce ourselves to the world characteristically strongly, and *distortions help when we need them*; they feel good, they must be natural.[16]

---

15 Thurman, 125–126.

16 Tyl, *Synthesis & Counseling*, 65–102.

I think that how we cope with disappointment, frustration, and pain in child-hood is often helpfully described through the mode and element of the Moon Sign. The *competitive character*, with the Moon in a *Cardinal* Sign, most often will pretend not to care about difficulty, and this can lead to resourceful self-protection or dra-matic extrication.

When the Moon is in a Fixed Sign, the *controlling character* will most often blame or make excuses when power is threatened. It is a conspicuous sign of maturity, howev-er, when this is reversed, when the Fixed Sign Moon takes on criticism and loss with seasoned poise.

The *dependent* need complex headed by the Moon in a Mutable Sign explores denial or another way of seeing things to protect against the loss of love and attention. Diffi-culty just can not happen here, it's too much to bear!

With the Moon in a Fire Sign, we tend to exaggerate and brag when we are not sure of ourselves: we tell everyone how important we are; we can easily distort the record in the process. I remember vividly visiting my close childhood friend John, with my twelve-year-old Leo Moon pumping strongly after the bike ride to his house. John came out and greeted me and passed on something his mother had told him that day—and I adored John's mother; my parents were divorced and my mother was problematic indeed—"Nolie, my mother says *you're insecure*! Ha, Ha!"

Now, neither John nor I knew what the word meant, but there it was. It sounded like a big negative (which John had picked up from the sound of his mother's voice). My Moon, ruling my Cancer Ascendant, vulnerable within my family situation at the time, instinctively went into blazing defense when I checked out the dictionary to learn the new word.

I set out to make very clear that I was captain of my own ship and that I was NOT insecure. Throughout my life, self-aggrandizement has always been something I have had to temper, watch carefully, and allow myself to earn. I did my share of blaming and made more than my share of excuses, but all of that sort of ironed itself out I think—yet, here I am indeed, writing about it still, fifty-one years later. These kinds of occurrences happen to us all, clients *and* creative astrologers!

The Moon in Aries will trumpet in *numero uno* terms, often masked in humor but meant with laser conviction. In Sagittarius, the thrust of opinionation to prove any point works to put any insecurity to rest.

With the Moon in Earth, the coping mechanism will be at best an assertion of self-sufficiency, keeping one's privacy, but it should be noted that hiding from the truth threatens to reveal a weakness in caring for oneself, in coordinating affairs efficiently.

The Capricorn Moon will drive on to make things happen; the Taurus Moon will resist change, bite down and bear the difficulty, and/or strive to make things as they should be ideally; the Virgo Moon will guard exactness or perfection as an unassailable protection.

The Water Sign Moon will fear imperfection: it must be emotionally significant and important to others. The Cancer accent under pressure will do anything and everything to keep security within embrace, to make it reliable; the Scorpio mechanism under pressure will be to command or attract attention, to control others somehow to dramatize personal significance; the Pisces Moon will reach for allegiance with all that is lovely and emotionally reassuring, idealized to perfection.

The Air Sign Moon is superb with outspoken denial or correction, changing the subject, getting away from the pressure or diverting it: in Libra, the effort will be to keep the peace and emphasize social grace, popularity; in Aquarius, establishing indispensability will be the way to cope; and in Gemini, pursuing options cleverly will usually allow a quicksilver escape.

While these considerations submitted here are framed in terms of the Moon, perhaps the most expressive emotional focus of what motivates our development, I think the considerations apply *in general* to the specific element families and modalities. For example, Bill Clinton has had to cope with an unimaginably enormous amount of legalistic pressure and character attack. His Moon is in Taurus, an Earth Sign in the Fixed mode.

His Moon in Earth suggests an assertion of self-sufficiency, keeping his own privacy, resisting change, bearing the difficulties, inviting an idealistic structure as the remedy of the situation (his counsel with "my family and our God"). As a *controlling character*, there has been enormous blame projected constantly onto a personal/political conspiracy to make excuses for the threats to his power.

But there is also the extraordinary Libra stellium at Clinton's Ascendant (Mars, Neptune, Venus, Jupiter)[17]: within the coping process, the Air emphasis functions with extraordinary denial and repeated attempts to divert the pressure.

Anger

Now, let us look at certain key emotional concerns—anger (frustration and aggression) and self-image feelings—to explore creative analysis of measurements.

Anger is a manifestation of adrenaline. It is energy that is devoted to defense. By driving the system to self-protection, anger keeps us alive. This kind of anger rises up

---

17 William Jefferson Clinton, born August 19, 1946 at 8:51 A.M., CST in Hope, AR.

to meet a threatening stimulus in order to eradicate it. Anger sets up boundaries for our protection. It is out-and-out combat for a cause.

We have to appreciate that anger is within us naturally at birth (Mars), that even *babies* show anger, usually beginning at the six-month period of age, just before fears develop, i.e., that what is provided to gratify the infant might not be there upon demand. Aggression forms as an expression of anger and to force gratification to occur.[18]

Another kind of anger is directed less to preserving life in primal fashion and more to protecting identity psychodynamically. This kind of anger usually masks an early hurt. *A swirl of emotions is attached to this hurt, to some event or pattern of events, and that complex enters memory; it repeats itself in response to certain triggers, over and over and over again in relationship with the environment.*

Since the mind works instantly and constantly to make everything significant, it will try to explain the painful early event or pattern of occurrences. The mind will file it all away for memory, codify it into dream symbols to preserve sleep, and set up vigilance about the complex into the future to protect against further hurt. The mind will even organize other hurts to add to the original cluster *to justify the anger, to make it righteous.* Think of the energy all this takes!

When this anger-energy, born in the past, is projected into the future, it becomes anxiety. This anger drains off energy from other activities in our life. When we project it onto others, when we displace our feelings of fear and upset onto our children, our mate, etc., *we disrupt our relationship with others.* In this way, we even unwittingly *perpetuate the pattern of anger* and its behavior into the next generation through establishing a behavioral model for our offspring.

We feel this complexity, so we try to still the anger and keep it bottled up as frustration. When it is too much to handle—when it shocks us and threatens to disrupt our life—we change it into guilt feelings and we stew inwardly *against ourselves.*

This is a very demanding process for us all; it is all around us, in everyone else's life, in all our media messages. The most recent findings and estimates say that some eighteen acts of aggression are shown every hour on Saturday morning television children's shows(!) and that, by the time a child is twelve years old, that average child will have witnessed 100,000 acts of violence on television, let alone the rage of desperation transmitted in so much popular music! As adults, we continue to lean toward the dramatic, catastrophe-laden, violent "realism" films for our own enjoyment.[19]

---

18 Bridges, K .M. B. 1932; Schmale, A. H. 1964. Also, Tyl, *Synthesis & Counseling*, 725–729.
19 Aronson, 265.

We need only appreciate the difficult aspect between Saturn and Mars, where controls (conservatism, tradition, and authority) work in awareness of energy (aggression, decisiveness, and impulse), to understand the dilemma and drain of anger. While our older textbooks suggested that Saturn would always win in the battle with Mars (a reflection of earlier society's intolerance of interpersonal aggression), I think our creative, modern resolution (in a time of fire expression) of this black and red conflict is to see the controls as *necessary for efficiency* and the energy as *essential for progress*. We should merge the two in wisdom, as a reflection of our society today. This wisdom, of course, is developed over time, through trial and error and learning.

It is important to add here that the long-held conventional wisdom that intense physical activity—an exercise program, for example—reduces aggression and releases frustration is wrong. In fact, studies have found that strong physical activity leads to quite the opposite conclusion. Even *watching* aggressive games (the national fascination with football, boxing, hockey) temporarily increases aggressive behavior.[20]

The relationship between anger and sex (Mars for both) is that each state is a psychologically aroused state. There is pleasure in being excited and *focused*. We feel potential at that time. Anger or rage sets boundaries and organizes who we are, disruptively usually, but it does serve a purpose as an escape into meaning, into action. The problem is usually the excessiveness of the anger, the disruptive explosiveness of it, and of course the hurt inflicted through it, the retarding of progress.[21]

The creative astrologer must be aware of where the tension of frustration, the emotional swirl, goes within the behavioral system. When the environment does not cooperate with us in the fulfillment of our needs, we are frustrated, emotions drive us to anger, externalized as aggression or internalized as hurt, guilt, or depression. There is an *Accumulated Developmental Deficit* created as we grow older. Within the aging process, these depositories of frustration, the sites of the accumulated developmental deficit, become the focal points of somatic and systemic breakdown.[22]

Case Study: David

When David arrived for his consultation with me, he seemed happy but apprehensive. He said he had seen me on television, heard me talk about astrology and its helpfulness, and looked forward to the experience of the consultation. He was friendly—*but clearly,*

---

20 Ibid, 259.

21 Ratey and Johnson, 59–62

22 This concept and the research illuminating it is thoroughly presented in Tyl, *Astrological Timing of Critical Illness*, through over seventy case studies.

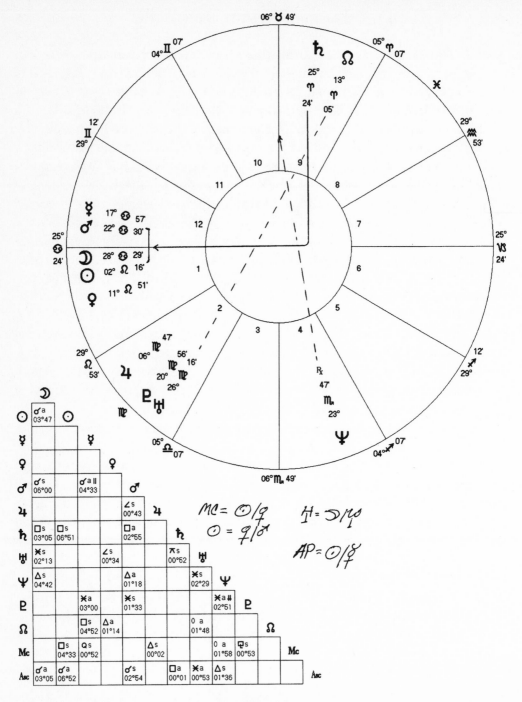

Figure 3
David

he was accustomed to being withdrawn. I thought he was pre-sold on the consultation and was behaving more openly than he usually did.

The immediate first impression of David's horoscope is of defensiveness (Eastern hemisphere emphasis) related to unfinished business in the early homelife (Northern emphasis). While the significators of the parental axis did not offer any clear corroboration of this first impression, Saturn's square to Mars, the Ascendant, the Moon (especially in Cancer), and the Sun did: here was a father situation indicated, quite similar in detail and reliability to the Saturn retrograde phenomenon we know well.

Looking a bit further with regard to the parental axis, I did note Neptune in the 4th (something is other than it seems) and this Neptune was quindecile to the Midheaven (a great deal of confusion in the early home, which has undoubtedly entered into his unconscious disruptively, even obsessively). I also filed away the suggestion of the Neptune-Midheaven contact, with Venus ruling the Midheaven and the natal Midpoint picture MC=Sun/Venus and Sun=Venus/Mars, to suggest the arts as a profession. Additionally in this regard, Mercury was quintile to the Midheaven.

The Nodal axis also provided a very strong signal about crucial maternal influence (the axis was quindecile Uranus, a very intense relationship indeed).

The Midpoint picture Uranus=Moon/Neptune seemed to bring together the *Uranus*-Node, *Moon*-Saturn, and *Neptune*-MC deductions into a unit of synthesis suggesting "temperamental and emotional unpredictability."

I noted that David bit his nails (internal anxiety, frustration, preoccupation), and when he spoke—as if he knew something was coming all too quickly from me—he guarded his mouth with his hand.

The Sun-Moon blend—an important guide to what we *should* see in the life, naturally, eventually—was very telling in terms of the profile I was developing from the measurements in the horoscope. There were problems: "The personality has the sensitivity and instincts to dramatize itself congenially. The emotions are well organized and intense. *Usually, the self-worth is assumed and does not require constant attention . . . love and family are very important.*" David's self-worth was probably in bad shape (the Sun, ruler of the 2nd, was squared by Saturn, and the Pluto-Uranus conjunction was in the 2nd); Mercury, co-ruler of the 2nd was conjoined with Mars in the 12th. His Leonine energy was nowhere to be seen!

There was no idealization process rescuing David, in my opinion. Instead, I thought that *David was angry*; anger was his escape valve from the trauma and his anchor to it in his early development. I know that, almost invariably, with Mars in the 12th House (usually within 8 degrees of the Ascendant)—here especially conjunct Mercury, fighting with Saturn and involving the Moon in Cancer, wanting security at all costs—*there is deeply rooted anger to be discussed in the consultation.* Emotions will have swirled into a complex of some kind early in life and been carried forward to explain pain and defend against further accumulation of upset. I could expect repeated and depleting expressions of anxiety in David's life. I had to find the source of these hidden feelings, the anger I was sure was there.[23]

David obviously saw his horoscope in front of me with many measurement markings and notes. After some pleasant small talk, in a very relaxed manner, with a light smile, I simply said, "David, what's all this anger I see here?"

David was caught off guard. He laughed nervously; his hand went to his mouth. He was shaking his head side to side, as if to deny, while he said, "you're absolutely right!"

I decided to put all my deductions into several introductory paragraphs, something like, "And this anger plays out in the midst of lots of defensiveness. When I see this kind of pattern, I look for a cause, something we can talk about in a rewarding conversation." NOTE: I was promising, *if we can talk about it, it will be rewarding for us.*

Also note, please, my words "When I see this kind of pattern," obviously referring to the horoscope drawing: this *objectifies* what I am going to say. It is not *David* I am describing; it is a *pattern on a drawing* that I am interpreting. *David* is not being painted into a corner; astrology is not accusing him, evaluating him negatively ("You are this, you are that . . ."). In this case, it was very important to objectify in this way since so much observation was tumbling out from me all at once to get our conversation going quickly. David's congenial demeanor and agreement with the anger deduction made this approach practicable.

I continued with the scenario we have just reviewed: "It all seems tied up with the early homelife, especially the years from three to eleven (David reacted in astonishment, still smiling), and it involves a heavy parental influence, *a father* somehow probably out of the picture, and *a mother* who is very much the opposite, deeply influential and uncomfortable. It is suggested here that this undermines your self-worth development, tends to defeat your pride—even today—(another smiling acknowledgement from David, in surprise), and it makes relationships very difficult. There's also the high probability that these concerns got you off the track, caused an

---

23 Please look back quickly to Marie's horoscope, page 23: her Mars was also in the 12th, opposed her Moon, and that axis was squared by Saturn. Indeed, there was much anger in her, in relation to her mother (Mars square the Nodal axis); she had several tattoos and had a history of rebellious behavior. I did not lead the consultation with discussion of anger since her idealization process was so emphasized, as the defense of first choice, if you will.

interruption in your education (significator of the 9th under high developmental tension, i.e., Mars squared by Saturn also in the 9th), etc. David, we have lots to talk about."

David was extremely complimentary about the deductions that had come forward so quickly in approximately sixty seconds. As I had seen so often before in this kind of approach, he was quickly relieved; *things were out in the open*: he could talk about these difficult things. He said something like, "I knew this would happen; it's sensational, *really*!" Residually, that is a very positive remark. David's door was open.

David's story was right to the point. I guided it with simple cues like "What about the father relationship, first? I was eager not to perform further deductive "gotchas" from astrology but to learn more about the connections I could make among the swirl of hidden feelings within David.

David's answer recalled a trauma, it was perhaps his earliest memory: he was a tiny baby, but he saw his mother, who was holding him, TURNING AWAY from his father. This short, powerful glimpse of memory was at the ready for him during our consultation *because David had fished for it hundreds of times in his life*, when circumstances went back and triggered the recall. He himself had probably given this physical image to the mental construct; the former was necessary to justify the latter.

The point was, David's father was shut out of the family by David's birth. David was preferred. His father was then away so much of the time. I asked David: "Why is this so important?"

This seems like a wasted question since we know that this feeling-event *is* very important, and the reasons are obvious, but the point in creative consultation is *to bring the feelings out from the client*. We need to learn more about this to understand it better. "Why is this so important?" is a subtle and powerful probe.

David explained that his mother's father, a "great man," the headmaster of a school, had long wanted a son. His daughter had presented him with two granddaughters before David came along. Finally! David was IT!

"And what about your mother, David?" this was an intentionally open question for David to fill out any way that was significant at this point of the discussion.

"I was terrified of her. She was so harsh . . ." David clarified that his mother was harsh to his father, that he (David) feared her harshness too (gender identification with the father, wanting to be like the father?).

Now, let us appreciate how much had emerged from this client conversation in just about five minutes. It was not difficult. It was based upon the clear horoscopic outlines of a developmental scenario *the likes of which are happening around us all the time in Western culture*. Creative astrology sees it as such. Creative listening brings islands of deduction together and stimulates further conversation. It is not for us to enjoy the conversation; it is for the creative astrologer to mold it.

In the preparation for the consultation, *measurements of time* reinforced all these deductions as well: note that Solar Arc Saturn developing from 25 Aries to the Midheaven at 6 Taurus (11 degrees, just about 11.5 years) makes successively the square with the Moon at age three and the square with the Sun at age seven. Note also that, *at the same time*, SA Mars developing from 22 Cancer to the Sun at 2 Leo in 10 degrees/years makes successively the conjunction with the Ascendant and the square with Saturn, then the conjunction with the Sun at age ten.

Was David angry with his father for not standing up to his mother, claiming his rights, so to speak? Or was David somehow identifying with his mother's ostracizing of her husband; were they *both* angry with the father? Or was David angry with the father because David was the light of his great-man grandfather's eye and was unconsciously drawn in with the mother trying to "get rid" of the father? Anyhow the father was rarely there, and David felt abandoned and was terribly angry about it. Very interestingly, the *grandfather* died with Solar Arc *Saturn*=MC when David was eleven years of age, and the mother divorced the father *the same year* (with tr. Uranus on the 4th)!

The job of the creative astrologer is to reflect back the picture of past development with illumination and relate it all to developmental time present and future.

David's confused anger emerged as anger with the world, with his lack of a father figure to lead him—after all, he deserved it, *he* was the preferred! His anger had caused a tremendous misdirection in his professional life. David had come to see me, coincidentally with his transiting Saturn, with all its personalized and fulfilled symbolism, "returning" at age thirty, with deep professional concerns.

For years in my astrology work, I have begun every consultation with the question "What do you do for a living?" In my preparation for the consultation, I always write down my analysis of the profession I think is indicated in the horoscope. When the person replies, I can then show written-down evidence of how accurately I had anticipated this, or, if the actual profession and my anticipation do not agree, I can start reworking the balances within the analytical scenario preparation—or, indeed, I can hold back my disagreement with the client's choice, waiting for the right time, when detours or blockages may be exposed. So many times, I have heard, "Oh that's just what I would long to do, but my mother *wouldn't allow me* to go to art school!"

My notes for David's profession were: "In the arts: Neptune quindecile MC, Mercury quintile MC, MC=Sun/Venus, Sun=Venus/Mars, AP (Aries Point)=Sun/Mercury, MC ruler Venus *peregrine*."

David's reply to my question, while we were making small talk was "I work for the government."

"What? Really?"

David smiled sheepishly and withdrew a bit, as if embarrassed.

"WHAT do you do in your government job?"

David explained that he worked with drawings, buildings if I recall, and the machines that reproduced the industrial artwork—something like that. The point is that we were getting closer to what I thought the horoscope suggested for his fullest expression, but we were still far from where I thought he could be.

The 9th House suggests continued education, after high school. When the significator of the 9th (the planet ruling or major planet within the 9th) is under strong developmental tension, the probability is very, very high that the education was/will be interrupted. This usually takes place at ages seventeen to eighteen, sometimes at nineteen or twenty: at the earlier time, the person does not go on to college; at the later time, the person leaves college, drops out, perhaps returns later, but the interruption is accomplished.[24]

Two things are very important in managing this measurement: 1) determining why the education was interrupted—a precipitous marriage? Why? Escape from the homelife? Why? Into the same kind of problems in the marriage? How is that described? and 2) How has the interruption undermined job resources, credentialization for choice of profession, job mobility, etc.? Is there resentment of this? Where is the resentment projected?

It is very easy to project arcs to Angles and check major transits for those critical age periods (when the significator of the 9th is under tension) to know with high probability the month of the interruption. For example, with David, tr. Pluto came to his 4th cusp at age eighteen, between May and October 1986.[25] David failed his examinations in school and relocated to another country. (Imagine empathetically with David how that would have embarrassed David's grandfather.)

Four years later, between April and August 1990, with tr. Jupiter conjunct the Sun and tr. Saturn conjunct the 7th cusp (opposing Mars, Moon, and Sun), David resumed

---

24 This is a most reliable and important deduction process in the American culture. It is slightly different in other cultures, depending on the societal expectations for education within professional profiles, etc. For the horoscope of a young person, this measurement can be critically important to introduce discussion and adjustment to project the best course of development ahead.

25 In the Appendix of Tyl, *Synthesis & Counseling in Astrology*, please see the "Quick Glance Transit Table" with the planets Mars through Pluto positioned for the first of every month for 100 years. With the Table, you can pinpoint transits more quickly than you can through your computer.

his studies in music. When transiting Uranus conjoined the 7th cusp in March and December 1994, I asked David about this change in his life: "I dropped out of the school, I was so *angry* with the teacher." And when he said this word "angry," about which we had talked, the room shook with significance!

"Why were you angry with the teacher?"

"He reminded me of my father . . . he was my father. I did nothing in the exam; I just sat there, and failed."

So, David had underachieved grievously for confused but intense emotional reasons, signaled by anger that emerged out of great ambivalence with regard to male authority images in his life. (I watched carefully lest I fall into that mold for him as his astrologer.)

As we spoke, tr. Saturn was returning to its natal position and squaring his Sun; tr. Uranus was opposing his *Venus, ruler of his Midheaven.* All of this was occurring in mid-1998, with tr Neptune=Sun/Moon also (a threat to relationship).

David and I talked about the high probability of a change in direction in his professional life, how maybe he did not need to use up any more energy with this amorphous anger, how dissolving the private relationship that was draining him would clear him up for a fresh approach. That fresh approach would certainly be in April 1999, with tr. Saturn conjoining the MC Angle and tr. Jupiter conjoining Saturn.

In projecting any horoscope into the future after understanding the developmental scenario out of the past, I recommend looking ahead for the most important measurements within a year or two, usually involving a contact (conjunction or square) with an Angle (Arc, transit, or SP Moon), and *working backward* from that time to illuminate the stepping stones of timing strategy to get there. In this case, April 1999 was easy to see, and I just worked back from then to see the build-up of measurements that would immediately follow the consultation. Those measurements would mark David's next steps.

David and I talked at length about his finding a better paying job in the private sector, out of the government, working in the arts—we settled on television production (which involved art and music, his specialties, and followed the natal Neptune symbolism); and how to prepare for that, getting contacts, going to places where people in that industry congregated, reading up about industry happenings, personnel, and the general politics reported in the television trade press, preparing his resume, etc.

Above all, I worked with David to begin to settle the past behind him, to set some process into action inside him to that end; to resurrect the pride of his Leo Sun. Not unconsciously, I worked through the loving authority of a father figure. We pictured his fulfillment in this exciting, highly probable career shift: and, by careful design and proper timing, as David and I were ending the consultation after an hour and ten minutes, I said firmly and ultra clearly, as my final words, "I think your grandfather would have approved of these things."

There was a moment of stillness as we shook hands, and I felt that David was beginning to come of age.

Depression

Depression has been discovered, formally named, classified, and probed by sufferers and therapists only within the last twenty-five years or so. And suddenly, within that period of time, we have seen depression grow explosively as a condition afflicting millions. We name the condition; we see it, we recognize it.

The rates of depression were lower for people born in 1900 (tabulated in retrospect) than for those born in 1920, and lower for the 1920 group than for those born in 1940. We do not understand the reasons for this. While almost 30% of the population reports a period lasting at least two weeks when they feel sad or blue, about five percent of the population report a major severe depression during their lifetime.[26]

Depression is twice as common in women as in men, slightly less among blacks as among whites. Evidence is growing that some forms of depression are inherited: when mood disorders exist in families, the children of a depressed person have a risk of approximately twenty to twenty-five percent of having the disease themselves, only a five percent risk exists among children of non-depressive parentage. The medical establishment regards depression as almost completely biological (genetically transmitted and chemically produced), as opposed to psychological, and therefore the paramount treatments are through drugs.

Some of the causes of depression are an inherited vulnerability. As we have seen, family history increases one's risk of developing the condition. Pronounced personality imbalances, especially experiencing low self-worth and being overly dependent, self-critical, pessimistic, and easily overwhelmed by stress increase one's vulnerability to depression. The abuse of alcohol is a concomitant of depression.

Depression is amorphous; it is hard to qualify. Feeling "down" is a normal emotion, it is not depression. A partial profile of the clinically depressed individual's feelings includes a deep and pervasive feeling of being alone ("depression is a disease of isolation");

---

26 Klein and Wender, 73.

feeling unsafe, hopeless; hating the self to the point of disconnecting from others; losing the ability to have pleasure (*anhedonia*); loss of energy and sex drive; and probable insomnia.[27]

It is key here for the creative astrologer to know that social interaction makes us human, and any dislocation, any shunning of connection, relationship, or intimacy, suggests that something is wrong. As well, we must know that even children can show symptoms of depression (monopolar or bipolar depression, the latter called *manic depression*), especially if one of the parents is a depressive, through drops in academic performance, increased social isolation, manifesting physical complaints for no sound reason, exhibiting dependent behaviors, moodiness, overreactions to frustration, or unrealistically low self-esteem. A childhood disturbance, crisis, or disruption can precipitate some of these symptomatic responses, and the feelings can swirl about for some time before gathering into a complex in later years.

We must be aware of a loss of interest in normal daily activities, crying spells, sleep disturbances, significant weight loss or gain, agitation or slowing of body movements, heavy weariness, thoughts about death, loss of libido, and mood changes. These conditions are often triggered by a trauma (divorce, death, loss of business, failed relationship); they suggest the emergence of depression.[28]

Case Study: Bill

"Bill's" horoscope presents a case where clear signals gleaned from conversation led to a referral to a psychotherapist.

The first impression of the horoscope is quite simple: there is a decided Western hemisphere orientation, giving the Self away to others (or leaving the Self behind); the self-worth organization is confused (the Sun, ruler of the 2nd, is squared by Neptune); the parental axis is strongly emphasized through Mars, ruler of the 10th, conjoining the Moon, and Venus, ruling the 4th, quindecile with Pluto.

The Moon-Mars conjunction is very much of an alert for us since the Moon rules the sensitive, home-security Ascendant, the conjunction is "locked away" in the 8th House, and Pluto in the self-worth 2nd opposes it. Additionally, Uranus, in mutual reception with the Moon, opposes Mercury retrograde, an intense, nervous second agenda possibility that is debilitating (Mercury rules the 12th, where we find Uranus). This is a perceptual condition; note that Mercury also rules the 3rd, the mindset.

27 Karp, chapter 2; Klein & Wender, chapter 2.
28 Medical Essay, *Mayo Clinic Health Letter*, October 1998.

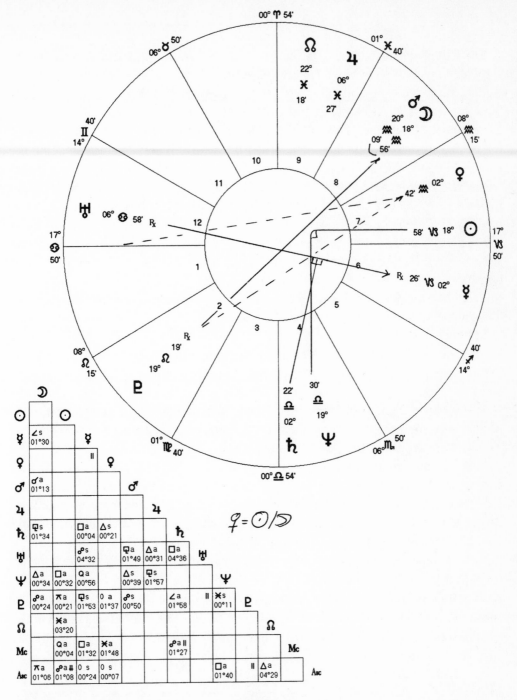

Figure 4
Bill

The Sun-Moon blend suggests the potential for "fresh applications for ambition through humanitarian or social service channels."

Bill's job is processing invoices for a large industrial company, not at all what we hope for from such a highly charged Aquarius Moon. The registration of "under-achievement," if I may, suggests short-circuits and detours in development.

Looking further, we see that Venus, ruler of the 4th, holding Saturn squaring the Uranus-Mercury axis and Neptune squaring the Sun, also rules the 11th, the House where we see love received, hoped for, expected. This Venus is quindecile with Pluto and the Ascendant. AND Venus is at the midpoint of Sun/Moon, a position that will dominate any horoscope.[29]

Here is a case then of *tremendous anxiety about being lovable*, high *self-criticism*, and self-announced depression. In pursuing a discussion with Bill, the anxiety about relationships (Saturn, ruler of the 7th, squared by Uranus; Sun in the 7th squared by Neptune), one hears of failure, being fired from jobs, not being able to relate easily, always living alone (age forty-six at consultation time).

In trying to nail down the Neptune manifestation, ruling the 9th, with Jupiter in the 9th trine Uranus and sextile Mercury (a positive, hopeful dimension), Bill told me that for twenty years he had been in a spiritual group, studying and working to transcend the ego.

Bill fit much of the profile for depression. He cooperated with my suggestion to return to psychotherapy. At the same time, he enjoyed quite a nice job promotion as we had predicted it together, with SA Sun=Jupiter.

Bill is a congenial, trusting, well-working man who is depressed and alone. He tries hard to improve his situation. One of the behavioral therapies that has been developed for mild depression is disarmingly simple, yet remedially reliable: have "people keep lists of activities they enjoy (or that they enjoy slightly, given they're depressed), and then consciously make an effort to engage in these activities more often."[30]

Case Study: Jane

Jane's horoscope shows us another profile of development that led through her particular vulnerabilities to clinically diagnosed depression. The Sun-Moon blend suggests that "the emotional energy of the Sun is focused within mental sharpness and nerves. There may be too much sensitivity stirred up about security; anxiety and fragility can be created."

---

29 Any planet conjoining, opposing, or squaring the Sun-Moon midpoint will dominate analysis, almost invariably.

30 Dawes, reporting work by Peter Lewinsohn, 215.

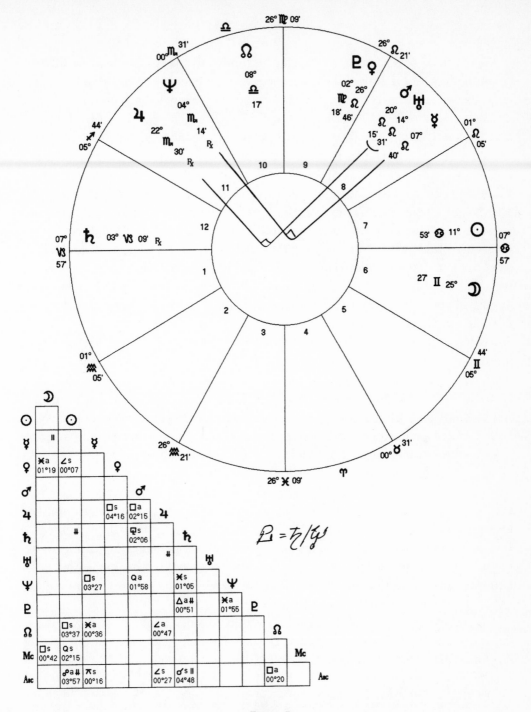

Figure 5
Jane

We see all planets above the horizon, threatening to sweep Jane away in a flow of circumstances. At the core of the horoscope, we have Saturn-retrograde at the Ascendant. The parental rulers (Mercury and Neptune) are square to each other.

Most interestingly presented here is that the Sun in Cancer is peregrine in the 7th and Uranus, ruler of the 2nd, is also peregrine! Security and self-worth issues should dominate developmental concerns, both as problems in development and continued expression of these values in working through relationships into the world. I thought she would be a nurse or teacher (note the Sun quintile the MC, the Moon *oriental* and square the MC; the powerful Venus ruling the 5th and being in the 9th).

Jane's father was absent, and her mother (note Sun square Nodal axis)[31] was decidedly problematic, "She was my other child (meaning 'earlier')." Jane had to care for the mother as if *she* were a child, when Jane herself was a child. This essentially led to a deep fear of failing *outside* the home, and she was eventually so depressed and fearful about relationships that she went to a doctor and was indeed evaluated as manic depressive.

Note here, please, the midpoint picture Pluto=Saturn/Neptune ("strong depression, feeling downtrodden; awareness of potential for loss, fear"). Additionally, the following midpoint pictures, when they appear in a horoscope, reliably accompany vulnerability to depression: Saturn=Neptune/Pluto ("the presence of grief, weakness, torment"), Neptune=Mercury/Saturn ("depression, a sad spirit looking for a ray of hope"); Neptune= Sun/Saturn ("sadness, loss of hope, delusions in relationships leading to aloneness"); Pluto=Saturn/Ascendant ("violent upset, deep anguish, being put down by others"; Ascendant=Saturn/Pluto ("feeling a loss of identity").[32]

When I followed up her Sun-Moon blend potential, mentioning her caring for others, Jane erupted into a flood of tears. She said, "It's such a sadness that I've punished myself for so long by not doing it!" In other words, Jane's depression, which could very well have been formed in the imbalanced household modeling, her caring for her mother with an uninvolved father, etc., had kept her away from helping *others*. Isolation was building. She added, "I see that this was a way of keeping myself unfulfilled. I pursued business to attract masculine approval."

The self-worth profile was fractured as well: note Mars conjunct Uranus, ruler of the 2nd and the 3rd, squared by Jupiter. The parental strangeness was corroborated by Neptune square Mercury, ruler of the 10th.

---

31 Indeed, the orb here is 3.37, a bit more than the rule-of-thumb maximum of 2 degrees, but instinct for the naturally evolving scenario of development encouraged me to include this aspect importantly.

32 See Tyl, *Critical Illness*, 32–38.

In addition to the depression, Jane has heart palpitations (Mars-Uranus in Leo), blood sugar problems and family diabetes history (Venus square Jupiter), and had developed hepatitis (Jupiter squared by Uranus and Mars).[33] So much tension had already backed up into her body, not yet forty years old.

Case Study: Jonah

Jonah's horoscope (page 46) is dramatically open to depression. Notice how the orientation of the planets is to the East, defensively, and the entire feel of the Sun-Moon blend is one of emotional sensitivity, needing family security desperately. There is a rampant idealism projected in that regard (Mercury-Venus conjunction in Pisces, Mercury ruling the Ascendant), and this idealism is quindecile with Jupiter, so obsessive, excessive, and vulnerable to impracticality!

As I began my discussion with Jonah on the telephone, after relaxed small talk, I simply mentioned the tremendous emotional sensitivity, the idealism about it all, and that "when we see something so pronounced, we suspect that it is usually overcompensating for something else."

"Yes, sir." Jonah was in his forties and a definite Southern gentleman.

"And that issue down deep seems to have much to do with your parents, both of them" (Saturn in the 4th square to the Sun, Mercury, and Venus, ruler of the 10th; this square was an alert to depression, aloneness, etc.; also, Mars was on the Nodal Axis).

Note as well his midpoint picture Neptune=Sun/Saturn (see page 46), and Node=Saturn/Neptune ("withdrawal from relationships").

Jonah corroborated what I had submitted: "My parents were divorced when I was born; my mother was distant, and my stepfather was garbage."

In discussing the emotional hurt in his adult relationships, Jonah said, "Every time I get near somebody, I let down my defenses and I get my heart ripped out."

Jonah had had a twelve-year relationship come to an end tragically with his lover's death from AIDS. "Even *he* used his illness against me in the end. I was there just to support him, and the love I offered just disappeared."

As Jonah and I talked, I could hear the growing isolationism, the dependency. His call to me was because of a new relationship potential with a much younger man, but Jonah's self-worth profile was in a shambles with regard to relationships (Mercury rules the 2nd and is squared by Saturn). BUT would the creative astrology here be keyed by his reference to a "much younger man"?

---

33 Ibid., many references indexed there, "Heart, Diabetes, Liver."

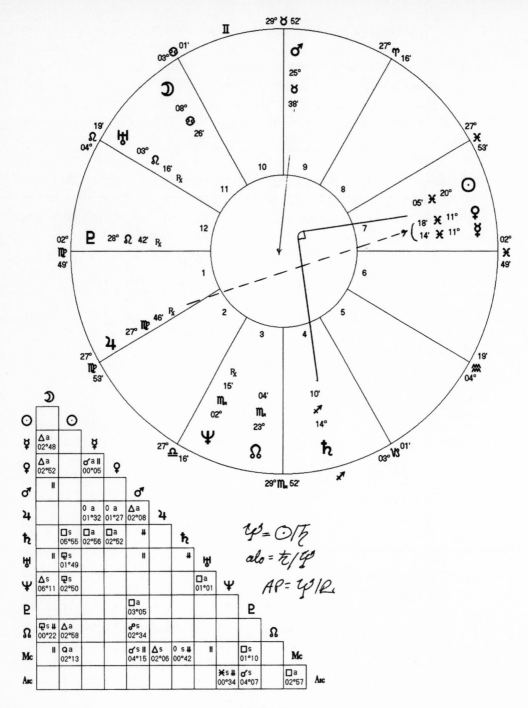

Figure 7
Jonah

"Why does he find you attractive, Jonah. Why does he love *you*?" I asked, trying to bring out Jonah's appreciation for himself.

"I show him love and attention . . . ."

"The same kind of love and attention you had hoped for when you were young? How will this new situation solve old problems?"

Our conversation was extraordinarily tender and altruistic with regard to the young man. Jonah was trying to relate, to keep from continuing as "a loner," to become significant in a relationship.

I suggested that education was the key to the young man's future (it had been interrupted, but Jupiter in the young man's horoscope was the ruler of his 9th *and was opposed his Sun-Moon midpoint*).

Jonah agreed emphatically. He had already thought of funding the program for the young man. As a protection against another crucial disappointment that could cause further alienation from others in the future, we attached a caution to the plan: a dateline, i.e., the plan had to be put into action with the young man's acceptance and cooperation by a certain date or the relationship would be viewed as infertile and *Jonah would walk away from further hurt*. Either way, Jonah would be stronger.

Self-Image and Public Image

Pride is the antidote to the self-worth crisis. Remediation of self-worth anxiety deals in the main with objective reevaluation of the social profile[34]: we rediscover with the client the attractive, fine attributes that form his/her image to others. Sometimes preparing such a list is like pulling teeth, but three or four attributes can usually be listed, and that is a fine start.

In short, we must find some source of confidence and pride somewhere in order to be helpful. When I am preparing a horoscope that has a Leo Ascendant, for example, I am immediately alerted to potential behaviors of importance and prominence, sources of confidence and pride that *should be* established: president of a school class, department head, owning a business, theatrical presentation, etc. Of course, the aspect condition of the Sun will modify the archetypal expectation, but that Leo Ascendant is *there*, and ideally it must be awake and active.

The creative astrologer can become so sensitive to this kind of expectation that, as soon as the client walks through the door, an evaluation can be made: is there a "short circuit" in what I expect, or is the flow free and clear?

---

34 Please see techniques in Tyl, *Synthesis & Counseling*, beginning page 729.

Indeed, this evaluation can be made with any Ascendant; I have chosen the Fire Sign Ascendant as the most brazen, if you will, in ego-transmission.

For example, my Ascendant is 00 Cancer 04.[35] Immediately, we are alerted to emotional considerations, security needs, sensitivity, the need to give and receive caring (recall page 28, please). Additionally, since the location is 00 Cardinal, *this trait will be given prominence:* zero Cardinals (all Cardinal Signs, usually within a 2-degree orb) are called "Aries Point" positions and carry with them a public thrust for any point, any planet configured there. Judy Garland's Mercury retrograde in the 12th was at 00 Cancer and her Saturn was at 00 Libra, both Aries Point positions; the square correlated with her deep depressive illness and the concomitant addictions, but, as well, brought her condition to the public, seeking the public as commiserator, appearing zonked in performance, on television, discussing her problems publicly, etc.[36]

Returning to my example with the 00 Cancer Ascendant: if I come to your office for a consultation, you are anticipating many things, one of which will be the Cancer feel. But I enter and you see an extremely tall figure (6'10"), weighing some 270 pounds, with a strong voice. You might have to remind yourself of the Cancer Ascendant! But you must seek it out for evaluation. With the Aries Point articulation, it should be/is indeed obvious.

The point here is that externals can cover over what we see in the horoscope; events in development can short-circuit their manifestation. The creative astrologer must stick to her guns many times in consultations, knowing what *should* be, what *can* be, and how important it is for the client to get there. Very often, in talking about such positive manifestation potentials, *the astrologer is the only person in the client's life recognizing what is within, what is possible.* In that moment, astrologer and client are together in a very special way indeed.

Case Study: Jack

Jack's horoscope shows the Sun in Leo (conjunct the Fixed Star Regulus, by the way; a reliable punctuation of prominence potential) with the Moon in Virgo. The relationship between the two is very close; it is clearly a New Moon birth. The New Moon shows us a Moon with little light, suggesting a form yet to emerge, and, as a result, there is often a slowness in development, some impedimenta along the road

---

35 Noel Tyl: born December 31, 1936 at 3:57 P.M., EST in West Chester, Pennsylvania.

36 Judy Garland: born June 10, 1922 at 6:00 A.M., CST in Grand Rapids, Minnesota. See Tyl, *Critical Illness*, 23–27, for full analysis.

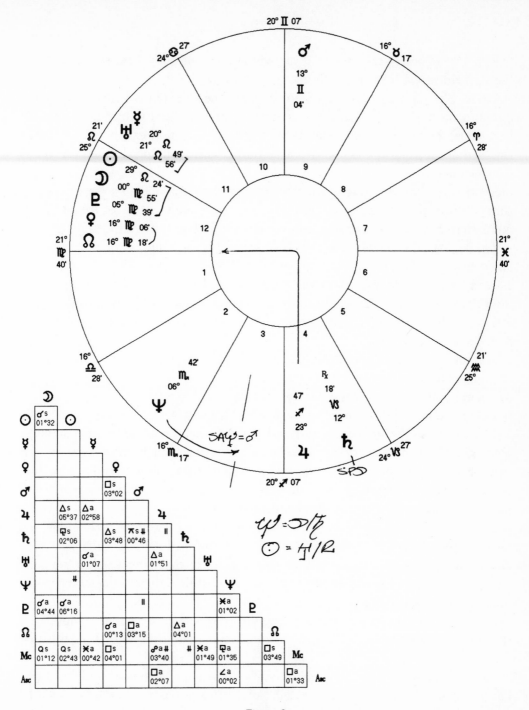

Figure 8
Jack

that are pronounced—shadowing, if you will. Additionally, this New Moon occurs in the 12th House, with quite a stellium.

We see Pluto conjunct the New Moon as well: whenever Pluto is conjunct, square, or opposed the Moon, we can expect a very important mother influence; in a female horoscope, the mother relationship is often competitive; in a male horoscope, often smothering. In Jack's horoscope, we have further corroboration through the Venus conjunction with the Nodal Axis and the Mercury (the ruler of the parental 10th) conjunction with Uranus. There is a mother concern here that must be discussed; it is surely at the core of the defensive, self-protecting structure we see from the conspicuous Eastern hemisphere grouping, and, indeed, the key of Saturn retrograde.

The Sun-Moon blend is going to subdue somewhat the energy to be recognized by an orientation to be correct, exact, insightful, and discriminating. This is corroborated as well through Mercury, *ruler of the Ascendant*, under high developmental tension from Uranus. Any time the Ascendant ruler is under such tension or is retrograde, we can expect difficulties in identity formation. The question, as always, becomes *to what degree, to what lasting effect?*

And finally, note that Neptune is exactly semisquare the Ascendant, and Jupiter, the final dispositor of the horoscope, is square the Ascendant. These measurements helped me to anticipate that Jack was somehow connected with the Ministry.

In fact, Jack is a church musician and a school teacher of music.

Jack gave me the conservative Virgo impression when he arrived for his appointment. The midpoint picture Neptune=Moon/Saturn (melancholy, inferiority) showed through as well (notice the three planets involved in this midpoint synthesis picture: the Moon is the mother situation, Saturn the father—and with Neptune in touch with the Ascendant, something is other than it seems, confused).

At the same time, I kept asking myself, "where is the Leo, where is the pride, the thrust to prominence?" Note as well Sun=Uranus/Pluto, "the urge for independence and freedom;" is this suggesting that Jack eventually must break away from the parental legacy—and whatever else that may have filled in those vulnerabilities—in order to be free and proud?

The self-worth condition (Venus ruling the 2nd) was influenced enormously by the mother, as we have seen through the conjunction with the Node. What was that influence?

I asked Jack about these things in a very relaxed manner. With poise and dignity, he corroborated so much. In essence he said, "My father was passive, he worked a lot; he was preoccupied . . . and an alcoholic; whenever he went away he'd return drunk."

"My mother . . . very supportive but . . . controlling. I needed to please her."

Jack went to music school (Neptune, Venus) and experienced there a terrible coercive clash with a teacher. In a vengeful gambit, the teacher told Jack he would never amount to anything as a composer (at the time of tr. Neptune conjunct Saturn). Because this trauma was so emotionally charged, Jack "gave up"; he went with a shift of his ambition into the school system and away from broader musical circles.

There is nothing unusual about this case, but Jack's pride was put to sleep. His vulnerability to this, to underachievement, was set up by the lack of involvement by the father (no authoritative love reinforcement), the mother control, and Jack's predisposition to melancholy. He was *blanketed by circumstances* (sometimes a very helpful phrase for understanding the 12th House, always a very difficult area to interpret; for me too).

The mission in our consultation was to anticipate and fulfill measurements tied to his SP Moon conjunct Saturn in September 1997, due one month(!) after our consultation. This would be followed by his SA Neptune=Mars ("Change of course of action due to dissatisfaction") and the transit of Jupiter opposed his Sun, three months later. This suggested to me strongly that Jack's pride could be awakened if his dissatisfaction could be brought out into the open, understood, and explained developmentally. He could jump on an opportunity being presented to him right away. He could make a new mark for himself . . . dare I suggest, in music, as a composer!

We talked about this at length. He was thrilled—inspired, is a better word—with this prospect.

The following are excerpts of a letter Jack sent me at the end of August 1997:

> *It was a pleasure meeting you this summer, your workshop at the conference was stimulating, and I'm really glad I convinced myself to have a reading with you! How's that for an opener? I've enclosed a copy of my latest creation—and I feel indebted to you for the inspiration.* [Jack's new piece of music, a choral anthem.]

> *After listening to the tape, I was stunned that I couldn't draw relevance to the period of May to September 1977, and again for July of 1978* [tr. Saturn conjunction Sun-Moon, just after SA Pluto=Asc]—*you saw that as a time in my life when I made a decision about my future, when I would have experienced an "I'm good at this!" feeling. In the summer of 1977, I had my first summer job as music director for a theatre company. I loved that job. It was the first time in my life that I felt like I really belonged to a group of people. I would spend as much time as I could down at the theatre (even though my mother resented it). That summer, the director asked me to rewrite the finale of the show. When my arrangement was first sung at a rehearsal, I*

had chills. Something that I had in my mind, something that I created, something that only I could imagine actually became real. I had never felt so satisfied.

As I told you, I auditioned at the _____ School of Music for composition but wasn't accepted. They put me in Music Education. That was rather devastating for me—I was always recognized as being the best. For years I never mentioned to anyone that I had this goal of being a composer.

Jack goes on in the letter to analyze his musical composition with reference "*to the bright shine of my 29-degree Leo Sun!*"

By the way, my school is having its Graduation ceremony on September 19th. This song will have its first performance then in (a major concert hall)! Now won't the Leo energy love that?!

I'm sure you'll recognize your influence in the words: "Give me courage to endure the path that I must lead; Set my sights, I won't surrender; this my strongest need!"

Well that's that. The ideas for this composition came during my drive home from my appointment with you, Noel. That's how much you gave me a "kick in the pants." Thank you.

I've kept Jack's music near me in my office for some fifteen months already. It inspires me in return.

The Self-Worth Profile

Self-worth that grows through obstacles becomes refined and clarified. Our language tells us about people who have "been there": "She knows what she's about; he is really centered; he has a way about him; she's got it all together." We show what we are proud of; what we are proud of turns out usually to be why we are loved, employed, sought out, and remembered.

Since the 2nd House is always square to the 5th–11th axis—the zones of experience, not the Signs on the cusps—the horoscope tells us that self-worth is *the key to being able to give love and to receive love*. The tensions among those Houses must be resolved, the self-worth strengthened from whatever debilitation may be encountered in development. Only then can someone traffic comfortably and securely in love—exchanging love, exchanging resources—with someone else, who, by the way, is involved with the *same* life process (the 8th House, completing the succedent Grand Cross of Houses, the second House of the 7th)!

Roberto Assagioli, a master of modern psychology in the line that runs from Freud through Jung and Maslow—as a colleague of all these men, a pioneer of psychoanalysis in Italy—provides us with an eloquent statement about the importance of self-love, the apex of self-worth: "If we love what is higher and best in ourselves, what we *are* essentially, if we love our potentialities for growth, development, creative ability, and communion with others, then this love, devoid of egotism, urges us to live a life of higher quality. This love is then not only not an obstacle to loving others in the same way but, rather, a powerful means for doing so."[37]

A very important point here is that our self-worth profile is constructed *in order to relate to others well*; relationship is the goal, the Western hemisphere is the essential complement to the Eastern hemisphere; it takes two to tango. Yet, self-worth development *depends* on interaction with others concerned about *their own* self-worth development, in order to grow and gain security and fulfillment. This is why the 2nd House is opposed by the 8th House (the second of the 7th). When two people meet, the unspoken evaluation is "what resources do you have that can benefit me?" Resolution of this axis is perhaps the greatest challenge we face in development; it is the heart of every horoscope.

Through fear, prejudice, and self-serving behaviors, people all too easily and frequently deprive one another of their rights, their freedom, and their due amount of fulfillment within this self-worth development process. Others push people into defensive behavior, sweep them away to victimization, exploit them, or keep them anchored to enduring problems. To counteract this, we look for friends (the 11th-House part of the Love Cross) who are similar to us, who think and believe as we do, who have similar skills and competency, and *who like us in return*.

Social psychologist Elliot Aronson in his *The Social Animal* puts forward much experimental evidence about this drama of liking, loving, and interpersonal sensitivity.[38] For example, people like us when we can provide them the maximum reward at minimum cost. People like us if we are better looking than not, because we provide an "aesthetic reward"; if we have similar opinions, i.e., "consensual validation reward." In short, attraction is supported by cooperation and good looks.

Extreme competence and, say, pronounced good looks—John Kennedy and Bill Clinton are fine examples—tend not to ensure popularity and being best-liked right off the bat. Because of excellence, that person may appear unapproachable, distant,

37 Assagioli, *The Act of Will*, 92.

38 Aronson, chapter 8.

superhuman. But, *when that person shows some fallibility*—John F. Kennedy and the Bay of Pigs fiasco, Bill Clinton and the Lewinsky scandal—*popularity soars*; that person is more accessible, more understandable, invites broader identification, and is liked more. Popularity increases.

The creative astrologer must understand that physical attractiveness—whether we want this to be true or not—*does* increase by far the assignation of the most desirable traits and the greatest prognosis for happiness. From early childhood on, we learn that beauty equates with goodness (Snow White, Sleeping Beauty, Barbie and Ken). Even as early as in nursery school, children have been found especially responsive to the physical attractiveness of other children around them. Less blame is attributed to the more attractive. In the workplace later, higher starting salaries are given to them. People who are physically attractive easily come to think of themselves as "good" or lovable *because they are continually treated in special ways*. The converse holds as well.

Agreement is important because it represents social validation. It has been found that our desire to avoid people who disagree with us is actually stronger than our need to associate with those whose attitudes are similar to our own. Disagreement introduces the possibility that we are wrong, and this threatens punishment. To defend ourselves, we create negative inferences about those who disagree with us; we bolster our own position as right.

Each of us—astrologers and clients—lives this social drama. There is a tactical concern here for the creative astrologer, to the expression of her/his personality in consultation: we must make ourselves and our work setting as attractive as we can (more about this later); we must practice judicial self-exposure (more about this later, as well) to encourage trust and exposure from our client. Our competence must be founded upon this base.

And further: we must know that the greater anyone's insecurity and self-doubt, the fonder that person will grow of the person who likes him or her. Therefore, it is extremely helpful with every client to find something that we genuinely enjoy, are attracted to, like, appreciate, honor, and support in that client and register that sincerely and early in our meeting. This does wonders to promote a positive feeling at the outset of the consultation.

For example, when going to someone's home for dinner, especially a new acquaintance, you would not think of *not* commenting favorably about something upon entering the host's home. It is like a peace offering. You say something nice and you know you will be better received. Just imagine the opposite: saying nothing at all!

Similarly, the host will comment favorably about you upon *your* arrival, how nice you look, what a funny joke you used as a greeting, how nice your thoughtful gift is, etc. This is the host's peace offering. This is how people get along together.

The dinner party, the consultation are micro-episodes in the macro-life process. Most often, client and astrologer are total strangers to each other. The compliment speaks of attractiveness, signals acceptance, and encourages comfort. Soon, the consultation will be probing deeply into possible insecurities and formative issues; *there must be trust and comfort at the outset*, to allow the development of agreement, confidence, and self-respect.

It is easy to see then, within the Succedent Cross of Houses, that self-worth development is a battleground in life. Everyone is involved in this process. People with the significator of the 2nd House under high developmental tension have been wounded on that battleground. If the significator of the 11th is under jeopardy, the feeling of being loveable is threatened (the 11th is the fifth of the 7th). Usually when both these Houses are upset, there is a difficulty in giving compliments—so the peace offerings are missing in social traffic. At the same time, that person can not *believe* a compliment received, so the person does not acknowledge compliments, and the compliments stop coming. Isolation follows.

When the significator of the 5th is under developmental tension to one degree or another, the ability to give love easily is threatened; there may be sexual dysfunction (in league with the 8th House similarly analyzed). When coupled with significator tensions referring to the 7th House, a fear of intimacy is suggested.

For the creative astrologer, all of these observations work together in conceiving and evaluating a scenario of human social development. This scenario is adjusted and enriched by the client, as the horoscope with all its suggestions is brought to the client's life with all its emotions, feelings, rewards and frustrations.

Case Study: Marilyn Monroe

Marilyn Monroe's horoscope is continuously revelatory in astrological study. Let us look at just a few details of this well-known study, along the lines of analysis we are developing in this book.

We see the Southern hemisphere orientation above the horizon and we see the anchoring, core-problem focus of Saturn retrograde.

This tells us that a severe problem with the father relationship propels Marilyn into a sweep-away tide of potential victimization. Initially, these suspicions seem to be

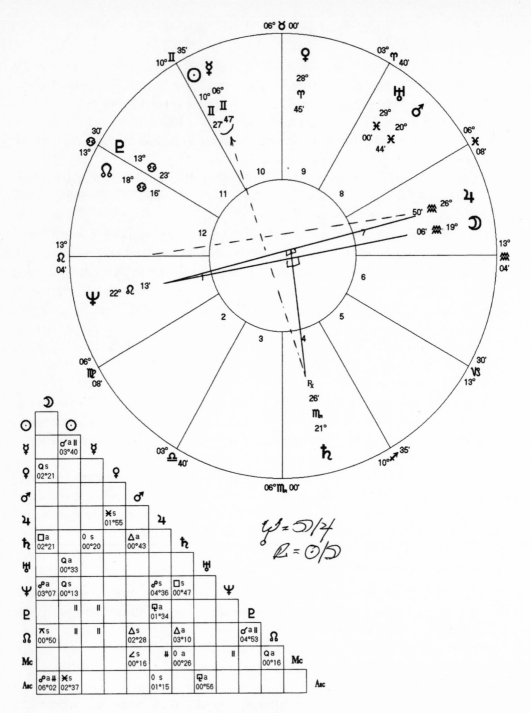

Figure 9
Marilyn Monroe
June 1, 1926, 9:30 A.M. PST
Los Angeles CA 118W15 34N03

rescued by the theatrical pride, the glowing Sun, ruler of the Leo Ascendant conjoined in the 10th with Mercury, ruler of the 2nd. Here is an ideal of some kind; dramatic and interesting. There is a peregrine Uranus, ruler of the 7th, a dominating adventurous trait that thrusts her before the public (conjunct the Aries Point). Is *all* this somehow overcompensatory?

We now check specific dimensions of personality development: Mercury is indeed ruler of the self-worth 2nd *and* the love received 11th, but Mercury is exactly *quindecile with the problematic Saturn retrograde*. Here is obsessive upset about self-worth and love deserved, hoped for, received. Both planets are located in the parental axis, linking the anxiety with the father crises. Additionally, Saturn is square to the axis of Jupiter-Neptune, the rulers of the 5th and 8th Houses, respectively, the key Houses in the sexual profile, the other Houses in the Cross of Succedent Houses. We know that the father problem (and the behaviors, including rape, and feelings that issued from the problem) will directly affect development of the sexual profile. It is well known that Marilyn Monroe was severely sexually dysfunctional throughout her entire life.[39]

Additionally, Venus in Aries (in males as well as females) tends toward flirtatiousness, testing the waters to see if one is attractive or not. Jupiter, ruler of the 5th, is quindecile with the Leo Ascendant. Sexuality, flirting were Marilyn's career. Neptune opposing the Moon reinforces her sexual public image, the smokescreen, if you will, that finally drove her to take her own life. We can note that Neptune=Moon/Jupiter, an eloquent synthesis of the components we are describing.

The older-man image, the man of power constantly figured strategically in her life (including Arthur Miller, Joe Dimaggio, Robert Kennedy, John F. Kennedy). This dimension of the development scenario certainly suggests the overcompensation for the Saturn retrograde legacy, *the midpoint picture of Pluto=Sun/Moon* (power relationships; relationships with power), and, finally, Uranus—ruler of the 7th—peregrine. With circumspection, we can hope that her serious relationships were with men caring about the wounded child within Marilyn, to offset others' strategic exploitation of her search for sexual/love fulfillment.

Case Study: Paul

This next example, let's call him Paul (see page 59), shows a tremendously focused projection of a severe self-image: Saturn, ruler of the Ascendant, is exactly conjunct the Sun in Cancer in the 7th, for all to see. The Moon squares the Sun-Saturn conjunction.

---

39 Please see full analysis of Monroe's horoscope in Tyl, *Synthesis & Counseling*, well indexed throughout the volume.

The Sun-Moon blend here suggests that "emotional security pays great respect to family and social structures, aesthetics, and graciousness. The personality should fit in easily anywhere. There should be a lot of creativity and resourcefulness, all calm and unruffled. One works to keep things secure and safe." There is a subtle, though important, dimension to the Moon in Taurus that should never go unnoted: there is a great need *to keep things as they are* to preserve security or to make them as they should be to achieve the ideal situation. (Very often the reigning need of Moon in Taurus works against advancement, to resist change, because of the fear of insecurity in transition.)

We see a dramatic Western hemisphere orientation, giving the self to others, and we immediately feel a projection of service to others for their benefit. The conservatism, the control, and the severity of all this is accentuated by the Sun-Saturn conjunction, which spills into the Moon's demand for idealized structures, especially in relationship (the Moon rules the 7th) and for the public good.

This growing set of deductions is corroborated strongly by the fact that Neptune is peregrine, suggesting a dominating rampant idealism in the personality.[40]

Venus, ruler of the 9th, holding Neptune, is peregrine as well, in Virgo (dealing with emotions without necessarily showing the feeling of them), and could call our attention to law and ethics as backing up the fastidious image that is building in public service. Mars in Virgo suggests a "passionate chastity" (Evangeline Adams' wonderful turn of phrase), and its square with Uranus, ruler of the self-worth 2nd, certainly sets up a private world battleground of ethical issues that parallels the projection publicly of such severity.

The sexual profile fits well with the scenario we are developing: Mercury, ruler of the 5th and Virgo in the 8th, is retrograde and conjoined with Pluto—a great intensity put under wraps, a perception that is intense and investigative; and the Sun, ruler of the 8th is overwhelmed by Saturn.

The midpoint picture MC=Mercury/Uranus suggests "a heavy thinker, winning through planning, mind over matter."

Every measurement carries with it an emotional reference to *abstemious principles*, indoctrinated in the early homelife, probably through the father (Saturn; Pluto, ruler of the 10th conjoined with Mercury), and all of these are projected publicly. There can not help but be a double agenda in the process: Pluto, ruler of the 10th, is conjoined with Mercury, and the conjunction occurs in the 7th House. Mercury is retrograde, suggesting a second agenda to the public presentation here.

---

40 Please see discussion of "Peregrination" in Tyl, *Synthesis & Counseling*, 155–190.

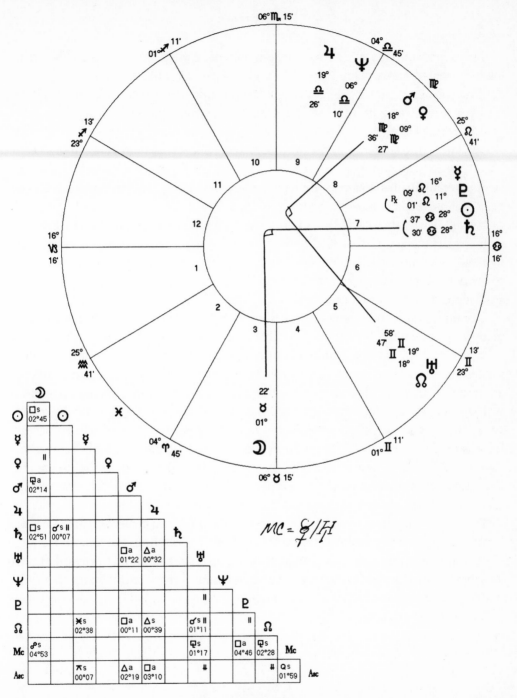

Figure 10
"Paul"
July 21, 1946, 6:56 P.M. CST
Vernon, TX 099W15 34N09

If Paul came into my office for a consultation, my earliest question, after the orientation prepared above, would be "Through its patterns, the horoscope suggests a developmental scenario for us to discuss. Here, please, let me ask you, what is all the tightness, the severity, if I may? Where does it come from? It obviously works well for you. Why is it there?"

Remember, the reference to the horoscope objectifies what I am going to say, i.e., it is not "*You* are really uptight, conservative, etc." My questions carry no value judgment at all. After all, Paul is dressed well; he is well-groomed; he is the head of his law firm; he is professorial in demeanor; he is obviously successful.

I would have learned that Paul's father was a preacher for the Church of Christ (an arch-conservative sect), that Paul himself had sold Bibles while in college, and many more glimpses into development that corroborate the private image that has been successfully brought forward into world view. This is the horoscope of Kenneth Starr, the special prosecutor in the Clinton cases.

It is interesting to note how Mr. Starr has been portrayed by the public media and many in government: a man on a witch hunt, an inquisitor into bedroom secrets, being sex-crazed, leading "sexual McCarthyism," a tool of the far-right radical conservatives out to get Mr. Clinton, and worse. This again shows us the collision course we all must run between self-worth patterns and public reward-punishment judgments.

There surely is someone born on the same day and near the same time as Starr with a very similar horoscope, whose strengths and pride *do not function as well*, as successfully as they do for Starr: if the Pluto in Leo were not square to the Midheaven, for example; if Jupiter were not square to the Ascendant, and Mars trine the Ascendant. This other person may indeed be suffering from extremely debilitated self-worth image and relationship difficulty.

The creative astrologer, in bringing the horoscope to life, *to the reality of the life being lived by the client*, must make adjustments continually, searching for cohesion among parts, within development within time, adjusting level to the attitudes revealed in conversation. We follow the formation of emotions around the measurements that symbolically track milestones in life development.

Chapter 3

Approaching Therapy: Making Creative Connections

IN PREPARATION FOR WRITING THIS BOOK, I HAD TWO SHORT questions sent out on the Internet to a random list of astrologers. People knew I was behind the question, but they were not replying to me. I thought this would keep the answers more spontaneous.

The questions were, "In ten words or fewer, why does someone go to a psychiatrist/psychologist?" and "In ten words or fewer, why does someone go to an astrologer?"

The answers from some forty people were labored, working with a nifty word here or there to differentiate *some difference between the two.* Think about the questions yourself for a moment.

My point is that there *is* no difference; people today are indeed beginning to go to astrologers for therapeutic consultation; they may not call it that, but the consultation with the astrologer is often serving that purpose. At least, we astrologers are proud enough of our skill to think that that *is* the case. If I were answering the two questions, I would use the same one word for both: *insight.*[41]

---

41 Indeed, there is the powerful added dimension about time structure in astrology; the thrust of the question was for overall benefit, not specific techniques.

There are several reasons that the two fields—psychotherapy and astrology—have moved so close to each other in the closing two decades of this century.

First, psychotherapy traditionally has been thought to take too long. Psychotherapy began in earnest in the United States after World War II and was led by psychoanalysts who espoused long-term, multi-year sojourns in the therapist's office. This practice gradually gave way to less time-intensive courses of therapy and criticism of the old "heavy" psychoanalytical theories, but the idea persisted that the "talking cures" needed time.

Now, in the computer age, information flows more swiftly than we could ever have imagined; psychotherapy has speeded up methodologically; people wanting help are more sophisticated and informed than they ever were; therapists are younger and faster-paced by generational model; and even costs figure in as a consideration for how much time is needed to achieve what results.

Single-Session Therapy

A new therapy has gradually been developed, called Single-Session Therapy (SST). Dr. Moshe Talmon is a leader of SST; he says that SST goes back for its roots to Freud and *his* occasional single-session client successes. Similar case records can be traced throughout American psychotherapeutic history over the last fifty years, full in the face of the idea of the long-term norm requirements.

SST has emerged; it has been discovered, not designed or innovated. It seems that people who drop out of therapy after one session have gotten what they want. It is not that they are disappointed with the therapist or the therapy. Many tests have revealed astounding results that corroborate this. For example, Talmon telephoned all of the patients whom he had seen for a single session (often even an unplanned one). He found that 78% of the 200 patients he called said that they had got what they wanted out of the single session and felt "better" or "much better" about the problem that had led them to seek therapy in the first place.[42]

Other researchers studied dropouts in a community mental health center and concluded that "The notion that dropouts represent failure by the client or the intervention system is clearly untenable. Almost 80% of the clients interviewed reported that their problem(s) had been solved, 70% reported satisfaction with the services rendered, and the majority of client expectations of the center were met."

Talmon points out that *just making the telephone call for an appointment* starts a process of self-study and healing within the patient. Tests show that those people who

---

42 Talmon, 9–10.

had to wait a longer period of time—say, a month—for an appointment *were more likely to show improvement* than those who did not have to wait! Talmon learned to take information on the initial telephone call and then, in the first session (the only session) listen again and evaluate how the problem had *evolved during the waiting period.*[43]

So the first reason that psychotherapy and astrology have moved closer together is that the public knows well that therapy (some therapy; most therapy) *can* be accomplished in one session. This knowledge and the awareness of astrology's enhanced sophistication have done much for the business and success of astrology as a therapy, as a resource for help.

The second reason is astrology's growing sophistication, as just mentioned. Astrology has indeed been enriched by assimilation of psychological discoveries, theories, and findings. As well, astrology has dramatically changed its public image from event-orientated fortunetelling to humanistic study and appreciation, and the public appears to have become more comfortable and has, in the main, accepted that image shift. The sophistication of astrology is continuously well publicized now. Many astrologers are psychotherapists; many psychotherapists are astrologers.

The image shift has been facilitated by the increase in the numbers of astrologers everywhere and the increase in their lecture activity, television appearances, books published, book stores opened, and favorable public media commentary.[44]

The third reason is that astrology does not call itself a "therapy," and this avoids the negative sense of going to a therapist for "mental health." While the social stigma can still weigh down psychological therapies, the absence of the therapy label for astrology elevates it in terms of getting some help that is not long-term in process or connected to mental health. And this brings up the point that astrology *should have* a label, *should* profess a helpful position within the scheme of social service, and this professional position should become clarified, known, and remembered through public repetition in media presentations and interpersonal accomplishment. Perhaps astrology offers "Self-Help Assistance." This label certainly reinforces self-empowerment, a key therapeutical concern, and is far from any institutional affiliation for mental health concern. Perhaps it is the field of "Insight Study for Self-Help Assistance."

---

43 Ibid., 18–19. A student in my Certification Course left a message for me to call her, that she had a very pressing question about her work. When I did call her, she said, "Ah! As soon as I left the message with you and hung up the phone, the solution to the problem came to me!" We can all recognize that experience.

44 We can note again that *LIFE* magazine, July 1997, presented astrology as its cover story, "Astrology Rising," and devoted thirteen pages to the subject.

The fourth reason is financial: clearly and simply presented, astrology is normally less expensive than psychotherapy, which, in combination with its sophistication and single-session time requirement, completes a most favorable positioning for astrology.

People want insight, help with their awareness of who they are. Astrology provides this. And astrology, only such Self-Help Assistance, is able to provide insight within the powerfully strategic developmental dimension of time.

Preparation for Consultation

Preparation for single-session success with astrology must begin with the contact made between client and astrologer to make the consultation appointment, face to face or by telephone. I need the sound of the client's voice giving me the birth data to feel that my preparation will be off to the best start. When I do not have that experience—when appointments are made for me by someone else setting up my schedule—I feel slightly disadvantaged.

I engage the caller in simple conversation: first to clarify the pronunciation of their name and mine, learn where the referral to me came from, and then describe my background a bit if they know little about me ("Where did you get my name and number, please? What has so-and-so told you about me?). These points of conversation establish who we are and bring out the comfort and reinforcement of an obviously positive referral (gratitude, possible relationship between referrer and referred, what will be expected from the consultation, the image held of the astrologer). A bit of personal background begins the important presentation of authority, learning, experience, and style for the astrologer *and* for the client.

During this process, we learn a lot: we evaluate conversational poise, vocabulary, courtesies, security, insecurity, and more; we can infer educational background, income level, confidence, and more; and we can often learn what the person feels the benefit of the consultation will be, specifically what is hoped for, expected, anticipated.

The telephone discussion allows the astrologer to say her or his piece, to establish the fee and what is to be accomplished. Here is what I say: "My fee is such-and-such. Our time together will be about an hour—more if necessary, of course—and we'll have quite a discussion together, about your whole development. We'll find out what's really important in the past, and what's going on now and in the time ahead. The discussion is usually very rewarding . . . for both of us!"

Often the client will ask, "Well, can I tape it?"

"Of course. But please know that this is not a performance by me; it's a discussion by the two of us *together*."

This statement starts *the client's* preparation for the consultation. The client knows it will be a *discussion*—so the client must be prepared to contribute. The client knows that the discussion will be going back into the past—so the client starts thinking about the past, in developmental terms.

The creative astrologer is sensitive to so much nuance in this initial exchange. It is extremely helpful in establishing the level of analysis, for relating the horoscope to the client's reality level measured sociometrically. For example, we will have to think and communicate differently for someone clearly well educated than for someone who clearly is not; for someone who perhaps still has an old-fashioned view about astrology in event-orientated, fatalistic terms; for someone obviously under tension and upset; for someone who is simply la-tee-da curious.

What can you infer about the socialization process around the date of birth at the location of birth: 1925, 1942, 1967, for example, in Scarsdale, New York; in Los Angeles; Billings, Montana; Enid, Oklahoma? Does the client still live where he or she was born? What might be inferred about the culture shock (in early experience) in the new location? Geography is very important in development: going to college in a distant place, for example, is often regarded as part of the rite of passage into one's own life.

Are there reality issues that must be assimilated: a speech impediment, race/culture conditions, lack of humor, a confrontational attitude, lack of response, nervous laughter, etc.

As much as we possibly can, I think we should give clients free choice for appointment date and time. I feel that it is their *election*, and time after time after time I have seen the appointment-time horoscope where I am to be located to be helpfully revealing in relation to the client's natal horoscope. I have seen appointments changed, one time, two times, three times, in an apparent push into being the proper consultation chart, into a revealing configuration tying in with the client's horoscope (most importantly the Angles and Moon of the election chart).

Most recently, a psychiatrist came to my office fifty-eight minutes late for an appointment. There was no clear excuse offered. We were lucky that I could accommodate the delay. When I saw the new appointment chart, I knew immediately why the doctor was there, why this delay had occurred(!): the Angles in the appointment chart were brought into relationships in his horoscope and in his wife's horoscope. The shifts were extraordinarily helpful analytically at the outset of the session.[45]

---

45 Just two measurements as an example: the appointment chart Ascendant was conjunct his wife's Uranus, ruler of her 7th, and the appointment chart's Mars was conjunct the husband's Sun. There were more, all suggesting the tension potential of a marital separation.

When the appointment is being set for a telephone consultation, the initial exchange will necessarily have to substitute for seeing the client that short time before beginning the consultation. Perhaps a bit more conversation is needed to "get the vibes," if you will.

With the horoscope itself, all astrologers have their own style of preparation, of course, but the essentials must be covered: a clear overview of the natal horoscope, a time structure that comprehensively covers development from birth to the present, and a projection of present conditions into the near future. The timeline development past to future is best shown through major Solar Arc development, articulated and punctuated by strong transits and the Secondary Progressed Moon, *especially through conjunction or squares with Angles.*

The horoscope papers and notes ordered on the desk before the astrologer are flattering to the client: the astrologer has done his or her homework and is prepared to take this consultation somewhere; the astrologer is organized; "This is more than I expected; it's all about me!"

Case Study: Henry

The horoscope here (page 67) belongs to Henry, a psychologist. It is marked with major aspect pictures, *rapport* measurements showing approximate Solar Arc development (especially in the early years), and expanded with transit activity of anticipated strong importance throughout development and into the near future.

The orientation to the horoscope comes quickly: the Sun-Moon blend (Capricorn-Taurus) suggests "people management, administrative drive, and social sensitivity within solid structure, a movement, an institution." As a psychologist for the state, Henry certainly expresses these potentials, with his change to administration late in 1994 (tr Uranus and Neptune conjoining Sun and Mercury in the 10th).

It is impossible to overlook the emphasis on the parental axis, and on the mother specifically (10th House-4th House axis, Sun precisely conjunct the Node, along with Mercury and Venus, idealism; the Moon squared by Pluto). The influence of the family/maternal situation is probably intense, and obsessive, since the Moon (mired into preserving the status quo, Taurus) is quindecile with Mars in Scorpio, ruler of the Ascendant. This is a potentially overwhelming focus indeed, with obvious sexual overtones to be considered somehow. Additionally, Mars is peregrine (not making a Ptolemaic aspect in the horoscope) and, by definition, will threaten to run away with its energies (deduction, analysis, sexuality, obsession).

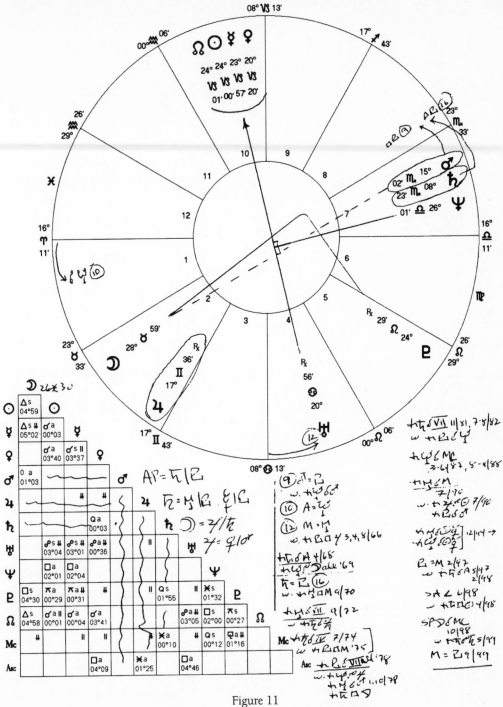

Figure 11
Henry

Saturn is peregrine (a father figure of dogma, perhaps ministerial, unanchored); Jupiter, ruler of the 9th, is peregrine (education must be all-important). We see the midpoint picture Moon=Jupiter/Saturn which suggests a dogmatic stance, a proving of a point (always in the relationship between Jupiter and Saturn), perhaps flowing into the idealism suggested by the Moon in Taurus, the way things should be, could be, might be, could have been, etc.

The Aries Point (AP)=Saturn/Pluto (00 Cardinal, here Libra, is at the Saturn/Pluto midpoint.[46] This suggests bringing forward some enormous breakdown, degeneration, collapse, to discharge it all to start anew. It is also an index of disclosure potential, even about upsetting issues.

The midpoint pictures of Saturn=Uranus/Pluto and Mercury/Pluto repeat an insistence on one's own point of view, *unrelenting self-assertion*. Something so prominent is usually overcompensatory; here defensively . . . for what?

As soon as we can, as the measurements accumulate in our consciousness, we begin to create a developmental scenario, much as a playwright assembles threads of a plot for a play. It is conjectural, but it prepares us for analytical discussion and adjustment during that discussion as we bring the horoscope to the client's reality.

We have an administrative people-manager type, with more than his share of idealism (the Moon in Taurus always brings Venus into prominence, ameliorating the Capricorn energy constructively). All of the tension seems wrapped up in an intensified, avant garde, maybe "off-the-wall" or eccentric situation with his parents (Uranus opposed the 10th House group), the mother in particular (Sun conjunct the Nodal axis, Moon squared by Pluto). There are decided sexual overtones here and there (5th and 8th Houses brought into the tension structure; Scorpio emphasis); could there have been sexual abuse by the mother? How does the father fit in, if he fits in at all (Saturn peregrine)?

All of this will have affected my client's sense of being loveable (Uranus rules the 11th), his self-worth core (Venus opposed by Uranus rules the 2nd holding the Moon), his comfort with and ability to give love (Sun rules the 5th), and, very, very definitely, his relationships (Venus rules the 7th, holding Neptune Saturn and Mars). There could well be a fixation here about whatever this is (Mars in Scorpio quindecile the Moon; Mars and Saturn, also in Scorpio, both peregrine). Henry will surely find it easy to talk about the situation (AP=Saturn/Pluto).

---

46 Normally, with midpoint pictures, it is most practical to observe an orb of 2 degrees, but here, while beyond 2 degrees, instinct led me to allying the Aries Point with Saturn/Pluto. It fit the emerging scenario, i.e., Henry's consciousness (orb) reached out to accommodate this picture.

Now, by any standards of humanistic analysis, that is a startlingly rich profile of surmise from the astrological measurements.[47] We all understand it, how the potentials were derived, but, before we take too much of the credit due, a tiny voice inside might say, "But it is not specific! Just what *is* the problem Henry had and may still be having in his development? Shouldn't astrology be able to define it *specifically*?"

This small voice is the voice of old-time, rigid, codified astrology searching to define and control everything in detail; astrology presented and explained as a pseudo-science.

Astrology is no more a science than psychology is, or architecture, or religion, or love. Astrology uses scientific measurements, to be sure, but the organization, translation, and interpretation of those measurements establish it as an art. It is impossible to define this drama of Henry's development in specific, exact terms before the fact. We could add something like "flavored with the spiritual, mystical, or neurotic," incorporating the Neptunian square to the parental-axis spine of this horoscope, but we simply do not know more detail, *and we do not need it ahead of time to be helpful in the consultation.*

Making Creative Connections

When we go to a doctor, we are asked about our past, in a search for our predisposition to certain conditions of illness, reactions to certain drugs, etc. In psychology, the questioning of the past is intended similarly, and the process has been structured in many, many texts. (Just study Assagioli's "General Assessment and Exploration of the Unconscious" to learn the example of his techniques of questioning![48]) In astrology, *as we work to relate the horoscope to the reality being lived by the client*, it can be no different. Questions discover the substance of development on an infrastructure of time, and that substance comes from the client's life.

What comes from the astrologer's brain are creative deductions conditioned by learning, experience, and inspiration. These deductions are connections we make among occurrences, the "stuff" of the measurements. Initially in the consultation, the creative astrologer is confirming what is already known down deep by the client and, very often, as the scenario develops, reveals *what is there in the development but has been overlooked.* Within the consultation, the client is like a candle before a mirror; after a while the source of illumination is lost.

---

47 In fact, we can add definitively that through no other humanistic discipline would such a profile of pre-consultation deductions be possible, and this is before the inclusion of time structures.

48 Assagioli, *Psychosynthesis*, chapter 3.

Henry was right on time for his appointment, was dressed very well, was businesslike, courteous, quite good looking, and very alert. He knew a good deal of astrology, so, after getting adjusted to the hotel room, the arrangement of chairs, etc., we could get down to what was important. The single-session nature of astrology, for the most part of our work, requires us to be brief, to get to the point, to know what is important. This is the hardest thing in the world for inexperienced astrologers to do, early in their career. They will see the starting place, if you will, very easily, know the measurement guides to creative exploration, but they will not have the courage to dig in. That courage comes from seeing over and over and over again the *applicability* and *reliability* of key measurement concepts, like those being dramatized in this volume.[49]

"Henry, the horoscope *suggests* (a terribly important verb, which does not assert definitively nor attack unequivocally; it is a protection for the client and the astrologer as the consultation begins) that you are quite a people-management person, strong on the administration end, but with a tremendous sensitivity for, shall we say, idealism in the social condition?"

Henry responded about his work, that he was a psychologist and had recently shifted into administration duties for the State Health Department.

"And that seems to have emerged out of quite a swirl of difficulties in the early home-life (Henry smiled in professional recognition; he *knew* where I was going) . . . somehow focused upon your mother, a tremendous influence. Tell me about that, please."

Now, this is not a question, obviously. It is a command delivered in a gentle tone. It serves the same purpose as a leading question: it gets the client to build substance onto the infrastructure we have detected. The command clearly establishes authority and leadership for the astrologer; a story is going to unfold; the astrologer presides over its telling.

With excellent narrative flow (he clearly had told the story before, or thought it through many times), Henry told how his parents had been connected with mysticism, that his mother would have sex only with God—not with her husband. Henry said the whole family would be engulfed in this, that the father "was emasculated and spiraled to nothing."

In one large paragraph of description (just a minute or two had passed), Henry corroborated so much of our scenario for his development. I heard the problem, and the way he told it to me was adult, professional, dispassionate, objective. It was recited,

---

49 This point of consultation technique and poise and the advanced studies required in astrology are the points that are very difficult for us to manage in our image and work record since astrology is not yet taught in college curricula. The training is difficult to come by. This challenge was the motivation for founding my Master's Degree Correspondence Course in Astrology, for Certification.

rather than emoted. Why? Where was the feeling, the passion (the Mars rulership of his Ascendant, in Scorpio, quindecile with the Moon)? Were the feelings over with? Completely repressed? Was there just a routine belief that he was somehow to be continually preoccupied and demeaned by this?

I inquired about this objective delivery, and Henry loosened up, more details were shared with more emotional expression, and it was not difficult to see how harrowing all this had been to a young boy. The years of nine, ten, and twelve (see arcs and transits) were indeed times of trauma within the family neurosis (he had witnessed some bizarre sexual conduct), and at sixteen with Saturn=Pluto and tr. Uranus square the MC ("potential self-destruction"), Henry "flipped out on drugs (LSD)." This was a signal of emotional danger and an attempt to escape.

"How has this protracted experience within your family—indeed, 'way of life' might be a better phrase—how has it stayed with you now? You're almost forty-five years old. (And here we are alerted to the key time of the accumulated Solar Arc Semi-square.) What about your own personal relationships?"

"I can't get married. I can't do it. I'm disillusioned."

Now, the creative deduction here—and the anticipation of it is not too difficult (Venus is the ruler of the 7th and is in the extreme idealism complex in the 10th House, presided over by his mystic mother; Henry is adamant about how difficult marriage is for him)—just flowed easily into my next question:

"Is it that you're attracted to women like your mother?" (Usually it is not good technique to ask questions answerable by 'yes' or 'no,' since either of those answers stops conversation cold. Almost all other questions used in these presentations are purposely clearly open-ended or generalized requests for full information. Here, though, the drama of my statement called for a simplicity of deduction and reply.)

"Yes . . . and . . . to become like my father . . . it scares me to death."

"May I go a bit further with this, please, just a bit more intimately?" I wanted to assess how deeply entrenched this was with Henry sexually, since the peregrination in Scorpio (Mars especially) is so pronounced, and that Mars, ruler of his Ascendant, is quindecile his Moon. And clearly, the Sun, under so much tension, was ruler of the 5th and Pluto, square to the Moon, was ruler of the 8th, the two Houses of the sexual profile. How had all of this been assimilated within Henry's own sexual profile?

With Henry's permission, I went that one step further: "In your private erotic times, Henry, what is the general essence of your fantasy, what excites you, please?" In private erotic fantasy, as in dreams, so much emotional content is discharged in symbolism.[50]

---

50 Any sexual therapy book and most general therapy studies deal with this subject. See as well, Tyl, *Synthesis & Counseling*, 553–625.

Again, very promptly and objectively, he replied: "I'm watching my lover being seduced by another man." And he added, "And I've actually done that."

"Is that image mother and father? (Henry had actually seen his mother and father in sex when the mother had relented.)

"Absolutely."

Well, there we are. The horoscope eloquently led us to a deep appreciation of Henry's complicated development. More dimensions of the syndrome emerged as I inquired about changes in his developmental timeline. The major events we noted together also confirmed his birth-time accuracy.

In 1972, his education had been interrupted and then resumed shortly thereafter. In 1978 he went to graduate school—looking for answers to everything in his study of psychology.

In mid-1982, a powerful measurement cluster occurred: tr. Saturn conjunct the seventh cusp (a parental Midheaven or fourth cusp) with *tr. Pluto conjunct Neptune.*

Repeatedly, reliably, I have noted that with the transit of Pluto to Neptune, or Neptune to Pluto (conjunction, square, or opposition), or the *SA combinations* of these two planets similarly, we learn that strange happenings occur, occult experiences, bizarre, unusual, abnormal, religious, mystifying, frightening, haunting, extremely special emotionally. Usually, they carry with them a symbolic registration of deepest emotions, much as dream symbolism often does. The most conservative person might say (actual comments): "Oh, yes!!! I met this strange, fascinating girl, who intrigued me with casting spells. For weeks, I would learn about all this with her." What did that do for you? "It made me know what I really wanted to have happen around me."

Or "I was driving a car, we had a wreck, my date was killed; I decided to go back to college and start over, to become a doctor. If I took a life, I wanted to pay it back and save lives." His estranged father was a doctor, and this turn of events brought my client back onto the path of reconciliation, identification, etc.

Or, "that's when my boyfriend and I actually saw a UFO at the side of the road." In my opinion in this case, this description or that experience of something was a strong bid for importance, for specialness, since the self-worth profile was severely debilitated ("I feel I'm worthless"); her defensiveness was silence, and, as an adult, she "sabotaged relationships; I choose men like my father." The UFO could easily have been a device of private specialness; it was simply not important if it were true or false.

A tough, swashbuckling, extremely romantic California businessman experienced SA Pluto=Neptune at the same time he experienced tr. Uranus conjunct Venus: "Ah!!

That was just when I had met Susan; this feeling built up in me like a total aware-ness, hard to describe; that there would *never be* another woman for me, *never*. This was love, this was perfection, *and my life changed*. I also went into complete transfor-mation and buildup of my body and my spirit!" Believe me, no one would have expected these words from this ex-Marine Buccaneer-with-the-ladies!

At this time, in response to my question, "This may seem like a strange question Henry, but what was it that happened in mid-1982, that was strange, dare I say weird, unusual, upsetting . . . ?"

Henry explained that his father died in 1982. "It was a most powerful experience."
"Why?"

"(As he was dying) I told him, 'I love you.' And he replied, 'I love *you*.' That was the first and only time I had heard that in my life." (Recall that Saturn is peregrine and Uranus in the 4th rules the 11th.)

When tr. Neptune came to his Midheaven in mid-1987 and the fall of 1988, Henry said "My job left me isolated, disoriented, horribly alone." This is what normally occurs when transiting or arcing Neptune conjoins or squares an Angle. It is a highly reliable signal for ego-wipeout; a signal to get onto a new track, to start over, to be real . . . perhaps in Henry's case to have begun to let go of the family neurosis.

When tr. Uranus conjoined the Midheaven at the same time as Jupiter transited opposed his Sun, Henry enjoyed recognition and reward professionally. When tr. Sat-urn, Uranus and then Neptune conjoined his 10th House cluster, Henry was in excel-lent, stable condition, professionally. It seemed as if family things were left behind.

There was a breakup with a relationship with SA Pluto square the MC in February 1997, and there we sat with tr. Saturn trafficking on his Ascendant in summer 1998.

Forty minutes had gone by and, thanks to Henry's professional poise, practiced objectification, a bewildering story had been told clearly. I reflected it back to him *in terms of praise*, congratulating his objectivity, preparing him for common sense.

"You know, you really understand this whole situation so well. I congratulate you! The time coming up now is perfect for more of the same, *understanding this situation out of its existence!*" Here, I was *pre-selling confidence in the time ahead*, specifically the **accumulated Solar Arc semisquare aspect in June 1998, accompanied by tr. Sat-urn square to the Sun, the time of our consultation**. These measurements parallel a changing of gears in life, getting things sorted out, a culmination of second adoles-cence; and the time was immediately at hand.

Henry was settled in his job, with his particular bureaucracy not allowing much mobility professionally. The only area open for him, for further happiness, was this marvelous developmental tension complex affecting *all* his natal planets and points, with an added kick provided to the Sun, all projected into a new start, perhaps a new way of giving love, feeling love (Sun rules the 5th). With the strength of all his under-standing, it was time to be bored with the past, the personal relationship under-achievement, and to let go of the weights of the family neurosis. My job was to illuminate that potential, that timing, and contribute to his empowerment to accom-plish that new level of growth; especially in the face of the accumulated Solar Arc semisquare time of change.

We talked about specifics on that path, with some humor, with some embarrass-ment, with some wisdom, and with lots of determination: Henry would try carefully to start to change his private erotic fantasies to something else so that reinforcement of the early trauma would be broken up, especially in connection with sex. He would believe how handsome and smart he was, and really what a good catch he would be, unmarried at forty-five! He would develop compassion for his father, realizing that the father too had been caught up in something beyond his control, that his neglect of Henry had been simply because of his own preoccupation with self-preservation. His father meant what he had said on his deathbed. Henry *could* relate to a woman the way his father really had wanted to, to be himself.

As first introduced on page 29, the tensions in development meet with success (reward) or defeat (frustration) through interaction with the environment. The inner environment absorbs the frustration. Emotions and concomitant feelings swirl about to explain things. They tie themselves to events. They are triggered time and time again and form complexes that affect behaviors—and they affect health. Gradually, stored tension and frustration within the aging process key somatic and systemic breakdown. I call this "Accumulated Developmental Deficit."[51]

Astrology can find the weak places in the body by theorizing that "hard" aspects represent developmental tension, planets and Signs connote parts and systems of the body, and that the accumulated developmental deficit will affect these areas of the body sooner, more frequently, more drastically, and more reliably than other areas.

For example, with Henry, at the close of our consultation, I stated that I was not a medical doctor but that the horoscope indeed had ways of suggesting difficulties in development related to weakened parts of the body. I asked him about his knees, his joints (the Capricorn focus, with the Uranus opposition), and Henry replied with all

---

51 Please see a full study of this thesis, with seventy-two case examples, in Tyl, *Astrological Timing of Critical Illness.*

the medical terminology about *fibromyalgia*, a chronic (but not crippling) painful stiffness of joint tissues (often the result of emotional tension or stress); about his stomach (Uranus in Cancer, the Moon quindecile from Mars and square from Pluto), and Henry replied in detail about his hyperacidity, the enormous daily dose of medicine he takes against that condition.

Together, we had made so many creative connections. Insight had been achieved.

Questioning Techniques

Dr. Moshe Talmon says it very well: "the art of psychotherapy depends largely on therapists' ability to mobilize patients' resources to heal themselves." *Every* therapist says this, just as every therapist recognizes the personality of the therapist as the major vehicle for persuading clients that they are valid in life, that change and growth are possible, and that they have the power to improve their efficiency toward personal fulfillment.

We do this by getting quickly to the emotional core of development, the hidden feelings and events that form and propel behavior, the short-circuits that encourage excessive defensiveness and self-devaluation, that take us away from the ease we long for, the naturalness of being that is our birthright. It is learning to understand and manage the difficulties that makes us strong, to adjust value judgments in living situations.

Direct and Open-Ended Questions

The first techniques we use are *questioning* and *disclosure*.

Basically, we should be aware of four categories of questions and how to use them. The first category includes *direct questions*, which we can pose in three ways. First, there are the questions that invite a "Yes or No" answer. These questions, as we have already seen, have a finality and drama about them, and they should be used that way, i.e., in bottom-line circumstances, "Well, from our discussion, it all adds up to leaving this job, doesn't it?" But, except in special circumstances wherein you can rely on a client's talkativeness, the yes-or-no question threatens to stop a conversation cold. There is no development with a "yes" or a "no."

"Did you get along with your father?" might get a "No," and that's that. It might get a "Yes," and that's that. The astrologer appears to be groping for significances, appears unprepared. (Listen very carefully to top television interviewers; assess how and why they ask the questions they do; note the results.)

Asking the question as an "open-ended question" (the second way of asking a direct question) improves the potential of response greatly: "What about your relationship with your father?" or you can pose the open-ended question in the imperative: "Tell me, please, about the relationship with your father."

Outside your orderly preparation scheme, there is another time to pop such a leading question: by listening to your client's word choice, you will often spot a key moment into which to interrupt (the third way), building on the energy of the particular word. For example, your client says, "Well you know, I'm different from what you'd . . . ." "Excuse me, why do you think you're different?" And then, the client may reply something like, "Well, it's because in my home, it wasn't strict enough, and . . . ." "What do you mean by 'strict'?" And from that answer you would know what was absent in the guidance of authoritative love that our culture ordains comes from the father. You are taking the consultation along on the energy of the pivot-words and concepts of your client.

Assumptive Questioning

The fourth way to ask the direct question is what I call the "Assumptive Question": "What was the big difficulty, the estrangement or fear here, in your relationship with your father?" might elicit something like, "My father was garbage. He was never there when I needed him, and when he was drunk he would beat my mother, and . . . ." or "Can you imagine that I was the one sent out to find him when he didn't come home . . . that drunk . . . it was horrible how . . . ." (Actual responses.)

In the "Assumptive Question," I am *assuming* that the relationship with the father in the case at hand was problematic, and the words I suggest here, "estrangement or fear," cover the three general variables in Saturn-retrograde situations (or, indeed, squares from Saturn to Sun or Moon), being out of the picture, there and passive, or tyrannical. By *assuming* that this is so, the astrological process gains authority and the astrologer can gain credibility.

The assumptive question also avoids the defensive first response that is often given by clients not being readily honest about the paternal feelings long past (or any other issue): "Well, my father worked so hard and he was always tired, and . . . ." When I have had to let that defense register, I knew that I would return to the same issue later, when the discussion would have loosened up (trust, disclosure). I can say without any exaggeration that the Saturn-retrograde insight has been valid for 98% of all relevant cases in my experience—*significantly*, not just more or less—in the last twenty-five years.[52]

---

52 Of course, there *are* exceptions. The astrologer goes on to the next point.

Recently I shared a consultation with a client with the Moon in Cancer in the 4th House. This Moon was very nicely sextile to Saturn. But Saturn, ruling the 10th and the 11th, was squared by Mars (ruler of the Ascendant), and Saturn itself made a quindecile to the Ascendant. There is tension here in the early homelife, impeding the champing-at-the-bit ego-development potentials with an undercurrent of anxiety about being lovable, self-worth problems, etc. This lady defended her family at incredible length, with enormous understanding; she went on and on. As the defensive statements continued, the protective words began to evaporate; what then started to emerge were statements like, "My father was scared of opportunity, and that goes back to his parents. Even now, in his seventies, he says to me, his college-educated daughter doing very well, that maybe I should give up what I'm doing and drive a limo, because I have such a good personality and that job would be secure!"

My plan was to listen to it all, to let reality emerge. It was truly remarkable. This lady had her Mars (in Sagittarius, by the way; arch opinionation) squared the Nodal axis. I asked, "Alright, is there something to discuss about your mother?" And again, the defensiveness started: "Well, she did the best she could, and I understand now that I became a mother . . . . Of course, I love my mother, *but I do not want to be like her. They were afraid of everything.*"

My client was visiting with me about a major job plan (the 10th House issues of the parents became very important as background to the 10th House profession discussion). She had a history of underachievement that was extraordinary. I pointed this out to her, and she replied, "I always put myself lower than others (total Western orientation). I then suggested, "All this defensiveness, all this rationalization is designed to preserve whatever security there was, because you need it so desperately at all times (Moon in Cancer)."

This was a primal explanation. She agreed. There was a way open then to objectify, and we went on to assess the state of security in the Now, and to plan strategy secure on that base *rather than on the base her parents had provided*. It seems so simple, but such deductions, such insight is often elusive. That's why my client had come to see an astrologer: she knew that somehow the astrologer could get to important insights.

Here is a sampling of "assumptive questions" for several key astrological measurement references; the answers will almost always be substantively revealing, leading strongly to significant disclosure:

2nd House: "What was the event or time period you would point to for when you started having self-worth problems? How do you see those problems related to the situation now in your life?"

11th House: "What was the event or time period you would point to for when you started feeling unlovable? How does all that focus now in your life, in your relationships? What has perpetuated those feelings?"

9th House: "What did your parents have to say about your education plans when you were nearing eighteen? Why do you think you had this precipitous marriage at eighteen (check arcs and transits at this key time of life), which interrupted your education? How did that time then set up the times now?"

10th House (besides the myriad parental references): "How does your job fulfill you? What is missing?"

7th House: "How does the tone of your relationships now fit the tone established in your early home? What was the model back then for the situation now?" Or, "How does your marriage fulfill you? What is missing?" Or, "What is it that you think you have sacrificed to keep your relationship alive?"[53]

Or, "What was the purpose of that marriage?" And remember, the parental axis is also the axis of the in-laws, another echo of a marriage and the spouse's parents extending one's own parental situation, i.e., the escape is not completed. And all of this, in marriage, is taken on within the vow to remain together for the rest of life.

Moon in the 6th (usually workaholic): "How does your overwork fit in here? How does your overwork tie in with your fear of intimacy at home (involving significator tensions among the 2nd, 5th, 11th, and 7th Houses)?

Tr. Saturn Return (looking back): "What were the currents of change, probably affecting your job, in this six-month period (leading up to the Return)?

Moon-Pluto, hard Nodal contacts: "What can be said here about the mother influence in your development—smothering, competitive? Please share that with me. What was the essence of the parental modeling in your early home?"

You can see the questions leading from evaluation in the past to reevaluation in the present. This is extremely important because, as the creative astrologer listens and learns the client's reality, she or he is making connections within a scenario of development, which must be looked at once again objectively. The creative astrologer will be asking for, reflecting, a new evaluation of these considerations in the light of information viewed afresh.

Of course—and it embarrasses me to have to write this caution here—the astrologer can not just make a list of questions, string them together, and expect to

---

53 Whatever part of Self, the individual-need profile, has been sacrificed is usually a powerful lure away from the relationship to regain that part.

have a meaningful (and ethical) consultation. There must be careful analytical preparation and an alert posture to make creative links among questions, to put feelings together with events. This shows the client that *you have a purpose in the development of the discussion.* I find myself saying often, "We are going to see that . . . .", and I regularly recall that objective; "It is important for the decisions that lie ahead."

The Radical Probe

Another important question category is the "radical probe," a key to depth-oriented brief therapy brilliantly presented by therapists Bruce Ecker and Laurel Hulley.[54] The objective is to find the hidden emotions—"the symptom's emotional truth"—which are completely the client's own creation but have no easily accessible explanation. *Recognizing what that emotional construction is* is what allows change to occur in depth-oriented brief therapy.

I paraphrase Ecker and Hulley in their brief-therapy treatment of a couple who have emotionally ugly verbal battles with each other every three or four days. The radical probe question must search for why the battles are important and not initially attempt to stop them. What makes it overridingly important for these two individuals to have fights that end the closeness?

The question then was given to the clients this way, with a fresh twist of phrasing: "If you were to stay close for long periods, weeks and weeks, as you want, there are ways in which that would be so good, so enjoyable. (Setting up the ideal.) But I want to know *in what way would it be, in some way,* **a difficult problem in itself to remain close and happy**, on and on?"

The therapist holds the focus on the question, at first strange, but then clearly highly charged with potential as the discussion develops. Soon, each of the clients experiences something new: being happy unconsciously represents *a loss of self in the relationship*, being passive, being controlled. Each of them thinks that *harmony equals submission*; each is vigilant against domination! Anger is a way of asserting the self (as we have seen).

After discussion and in followup, the couple said their fights were quickly fizzing out because "we're now so aware of what we're really up to!"

Astrologers can use the radical probe technique easily. After showing keen interest in a pattern of behavior, the astrologer can ask the client, slowly and clearly, "I see you want to help me understand the problem, and I am going to need your help further

---

54 Ecker and Hulley, 221–31, 158–167.

(enlisting support for the probe). Let me ask you something quite specific: just relax and even close your eyes if you wish, and think for a moment, *what would it be like if you **never ever felt again**—except to the degree that is normal for us all at one time or another—*if you **stopped** *feeling that you were unlovable, that you were worthless,* especially in your present relationship that's so important to you? What would it be like? How would you feel?" (The answer will *not* be, "Oh, just great!," I assure you.)

Or: "What would it be like, what would happen, what would you gain if you took away those controls from your sexuality, if you trusted that your wife (husband) found you desirable, even after your operation; what would happen if you showed love trustingly?" You could then follow up with the final section of this question, later in the consultation, slightly paraphrased, "What *will* happen when you show love trustingly?"

Perhaps the man feels he is overweight and that this is a point his wife might bring up, i.e., at the wrong time! Perhaps he senses a loss in erectile reliability; perhaps his additional weight makes his penis look smaller. Perhaps all of this is related to something else, an earlier failure triggered by present challenge. Perhaps the woman feels the same thing about her weight. Perhaps she is afraid to be criticized for her unwillingness to innovate sexually (the man looking for more stimulation), after all, "isn't the way it's been good enough?" Does this tap into earlier feelings formed around inadequacy?

Perhaps one of these two paragraphs is the precisely valid radical probe to arouse objectification, to break the thought patterns set up very, very early in life and triggered somehow by a husband's impotence, a wife's mastectomy, a loss of job, etc.

What about the radical probe question to a young child—an intelligent eight years of age—angry within her parents' divorce, compulsively touchy-belligerent to her father: "Connie, pretend for a minute with me, please, what would you feel like if things were peaceful with your daddy, if you were not getting all upset for whatever reason?" In other words, what is her belligerence saying *for* her? If that went away, how would she feel weakened? Is her behavior just arch self-assertion? Why is the extreme behavior necessary?

In short, the creative astrologer would use the radical probe, in a calm, conceptual, researching tone of voice, to ascertain *what makes the symptom more important to have than* not *to have?* Why is the behavior pattern that is externally problematic *internally rewarding?* "What would it mean about you (or your life, your marriage, and so on) *if the problem never changes?*" "What does it *mean* to you about your husband that he refuses . . . . Why are you comfortable with that?"[55]

---

55 Ecker and Hulley, 161–162.

The Focus Question

The fourth questioning technique is the "Focus Question," which I have adapted from the intriguing work of psychologist Eugene Gendlin. Gendlin presents the premise that the feeling-details are stored in the body: "Nobody can figure out, intellectually, all the details of a personal problem. No therapist can. You can't—neither for someone else nor for yourself. The details are stored in your body. The one way to find them is through focusing."[56]

Relaxing the client, Gendlin asks that the client be aware of what he feels, what he senses about the self at that moment, standing back in the mind from whatever emerges, just recognizing it quietly. He then asks that the client *feel all of that*, and allows about sixty seconds of silence for this. Next, he has the client focus on some special feeling within the whole, instructing the client to follow that feeling. Finally, he asks the client "to find some *new* words or pictures to capture what your present feeling is all about." He calls for "some fresh difference," asking the body: "Is that right? Does it *feel* right?"[57]

The client's description of the feeling is often extremely helpful for further discussion and understanding. The astrologer should push aside all the glib, routine, superficial answers about jealousy, for example, and probe for what is behind, observe how the feelings in the body emerge to illuminate the hidden crux, which might well be—in the case of jealousy—the feeling of being left behind, which is then related to an early home experience where a preferred sibling got all the attention.

Gendlin works from the observation that when people change, *they show it*, most often quite dramatically. If we ask the body to send us the message about feelings the body *will* respond. That release of information is a major step to freeing up the energy, and the body will register that in a different look. (Look what happens when you study meditation or Yoga, or when you own up to something! When you remove guilt feelings, you say, "I *feel* years younger" or "I *feel* as if a giant weight has been removed from my shoulders!")

This is very easy to appreciate every day: just watch during your next substantive conversation with someone: note when you see the other person shift position in the chair, move their arms across their chest, cross their legs, look away, and know that *this is the body speaking to the point you are making*. Inside there is a reaction that is not getting out easily.

---

56 Gendlin, 43.
57 Gendlin, 48–49.

Experts in communication skills state that over 50% of a message's impact comes from body movements! They say that body language is often more believable than verbal communication. And we can see body movements occur in clusters, linking the thoughts being expressed—or being masked.[58]

I have adapted Gendlin's "focusing" technique into the "Focus Question" in this way: I ask the client to still him- or herself, exhale, relax, and then I say, "We've been talking about this difficult swirl of emotions inside, and we're making progress with understanding them. Now, very sensitively, look inside, find where all this hurts . . . where do you feel this difficulty . . . where specifically?"

The objective is to get at a planetary complex, a psychological disposition, through body registration.

Case Study: Gayle

The horoscope shown here (page 83), for Gayle, is a clear example of the Focusing Question at work following up an Assumptive Question.

Gayle's horoscope shows conspicuous Northern Hemisphere grouping below the horizon (unfinished business in the early home); the Ascendant ruler, Mercury is squared by Saturn, and Mercury also rules the 4th (corroboration of the hemisphere deduction); Mars is conjunct the Sun in the 4th, the Sun ruling the mindset 3rd (further corroboration, with the intensification of the mental process involved, especially with Mercury being the final dispositor, etc.); and Pluto conjoins the Moon (even more corroboration, introducing the competitive-mother potential, echoed here by Uranus square the Node).

In a flash, quite literally, armed with confidence in our orientation to key measurements within the first impression, we have a profile of this horoscope that can lead a rich discussion: there is an extremely cerebral, conservative, and perhaps idealistic defense against problems in the early home, focused primarily on a highly influential mother, who probably competed with the daughter. This mother relationship probably impedes easy identity development, affects the self-worth profile strongly (Moon rules the 2nd), introduces anxiety about being lovable (Mars rules the 11th), and focuses much, much tension into the realm of relationships (Jupiter, ruler of the 7th, quindecile the Midheaven; Mercury quindecile the Midheaven).

Vocationally: the MC=Mercury/Jupiter midpoint picture (classically, a writer) is very close and very strong (the tight orb, the nature of the quindecile). This observation,

---

58 McKay, Davis, Fanning, 53–58.

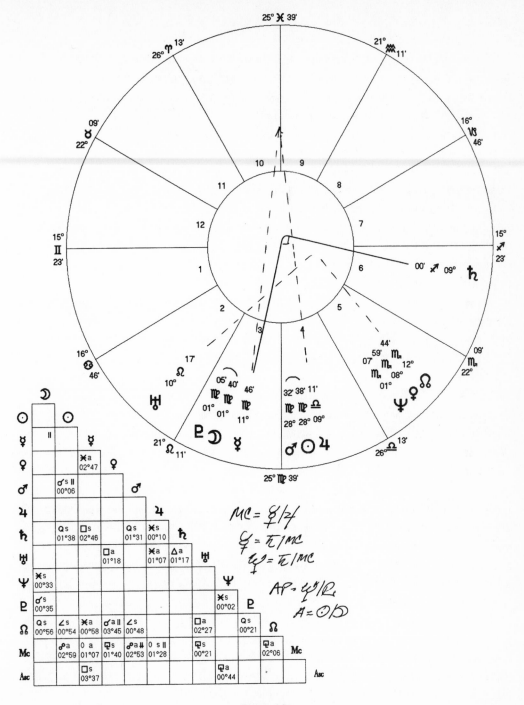

Figure 12
Gayle

along with the strong 3rd House and Mars oriental suggested that Gayle was a writer, promoter; manager of information, instructor, with conspicuous creative talent, artistic talent (Venus-Neptune conjunction, squared by Uranus, sesquiquadrate Midheaven; Neptune sesquiquadrate the Ascendant).

Gayle was indeed in technological information management, teaching secret weapons deployment and management by computer, and she had been a writer for an advertising agency. But where was the artistic nature? Gayle did not "look" artistic, but this dimension was there, locked away somewhere.

Gayle corroborated every word of my initial first-impression, "the-horoscope-suggests" statement. She beamed with surprise. She mentioned it had taken her therapist months and months to put these things together.

Her father had been passive in a home dominated by her mother who indeed "competed with me for my father's affection."

Gayle had learned to objectify very well, surely thanks to her therapy. She was cheerful, robust looking, chunky, yet tallish in appearance, had short-cropped hair, and had obviously chosen not to make a show of femininity. Here she was forty-one years old and obviously caved in with regard to relationship potentials. Venus, ruler of the 5th was conjoined widely with Neptune, in Scorpio. Again: where had the sensual fantasy gone? Saturn rules the 8th and was square to the key Mercury, ruler of the Ascendant and the 4th, the core of her mental construct.

"Are you being medicated for depression?" My question was a dramatic yes/no probe loaded with assumption, some five minutes into our consultation (Mercury square with Saturn, Mercury=Saturn/MC, Neptune=Saturn/MC, feelings of fear; incongruous resigned comfort with the situations we were discussing). She was indeed under medication for depression. If she had said "No," I would have asked, "Have you ever been?" This was important to determine how deeply the problems had imploded on her mental state.

After the initial section of background corroboration, I said, "Gayle, so much of this seems dry, emotionless; even your work. Cybernetics is so cold. The horoscope suggests that some emotion should be *allowed into the process*." (Notice my word choice: why wasn't emotion *allowed* into free expression? Did her early emotional expression originally put the father in an awkward position, did it frighten/challenge the mother? Did the early modeling situation in the home drive the emotional expression underground into a fantasy world, compounded then by enormous insecurity?) I concluded with: "Writing and illustration are strongly suggested here."[59]

---

[59] I do not know where I got the word "illustration." This kind of inspiration, if you will, happens when sensitivity, concentration, and confidence work together a lot. I could have simply said "art," but the specific word "illustration" was precisely apt.

"*I have just bought two books on illustration!!!*" Gayle interrupted, sitting far forward on her chair, clearly excited. (Her art outlet was the way out *privately* for her Venus-Neptune in Scorpio conjunction, *squared by Uranus*.) Gayle was indeed an artist, had gone to art school.

My next question was again assumptive. I jumped for impact, from the excitement of discovering the art dimension, back into her insecurity matters and experiential aridity with regard to relationships and giving love, feeling lovable, etc. I wanted to make a connection dramatically. "How do you express your sexual energy, your longings? Through your art work? Surely you draw scenes of enjoyment!"

Gayle was shocked with this detection. She had never ever admitted or shown this to anyone. She was thrilled with our discovery and with her *finally being able to talk about it!* (See "Disclosure" section below.) Some of the details of her drawings were extremely symbolically revealing for Gayle, *being forced to receive (believe) attention and love*.

I then followed up with a relaxed moment of looking back to the whole picture of development and the tight defensive behaviors we had identified in our conversation. I asked her a Focus Question that concluded, "All that hurt, all that tightness we've been talking about, *where* is it, where do you feel it, where in your body does it hurt so?"

After about twenty seconds of introspection, Gayle said, "From my head to my stomach."

"Not the genitals?"

"No, my stomach."

"Insecurity? That's the core issue?" (Yes/No question for bottom-line effect.)

With dramatic recognition and relief, "Yes, yes it is."

Gayle admitted that she never *drew people for others to see*. Interestingly this tied in with much of the AP=Neptune/Pluto image, her comfort with "strange things, strange books, pictures, and music." Gayle had a well-developed private world that was closely tied to the Neptune-Venus in Scorpio art realm.

And then there was Ascendant=Sun/Moon, which should promise personality beaming, even power galore. Gayle was beaming and delightful, but her Ascendant ruler was squared by Saturn and she was taking anti-depressant medication. How were we to refind emotional security and explore relationships in maturity? After all, Jupiter, ruler of the 7th, was in fine shape, astrologically. Gayle's separation from the relationship world had to be an over-extended defensive routine from long ago. The accumulated Solar Arc semisquare (a second adolescence, a second chance) was due in three or four years.

In our date review of the past, through a string of difficult relationship situations in her late twenties, we finally came to the arc time of Venus=ASC.[60] When Venus arced from 8 Scorpio 59 to 15 Sagittarius 23, a distance of 36½ degrees, she was almost thirty-seven years old. At the same time tr. Saturn was opposed her Moon-Pluto conjunction and then opposed her Mercury. It was a powerful hot/cold time for her development in relationships.

At mention of that time, Gayle shone with bittersweet recall. There had been a powerful, unforgettable, brief relationship, which had been unsuccessful and short-lived.

"Why did it fail, Gayle?"

"Fear . . . . I was afraid. He was willing, but I was afraid."

"What was the worst part of that fear?"

"I was . . . as you say . . . I was not lovable, *who* would want *me*?"

It is so clear that the focus question we used earlier had exposed "insecurity," which is the Moon, in the Pluto conjunction. The astrologer can immediately see the connection between Gayle's not feeling lovable herself *and the competition the mother had with Gayle for the father's (a man's) attention*. Gayle generalized this suppression of her emotions to not allowing herself to relate to *any* man, except through her aesthetic fantasy world. (At one point she had said, "I have a resistance to drawing people." But not in those private pictures? "Right.")

That relationship failure did it! Since then, Gayle could not continue with the fear. Even the Sun=Venus and Mars=Venus arcs went by four years later with no knock on any door.

There we were together, facing an extraordinary opportunity: SA Sun=Uranus 10/99 with tr. Pluto conjunct Saturn. Here was time for "an independent, even revolutionary spirit; being oneself and getting away with it" and the fall away, the destruction of the values barrier set up by all her conditioning (Saturn rules the 8th, other's values, etc.; Pluto coming out of the conjunction with the Moon, ruler of her 2nd). Here was the time toward which Gayle could build with confidence, for a new image, a gradually developed new freedom, relating her creativity to people and gaining their appreciation for her art.

Gayle felt extremely empowered by our consultation. She stated her plan to leave her therapy very soon and draw her own future to her.

---

60 In Solar Arc terminology, "=" means conjunction, square, or opposition (semisquare, sesquiquadrate); and angular references are key to the Ascendant and the Midheaven, so as not to introduce other planetary aspect references. In this case it is clear that SA Venus on the 7th cusp "equals" the Ascendant (opposes), at age 37.

Essential Techniques

Disclosure and Objectification

We must remember that planets do not do things. People do. Understanding a planet does not reveal a fact; understanding a planet gives us a direction, a direction to follow to appreciate an individual's reality. Disclosure brings individualized substance to the planetary principle.

Society conditions us to be anxious about self-disclosure. Very quickly in life, we learn to hold back what we feel and who we are because of our fear of disapproval or rejection by others, by the outer environment. On the other hand, self-disclosure is the essential springboard toward giving love and establishing intimacy; it is what normally makes relationships exciting, makes them close. The bottom line then is that we have to take chances with showing who we are for the reward of relationship. Otherwise, we face ever-increasing self-protection and isolation, the concomitants of depression (see page 39). *Giving love* is as important to good mental health as is receiving love.

Sidney Jourard asks if we can assume that people come to need help because they have not disclosed themselves in some optimum degree to the people in their lives![61] There is a definite correlation between what persons are willing to disclose to other people in their life and what these other people disclose to them. Ideally, there is a reciprocity in self-disclosure.

Self-disclosure seems easier for people with an Aries Point configuration with a planet or Angle. For example, my Ascendant at 00 Cancer 04 suggests that I will deal openly with emotions; they will be pushed forward in my life. I can not count the number of times I have said, "I get paid to show my emotions." I felt this not just as an astrologer but, as well, during my twenty-year career as an opera singer. For the longest time, I felt it practically incomprehensible that someone could *not* be expressive, especially if I were ready to listen or if I needed to hear such emotion. I had a marvelous relationship between marriages wherein the wonderful lady told me once, only half in humor, "You don't really love me, you love the thought, the act of loving!" That says it too.

Now—right here in that last sentence—I have judiciously *disclosed* something about me. I have already done that two times earlier in this book to make a point, and I feel confident that you reacted to it both times: first when I talked about the "insecurity" experience with my friend John (page 28) and then again, very subtly when I mentioned

---

61 Jourard, 29, 13.

that the 12th House was always difficult for me (page 51). I showed myself to be vulnerable, specifically vulnerable. You feel that I trust you with that information. Through disclosure, we get closer together. We can identify with the same problems. We are more alike. I am accessible to you.

With Gayle's horoscope, *I knew* that there was AP=Neptune/Pluto, I knew she would come forward (Aries Point) with reference to something private, esoteric, strange, occult, different, parapsychological, etc., and she did. *No one had ever asked her before!* And THAT was why such a schism was being built in her life leading her toward isolation, a swirl of behaviors clustering around the painful competitive mother syndrome, which worked throughout her life to keep relationships at bay because she was not allowed to relate to her father; and this led to her feelings that she was not lovable in return. Fascinating, isn't it?

Ross Perot has AP=the enthusiastic Sun/Jupiter midpoint. Liberace had the charismatic relationship of Mars-Neptune precisely at the Aries Point (AP=Mars/ Neptune). Stunt daredevil legend Evel Knievel has AP=Moon/Uranus and Pluto/MC. Arnold Schwarzenegger has his powerful (and prosperous and resourceful) Jupiter-Pluto midpoint configured with the Aries Point. George Bush has AP=the popular, congenial Venus/Jupiter midpoint. Rationalist philosopher Rene Descartes had AP=Mercury/Saturn!

The creative astrologer should explore the potential of the Aries Point configuration as being *a way out from within*, especially in cases where there are swirling blocks of hidden emotions, clots of distortion that are defined throughout years of defensive overcompensatory actions against difficult, demeaning developments in the early homelife.

The rewards of self-disclosure are increased self-knowledge, closer intimate relationships, improved communication, lighter (fewer) guilt feelings, and more energy (since defensive, repressive controls are relaxed and energies are freed up to do other things).[62]

The consultation *allows* and should *encourage* clients to talk freely about themselves, reaching for insight with the astrologer. If initially it is difficult, disclosure can be prompted by *the astrologer judiciously disclosing first*. Very often, the client expects some kind of censure from the "all-seeing" or "mysterious" astrologer, from the horoscope he does not know anything about. When that threat does not materialize, when the astrologer's responses are non-conventional, fresh, selfless, when the astrologer is

---

62 McKay, Davis, Fanning, chapter 2.

opening up to the client, the client then *wants* to disclose as well, *wants* to share in trust, wants to lift the weight off his or her feelings.

But when disclosure continues to be difficult to one degree or another, it may be reflected by the symbolisms of the 12th and 8th Houses. Anytime the Sun or the Moon is in either of these Houses, there is most often a line drawn, a curtain pulled, a one-step-removed stance adopted by the personality, especially when it is under pressure. A line of defense is at the ready. (Interestingly, the woman who talked to me about my being in love with loving, was actually drawing a line, wasn't she? This wonderful lady had the Sun in Sagittarius and the Moon in Leo, but the Sun was in the 12th and the Moon was in the 8th!)

Or, as in the case of Jonah (page 46) the 12th and 8th Houses are indicated obliquely: the Sun, ruler of the 12th, squared by Saturn (and the Sun in Pisces); Neptune, ruler of the 8th, square Uranus.

Remember, Jonah said, "Every time I get near somebody, I let down my defenses and I get my heart ripped out." He also told me "Everything I do is to keep away from my hope." (Here is the Jupiter tension within the hope/idealism figure, i.e., quindecile Mercury and Venus). Additionally, Jonah has the Aries Point=Neptune/Pluto, as Gayle does. I asked him about the paranormal, etc., and he replied, "Oh yes. I hear and see people. Their minds. I can tell if people are sick, passing on . . . ," All of these glimpses profiled Jonah's growing isolationism and incipient depression.

And finally, it appears that placement of Pluto in the 8th House suggests a very, very strong need *to benefit from disclosure*, usually through psychotherapy or deep self-study of some kind—including astrology, of course. Determination of the value perspective of one's own needs (2nd House) is accomplished best in recognition and awareness of the needs and values of others (the opposite 8th House).

Disclosure brings out hidden emotions, distorted emotions, "emotional facts," formative source events, and value judgments that so often precipitate trigger-fast recall of the past.

Think of the culturally obvious masculine image of impassiveness, not just in America, but in the Netherlands, Germany, and South Africa (German and Dutch inheritance), particularly. The man who shows little emotion is the strong man, the provider who has prevailed through thick and thin. These men are proud, stoic, guarded, prepared to defend themselves to the death. And the family must be content with that—"After all, I pay the bills, I keep us alive!" *His* father was that way, and you should have seen the grandfather! And unfortunately now, look what the absence of sharing, of disclosing inner feelings causes for the future, the father's being taken out of the children's life early on, one way or another, being there but passive, stoic, or so tyrannical, any combination of these, so as never to have shared the guidance of authoritative love. How is this being passed on? *How can we objectify this for our client and gain some distance from that situation?*

The opportunities for the astrologer to disclose her- or himself, to set an example, to invite a bond of trust should be explored judiciously. The consultation belongs to the client, not to the astrologer, who can all too easily find herself/himself talking at length about some personal point that takes the moment far away from the client's benefit. (When this happens, the astrologer has lost the client. Trust and rapport are not easily retrieved.)

A simple statement like, "I went through a similar experience long ago and far away! (By emphasizing distance, we are saying, "I've outgrown it" or "It does not affect me anymore.") My father was entirely out of the picture. What *did* happen in your relationship with *yours*?" Just enough disclosure is offered to help your client not feel alone, to begin a closer level of relationship with him or her.

As the creative astrologer links islands of disclosure, guided by the configurations in the horoscope, a developmental picture is created. It is there, over there, out there, it's up in the air, it's on the desk. You and your client can talk about it *objectively*.

You can point out that the parents had their own problems in life and with each other and that, "*It's fair to say* you got caught in the traffic pattern." Such a simple statement, but so effective! Objectification is established, a traffic pattern back then, and the client got caught up in it, but "*has indeed escaped, relatively unhurt.* Eh?" That's a fair statement to all concerned. The distance established even invites *compassion for the parental situation*: from "Boy, they were a real mess," or "You know?, when I worked that out for myself, it was beautiful; I was able to be with them at Christmas and actually not be affected by their stuff anymore!"

The Grave Farewell

The ultimate objectification process is the farewell, the cessation of relationship, acknowledged in death. Very often a parent, sibling, or spouse who has become a repository of problematic memory will have died *before* things are settled. This leaves the client *with a permanent tie to the problem cluster and time period,* to the memories and feelings. Some break must be made to allow freedom.

I have lost count of how many times I have helped expedite such a break this way:

Well, we've discussed this situation thoroughly, and I think we both agree that we understand it. It's too bad this kind of understanding didn't come up long ago, but that's the way it is. Now, there is something that can still be done though, and I think you know what it is.

This statement puts astrologer and client together in understanding, resignation, and finality, except for one more "something." The final phrase really involves the client, and, with his mind racing to tell him the answer, he will often anticipate what you are going to suggest.

Where is your father buried?

Now, if the father (or mother, etc.) is buried in the city where your client lives, there is no problem. If the father is buried in a nearby city, getting there should not be difficult. If the city is far, far away and the client can never get there, a church or synagogue can substitute. The point is *to formalize* the visit solemnly.

> *I want to suggest* [leaning forward intently] *that for four days, at the same time every day—tell me a time when you are alone, safe from interruption, for say ten minutes. OK, at that same time, privately, every day for four days, please sit down in complete concentration—take the phone off the hook, put your pet away, arrange silence, set a timer for ten minutes, reviewing what we talked about today, what pains you are preparing to leave behind, what compassion you now have for your father's situation, the appreciation you have for his having done his best.*

> *After four days of this wise meditation, I want you to go to your father's grave . . . alone . . . and I want you to say farewell to him. Say good-bye; thank you; good-bye. Feel this deeply, throughout your entire being . . . . Then leave the grave, and return to your life, a freer life, a life of importance to your own family and your own future! And please, call me up; tell me* **it is done.**

This is closure based first upon objectification and second on will. The will is alerted to a projection of purpose: *this is clearly the way I can be free.* This is of real value to me and my family, and indeed to my future development. *To do other than separate myself from this, from the routine I have been living in, now that I understand it, would suggest that I don't want to change!*

Maybe the client needs to understand more deeply than the astrologer can facilitate. Maybe more protracted therapy is needed, and the astrologer should be prepared to make a referral to a psychotherapist or two nearby.

But remember, maybe the negative behavior pattern is dynamically *more important*—even though the tie with the parent, for example, is severed—than adopting *new* behaviors (recall the Radical Probe discussion, page 79). For example, staying grossly overweight—while clearly linked to the insecurity problems engendered, say, in the mother relationship early on and routined in overeating for years thereafter—is still important because it works against relationship just fine and prevents intimate sharing. For example, the disclosure might reveal morbid fears that have developed about having a child who might be birth-impaired the way the neighbor's child was, the neighbor who was mother's best friend and who was constantly criticized by mother. (The criticism then would flood down onto the daughter.) Getting at such hidden feelings and sensibilities might then expedite objectification.

Normally, the closure at the grave is an excellent help for the client, with the four days of ritual meditation being key to building the importance of the event.

It is helpful to note that Assagioli's well-developed work with suggestive techniques in his awakening and manipulation of will[63] is so very close to hypnotism as therapy. The client is brought into a relaxed state and suggestions are made with many different word devices used to plant the seeds of change. One factor must remain clear within all our work and that is, as in hypnotism, no person can/will do that which they are not predisposed to doing. The self-help dimension we explore in astrology, just as in psychoanalysis, is conditioned upon the core desire of the client to change, to develop, to get on with life differently, more efficiently, more fulfillingly.

Many, many times, I have had clients comment that I give them "a hypnotic feeling." I *have* studied hypnotherapy, and those techniques do sneak into my voice and turns of phrase, but what is really being said here by these clients is not that I am using hypnosis, but, rather, *that I am keeping my client's attention, I am forcing focus,* I am offering (most of the time, I hope) a sense of empowerment. I think this means that they retain significantly the content of our consultation together.

Very often when the client is ready for change from the routine of underachievement (or what have you), *the astrological parallel measurement, the background that would support that change, is lacking.* I have often found that, even with the best intentions, anticipation of change is futile or inoperative or incomplete *unless* it can be tied to a measurement in the near future.

In the cases we have studied so far, I have shown *the imminent measurements to which we could tie the energies of the consultation.* Those measurements are usually an Arc or the SP Moon conjoining or squaring an Angle, the Arc of an Angle into strong planetary contact within the natal configuration, a transit of Saturn, Uranus, or Pluto to an Angle, a strong Arc or transit to the Sun or the Moon (except for Neptune). There is

63 Assagioli, *Psychosynthesis*, chapter 4.

the very important accumulated Solar Arc semi-square (as we saw in Henry's case). With any such Arc, there will almost *always be a strong transit to trigger development specific to the month.*

I have found that when people seek me out for appointments, the pressure is on in their life. I do not attract the simply curious any more. One can see the developmental tension immediately, tied to the moment just past, transpiring, or building. When I am in some other location lecturing, appointments are made with me because I happen to be there; it is an opportunity rather than an elected strategy, and I have found that the horoscopes are usually more difficult to tie to imminent dateline energies. This should be an observation relevant to your practice as well.

Time-Target Technique

We all know about New Year's resolutions. Why are they so popular? The significance is that *the specific date reference ties motivation to probability:* I set a date for it and *that means it is going to happen.*

Now, indeed, many people set dates for things and then ignore them. How many repair people come to your home an hour or two late, a day late for contracted repairs? How many builders come in over budget and beyond deadline? Many resolutions are forgotten by the second week of January. There are people who make a lifestyle out of making promises, projecting completion times, and failing to meet them: the specific projection makes them feel important; the failure is always someone else's fault, and the process repeats.

But then again, there are people who do stay on time with projections, who *do* make things happen in finest Capricorn fashion. The sense of Saturn as symbol for *necessary* controls is a very real manifestation of a sense of responsibility, feeling good (significant) about having to answer for something. The point is that *assigning time to change* can be a very helpful technique in client service. Time somehow promises change, triggers motivation, ensures results.

For example, a female client (at fifty) was totally distraught. Her longtime significant other had suddenly ended their relationship. He had broken the news through a long-distance communication—there had been no face-to-face discussion to ameliorate the shock. It had been done impersonally and, for her, traumatically. It was over.

The extremely intelligent, poised lady was hit hard. The month was mid-April. Her anguish was unending, and it disrupted her efficiency, her confidence, and her ability to see ahead.

The planets may have paralleled this disruption in her life—but the configuration was nowhere near as dramatic as would normally be shown, at least in *her* horoscope (perhaps his)—but how could the planets be expected to rescue her? The only thing that would rescue the feelings of this strong, sharp woman—beaten and demoralized—would be her own mind, her perception of herself in life at that time, her seeing a road to travel into the future.

Societies everywhere, in the face of death (the end of a relationship is a death as well), culturally prescribe mourning times. These times have evolved as the perfect way to allow time in which to lament loss and then to establish a cut-off date when the pain is supposed to cease. In self-help books and in formal therapies, this mourning period is the time period during which one prepares and plans to "let go."

Key to assuaging any suffering is, first of all, *to allow time for the suffering to exist.* Give yourself or someone else permission to grieve. But then, there must be a time set, ahead of time, for the suffering in the main to be over. Every transition begins with an ending.[64]

I said—and I made quite a production of this for maximum impact—"Annie, this is simply terrible. I commiserate completely, and I want to be here for you any time you want to go over it. But I have an idea that will help you a bit later, after about two months of really feeling and working in and out of this pain.

"I think it is important to set a date when this pain will basically be over. Sure, it's a time of letting go—easier said than done, right now, of course—but we can set a clear cut-off date. Beyond that date, *it's got to be a new you.*"

Annie was listening intently, but there still were nervous intrusions of the painful thoughts she was feeling.

"I suggest . . . how about . . . the 4th of July—INDEPENDENCE DAY—as the cut-off date for all this. July 4. July 4. That's the end of this pain. July 4, and I'll help to see you through it."

Of course, the date being Independence Day was niftily fortuitous for a broken relationship, but there are lots of devices to use when such a remedial challenge presents itself. (When you think about employing this helpful technique, you will delight yourself with your own creativity within the circumstance that presents itself.) I saw Annie several times in the intervening period, all times of tremendous pain for her. But she indeed was back on her track after July 4.

Setting a time target can be linked with behavioral modification (rewarding oneself significantly for maintaining a new way of doing things; a great bottle of wine on

---

64 See Bridges, chapter 1.

every Saturday, *only* after I have actually spent quality time every day of the week with my son).

I have helped many men stop smoking by telling them in all seriousness (without a shred of formal evidence from the Sorbonne, but based upon known research data) that, "You know? There is an extra bonus you will get from this effort to change, to stop smoking. There is very strong research data from the Sorbonne (sounds impressive, authoritative) that says, when men stop smoking, within two weeks—at two weeks (time to get the abstinence program past the torture time)—their vascular system allows more responsive, stronger erectile capability and better sexual performance."

Self-Talk

I easily recall many times when I have been terribly upset about something, been far away from the target of my upset, and decided to write the "mother of all letters" to that person to make my position known. What I was doing, of course, was venting my anger, getting out *my* emotional truth in furiously typed prose, on and on and on. When I was finished, I was too embarrassed by the excessive emotionalism in the letter actually to reread it—and it was usually interminable—and of course I could never, ever send it off. But the fact remained that somehow I was free of the tightened emotions, the block, the upset, the raging upset I had felt earlier.

What if I had not written the letter? How would all these feelings have come out? Upon whom would I dump the pent-up tensions? What would the tensions have done inside me?

These days, so much reckless venting takes place in response to e-mails: responses are not re-read, edited carefully, or even held in the hangar for a day or so, but are sent instantly in a knee-jerk reaction-fit with the press of a button, and the result becomes temperamental, awkward, painful, history. The dumping releases tension, but hurts someone somewhere else.

To get something off ("out of" might be a better adverb) one's chest is very, very important and helpful; just getting it out, not driving it home.

Journal writing is a well-known therapy. So is writing yourself a letter, or writing someone else a letter that is never to be sent. What comes out of the "chest" is most significant. Very often the streams of sentences are cries for recognition, affection, help; they reveal misunderstandings that trigger swirls of hidden and/or distorted feelings, BUT, since that is all brought out of one's Self, it *is* objectified, *it can now be viewed differently, more efficiently*. We can read it sensibly, objectively, and see how to help ourselves. I have recommended this to many clients about certain points we have discussed, and we have learned more later when reading the letters together. Original pain so often dissipates in objective humor. Try it!

Just this morning, writing these pages, having been at it for four hours, since 5:00 A.M., I got a telephone call from the bank that there was a problem that required my immediate attention. I was so wrapped up in my writing that I resented deeply being torn away from my work.

I left home to go to the bank and solve the problem, and en route I stopped by to leave some things with a printer to have completed overnight. Standing at the printer's desk, I had to wait for a young man to complete his business with an interminably slow clerk, before I could do my business.

Meanwhile, my mind was racing with ideas relating to this book. I was building up an intolerance of the situation of waiting, which was all too tied to my Moon in Leo. I decided to give myself some therapeutic instructions; I silently talked to myself: "This fellow can't help his fumbling around. I *do not* need to get out of joint because I'm being held up a minute or two. If you asked my daughter what her Daddy can't stand most, she will tell you 'standing in line.' And here I am! Stay composed. Don't fidget. Don't show displeasure. Don't be so selfish. None of that will help anything. This situation doesn't have to prove how important you are. You know that. Patience is part of being a Capricorn, isn't it? You can't expect everyone else to clear out of the way when they see you coming!"

Those were my thoughts. That Self-Talk therapy made me a patient customer, not only at the printer's office but later at the bank, where I could easily have been ballistic! I performed more efficiently; I was pleased with myself.

Now, what if I were someone working out a deeper problem in life rather than the fleeting egotism of a fire-sign Moon; what if I were an alcoholic trying to recover, someone on the third day of stopping drinking? What if the frustration and tensions suddenly had triggered again the need to drink, to calm myself, to escape, to hide the fragile ego fears? The plan would have been hatched to leave the printer's and go to the bank as quickly as possible and then to go to the store to get a gallon of wine, knowing I would return home, darken the bedroom, go to bed, start drinking and forget the world until, maybe, tomorrow. Such a little thing as being pulled from work (away from the preoccupation that was diverting me, say, in my recovery tension) and waiting in line under the bank tension yet to come could have caused someone *a relapse to any previously routined dysfunctional behavior pattern*. (Notice how defense against deep pain would have overwhelmed the involvement in work for the future, i.e., the breakdown of progress in life.)

The creative astrologer can help the client en route to changing behavioral patterns or negative emotional focus by *creating during the consultation (or having it prepared ahead of time) a powerful subtext for the client to learn and use (a kind of therapeutic mantra) when pressure mounts up in everyday life situations.* Something like, "There it is: that need to hide in wine. I do NOT need to do that anymore. I UNDERSTAND why that feeling is there and I hate it. Oh God, help me help myself! NOW. NOW. I am defeating this. I AM VICTORIOUS. I want the best for these people around me. They want the best for me. I am going to be patient and so proud, so proud, so PROUD to go home and continue with my wonderful work. Exhale, exhale, get it out and live."

Or "I simply do not *need* to scream at or hit or punish my child in any way now; this is just a normal, natural five-year-old thing that he or she has done; my parents wouldn't have understood it, but I DO," can be so helpful.

McKay and Fanning take this technique into the consultation proper. They call it "Cognitive Restructuring for Self-Esteem."[65] They ask the client what he or she was thinking of, saying, during an episode when the client felt worthless, indulging in self-reproach. When whatever that was is established, they introduce the identification of that "voice" as that of the "arch critic," the shark, the bully, or they give it the name of the mother or father (the original source), for example. The point is the voice *is identified* so that whenever it speaks up again, *it can be identified as NOT belonging to the client.* Distance is achieved.

Then, with logic, now that the critic's voice is out in the open, you can establish another voice, the "healthy voice." This voice personifies your client's ability to think realistically, the common-sense foil to the critic. This is the source of the rational, the compassionate, the caring. "By creating this dichotomy between the critical voice and healthy voice, you can encourage the client to confront his or her critic."

The next task (or perhaps this has already been ascertained in the consultation) is to identify the critic's voice, *where* it comes from, *how* it was formed, what purpose it continues to serve, etc. A few artful question will establish this, corroborating the guidelines dramatically presented by the horoscope. Just think how valuable the self-help of Self-Talk can be!

The Consultation Process

When the creative astrologer understands, practices, and explores these techniques, they fit easily into a smooth consultation process. The client is empowered in terms of

---

65 McKay and Fanning, 8–9.

the astrological guidelines, e.g., anger is controlled better than before through Self-Talk, it is understood better in terms of its formation because of the results of the radical probe or assumptive questioning, and a dateline can be set for adjustments in present behaviors, all linked to change ahead. The client has a meaningful development schedule when she or he leaves the consultation.

A very important point here is that astrology and astrologer are not curing anything. The creative astrologer is using astrology and helpful humanistically sensitive techniques to release client energies that have been tied up within overcompensatory defensive structures of behavior—the Grand Trine is another reliable example of a major defensive construct (see page 13). Objectification leads the way to understanding, to changing the shape of problems, altering the balance of their importance. Astrology and astrologer help the client to improve the quality of effort in life.

Moshe Talmon's research in SST therapy includes a fascinating test report: forty-four patients who were seen for initial consultation but never received treatment (in psychotherapeutic terms) actually *improved*, according to introspective tests given to the patients. Some force or set of forces helped them. The inference is that somehow single session therapy (or anticipating SST) awakens the following list of nine different therapeutic mechanisms; and *so does the astrology consultation*:[66]

- Insight

- The capacity for self-analysis

- Working through feelings with the people involved

- Normal maturation and growth

- Therapeutic relationships, especially marriage

- Taking responsibility for their own lives

- Breaking the vicious cycle between the patient and his or her environment

- Genuine reassurance

- Direct learning

---

66 Talmon, 65.

The conclusion is quite simply that we should never underestimate clients' capacity to change, to use their minds to that direction. Again: planets are not doing anything; people are. The planets are guides for us all, and they are witnesses to people helping themselves.

The Thinking Astrologer

In his book *Focusing*, in the opening chapter titled "The Inner Act," psychology professor Eugene Gendlin reports the findings gathered over fifteen years by a group at the University of Chicago: "We have been studying some questions that most psychotherapists don't like to ask out loud. Why doesn't therapy succeed more often? Why does it so often fail to make a real difference in people's lives? In the rarer cases when it does succeed, what is it that those patients and therapists do? What is it that the majority *fail* to do?"

Gendlin and his group studied many forms and techniques of therapy, from classical approaches to recently developed ones, and, as well, thousands of therapist-patient sessions recorded on tape. Their studies gave up results that were "very different from what we and most other professional therapists expected."

First, they found that a crucial difference was *not* the therapist's specific method or technique, nor was it what was talked about in the consultation, but in *"how* they talk." This was *an outward sign of the real difference*, which is "what the successful patients do inside themselves."[67]

Indeed, this study relates closely to the nine points presented by Talmon (page 98) and to the classic George Mora study (please recall and memorize the finding earlier, page 17) highlighting the personality of the therapist as key.

Another major discovery by the Gendlin group was that "the process of actually changing feels good . . . . The change process we have discovered is natural to the body, and it feels that way in the body. The crucial [therapeutic] move goes beneath the usual places where we are afraid and where we experience personal areas of ourselves as painful."

We begin to see how powerful the tool of astrology is in guiding our thoughts and our work with clients *to get to where it may hurt*, to get inside and beneath difficulties that may be there, to locate and objectify the swirl of emotions and distortion of feelings that may be tied to some occurrence(s) in the past. Astrology also gives us

---

67 Gendlin, 3–11.

uncannily well-defined time references, past and future, to test personality responsiveness and to guide strategy, to spot developmental tension focusing in particular zones of developmental experience. Astrology can help any client who is eager to do so, to adjust any routined expression of personality development to get to a state of greater efficiency.

Astrology quickly and reliably identifies the needs and the presses upon them that propel development. The astrologer brings that plan to the reality disclosed by the client. Together, astrologer and client achieve insight, rebalance judgment and values, and affect change. And it feels good.

Presentation Skills

How astrology does this is not found simply in some magical arrangement of planetary symbols, but in how *the astrologer relates these planetary guides to the reality of the client,* how we talk the scene. Developmental considerations as yet unknown to astrological symbolism must be ascertained—sociological matrix (gender, race, family income, regional influences, cultural lineage, education, religion), appearance, height and weight, the sound of the voice, inherited disease, injury, accident and more—and assimilated into the archetypal astrological delineations.

For example, how does my appearance before you in your office affect the preparation of my horoscope that you have done before seeing me? I'm six feet, ten inches tall, and weigh 270 pounds.

For example, how does the sound of my voice (trained for twenty-five years in the opera world) affect your inference of how I traffic with communication in my world; after all, my Moon in Leo is in the 3rd House? What if I were using two canes (I'm not, yet) to support severe joint difficulties? It would not be enough for your mind to say, "Aha! He's a Capricorn, and Saturn is opposed by Neptune, and THAT's his knee problem"; rather, you would better extend that thought to how has he managed that problem in the light of his prominence and his vanity (Moon opposed Venus, Jupiter conjunct Sun); has there been a breakdown from "leaderissimo" self-sufficiency in the past (Moon in Leo); does the condition make him feel less effective (appear older), his facility to keep the exchange of resources in relationships active and interesting (less attractive?), etc.?

In short, how might a physical problem have affected the client's development at that time of life? How does this introduce concerns about the aging process?

The creative astrologer must be very, very alert, ever perceptive, to bring our astrology symbols literally to life. We can not allow old teaching and narrow rules to confine our art. When we do look around, we do see a lot. Through astrologers, astrology must continually come of age.

Knowing that the astrologer is key to the process of helping others to help themselves, we should inspect what the astrologer (and any therapist) uses to be effective. There are three things in the main: *appearance, knowledge*, and *communication skill*. Within these three, we have subdivisions of image, authority, and voice; caring nature (empathy), sincerity, and persuasion. This could be broken down to many levels, of course, but the point is made: to be optimally effective we have to inspect our appearance, our knowledge, and our communication skill very, very objectively.

What about you is most attractive? How do you present that?

What in your work area shows your learning and experience to the newly arrived client? How are your books displayed, for example?

What shows your sense and practice of organization and order? What is the impression your client gets of your work area?

What do your word choice and grammar suggest about your intelligence, upbringing, and education?

What discloses a bit about you, *your* personality, your pleasures, your indulgences? (Pictures, art. Antiques, trophies, etc., so the client can get to know you a bit indirectly; start to close any distance between you.)

How does your voice sound (listen to a tape or two)? What are the *delays* and self-protection devices in your speech that you may be inflicting upon the consultation session? What are the speech "fillers" that easily manifest as insecurity when you search for words? I recall a businessman who would say "and all that garbage" when he meant "et cetera" or "and so forth." He was insecure about his grasp of his subject; he demeaned the details he did not understand and certainly did not want brought up. It was the signal of why he eventually lost his job.

How fast do you speak (speed suggests agitation, an aroused nervous system; performance rather than sharing)? How slowly (slowness suggests confusion or deliberation or remoteness)? How loudly, how softly, how clearly?

You do *not* use jargon, do you? I submit that any "astrological talk" the astrologer uses *is a defensive ploy* by the astrologer; it means nothing to the client; it is substituting inaccessibly arcane mumbo jumbo for practical information, in order to establish authority. Take out the jargon, which does absolutely no good whatsoever in the consultation, and *discover the time then opened up in which to say something important!*

One of the great lacks in the profiling of astrology as a profession is its lack of educative guidance and accreditation. All astrology organizations are trying to help with this in one way or another—as I am with my Master's Degree Correspondence Course for Certification—through teaching, testing, and challenge, and reward reinforcement. The weakest area by far for astrologers is the training in consultation techniques.

In my work with astrologers, I hear three weaknesses almost always in the first tapes of their consultations: first, even when the astrologers (who are indeed quite advanced at this point, accustomed to high-pressure challenge from me) can show the most comprehensive and clearly on-target preparation work ahead of time, they show fear—and thus a delay—*in getting to the core of discussion*, getting to a major point within the first minute or two of the consultation. The introductions into the consultation are often interminable, sometimes twenty minutes in length. Astrologer and client jockey about for comfort. Each is insecure, and neither offers the other an organized space. The astrologers are deficient in establishing intelligence, authority, organization, and purpose, neatly and smoothly.

A very important guideline here is: *Know what's important.* Anything we say that is simply generally descriptive without going somewhere significant in terms of development *is a waste of language and time* in the consultation.

Second, the sentences the students use tend to be loose, word choice tends to be vague where it could be keen, and speech fillers intrude, including *uhs* (sometimes ten times a minute!) and nervous laughter; and, amazingly, there can even be background distractions or interruptions, a dog or a cat, or radio or CD music!

Imagine how *you* would react (feel) if you were pressed in your development and you sought out someone for disclosure, discussion, and insight and you met up with these conditions and you were paying for it as well? What conditions would you like to have? *Make sure you establish them.*

Three, the astrologers seem embarrassed to deal with deep issues, i.e., disclosure, face to face, which says a bit about the astrologer's own poise with deep issues. Are you informed and balanced enough in your objectivity to put your own pressing personal developmental problems aside to talk meaningfully with your clients about theirs? What if you must listen to and deal with sexual issues? What about a man or woman who discloses that he or she was abused as a child? Can you discuss the resiliency adults can have out of such difficulties? *To what degree have you set out to learn about such specialized issues?*[68] What is your reading and study program monthly for the next six months? Think how much you will know and be able to share THEN! Just think about that!

---

68 For example: to start, set aside two hours; go to a large medical offices building; go into different specialists' offices and pick up the informative fliers and brochures that are openly offered on the waiting room tables; walk out, go home, and study. Keep the literature on file. Think of what you will learn, what further learning there is.

What is of great credit to the students and the way these issues are managed, though, is that *they are able to correct these situations with the next, the next, and then the next tape*; amazingly so, as night turns into day! The tape objectifies what we have too long taken for granted. We hear what we did not know was there. We are having a consultation with ourselves! The guidelines to make such repairs and to grow have structured this book. They work.

And then, there is perfection. One astrologer, "D.S.", normally working in a foreign language (for which I have special accommodations for training in the Course), worked very hard to send me a tape of a consultation done in English. It was such perfection, I could not believe it! The word choice, the changes of vocal color, the pacing, the patience . . . all were as beautifully managed as I have ever heard, and the consultation was an enormous success. Why?

Part of the reason—beyond her exquisite analytical talent—is that in the foreign language (English) she was choosing her words with care, enunciating them cleanly; and also in the foreign language, she was able to address emotional content without the words frightening her, i.e., the emotional value of the words was not as fully developed as the word values would be when translated into her native language.

This tells us that we must give especially attentive care to our speech and our word choice (which we so easily take for granted) in the consultation. We must edit our speech as we edit our written text. For example, listen carefully to people talking around you today and tomorrow, or to newscasters on television (some are absolutely deplorable in their sloppiness, and you do *feel* this when you are alert; their speech is a major factor in their performance and the image they create and are paid for): listen for the "g" in the participle ending of verbs and in certain noun plurals. If the "g" is there you have one impression of the person's intelligence, and if it is not there—if it is dropped in sloppy (often regionally conditioned) speech—you have a different impression. Listen for the unfulfilled "you," and as well, out-and-out bad grammar, "This means a lot to Bill and I." (To I?? You probably wouldn't write that. Always use the accusative case as object of any preposition: to, for, with, through, by, at, on, under, over, after, outside, inside *me, him, her, us, you, them*.)

"Listen carefully to the people talkin' roun' you."

"How ya feelin'?"

"I was gonna tell ya" or "I was going to tell you."

"You know about this better than me" is wrong. It is ". . . better than I (do)."

And then there is the incredible: "Me and you are going to have a good discussion" [*You and I* . . . of course] or "can't hardly" (double negative; *can hardly*) or ". . . care less . . ." (it's "could not care less").

This is not snobbism; being this alert to something so important simply is being aware, intelligent, and efficient. Improving word choice and sentence structure increases efficiency and improves image enormously, especially when you are talking about swirls of emotion in and development of a person's life, inviting disclosure and trust, forming creative reflections for growth, and charging for it.

Attentiveness to this communication dimension of language actually arms the astrologer against sloppy *thinking*, because it requires the astrologer to be maximally alert for an hour or so, at her highest awareness; it helps us to "dress up" and do our very best for the client.

The demand to concentrate, to listen creatively, to speak cleanly, simply, and memorably requires hard work. That's what tires the busy astrologer, the busy therapist. Our responsibility can not be taken casually. We must build interpretation muscles and consciousness stamina. Seeking out insight, bringing insight into being, is much more demanding than talking about last Sunday's ball game.

And finally, we are going to see vividly in the next chapter how language is the key to persuasion, to triggering the desire for autonomous change within the client.

On Creativity

Too many astrologers begin the study of astrology thinking that a book full of rules is going to give them a hold on the description of life. The shock comes quickly in this day of heightened individualism and enormous social mobility: it does not work that way. The fourth House does *not* mean the mother exclusively any more; the 10th House does not mean the father exclusively any more. A hundred years ago, the horoscope reflected the times then, the times when women did not have jobs outside the home, when boys almost always followed in their father's footsteps professionally, and the 4th and 10th Houses respectively showed a great deal of that. In our times now, none of that is important; *other* considerations in that axis are.

We must be prepared to break the rules! The consultation expects us to be spontaneous and improvisational, reacting and responding in the moment to whatever is happening, as the client and we bring the horoscope to life.

I feel that the astrologer must be enriched somehow by every consultation experience; it is in this way that the astrologer grows in learning and effectiveness, and freshness. The stimulating therapist, teacher, and writer Jeffrey Kottler feels that *personal growth and creativity* are synonymous in the life of a therapist.[69]

---

69 Kottler, chapter 9.

Even today, after some thirty-four years experience, I have periods of insecurity about certain clients I am scheduled to see (further disclosure at work here). I can not easily get a grip on certain configurations ahead of time; the scenario of development eludes me a bit here and there. But this anxiety perks me up; it reminds me to be maximally alert. Perhaps it is the fifth person I am seeing on that day, and I am tired of concentrating for so many hours, basically immobile in a hotel room in Zagreb, Jerusalem, Johannesburg, or in my office at home. I restudy my preparation, I look around and into my client over and over and over again, listening to every word, listening between the lines, watching every eye movement, body movement; I enunciate as clearly as I can to make myself clear; I realize I must cut to the quick, simply and directly, especially when using an interpreter, which consumes half the time of the consultation! And I know that, with my experience and concentration, more often than not, THE INSIGHT WILL FORM.

Kottler suggests that risk and fear are also synonymous, and every counselor must face them both. We can take risks and face up to fear, and this exercise of our faculties *allows us to be more creative*. We can "tinker" with the assumptions of our astrological guidelines ("This Nodal axis discovery, about the mother—it certainly could apply to *any* pervasive feminine influence in the early home, couldn't it?"), and instantly the mind can be flooded with scenarios based on new hypotheses. It takes practice to allow that to happen, but results come quickly.

We can make it a habit to look beyond the obvious; to play astro-detective. For example, yesterday afternoon, I had a telephone appointment with a regular businessman client, a man of flourishing life development. Much was brewing for him immediately ahead in the Spring of 1999: the measurements clustered around the Uranus transit of his fourth cusp, the Saturn transit of the seventh cusp, the SP Moon square his MC, and more, all within a month of each other. Marvelous energy focus. (Major developments in life seem, noticeably often, to depend on Angular and/or dramatic Sun-Moon activity.)

Things were right on track with regard to his own company's new product release (therefore he would not change jobs or be fired, etc.).

Out of the blue, George asked me, "Noel, do you think my parents are going to die then?" (George knows a good deal of astrology and was "up" on his measurements.)

Now there *must* be more to this question than what is on the surface. What am I going to answer? "Yes" or "No"? This man is extremely bright, but also exquisitely human. What was being said here *beyond the obvious*? What was stirring inside him? "George, recognizing how very, very old your parents are, and your mother being senile, we know they *will die soon*. They *could* die at this time (the angular activity), but there is nothing classical here to show this (nothing Plutonic, no 8th House "matters of death" showing, etc.). But what I would like to suggest to you is that your concern is actually "will their deaths—and we know statistically that when one dies, the other will probably follow in a matter of months—will their death get in the way of all that you are doing? Not meaning to sound harsh, just practical, since you are the executor of their estate, *how will your work be disrupted*?" I took a chance; I invited creativity through risk.

George agreed with that suggestion. He was clearly relieved; I could actually feel that bodily reaction on the telephone.[70] He started to feel "good." We pursued that business track. We felt that emotional preparedness indeed was important, but that progress at this time was essential. Keep the work going. Keep the schedule. Know the possibility; waiting around for the death(s)—being pro forma in our culture—would waste too much.

But there must be something *even more* to this! George is not so simple.

A second related question about his sister had been raised for me to study when he had called earlier to set the appointment (and indeed the call chart had the same Ascendant as his sister's Ascendant). Her chart revealed [now, read slowly] the Saturn retrograde phenomenon in the 10th . . . a heavy emphasis below the horizon . . . and Saturn retrograde quindecile the Sun in the 4th . . . with Mars quindecile the Saturn. Saturn here ruled the 7th. This is not hard to follow: let your mind think of it in this shorthand way, "Saturn-retrograde, obsession, parents, to the detriment of relationships." That's that. Now you know it *inside*; you feel it. Now we must assimilate this knowledge into the consultation as it was developing.

But also in the sister's horoscope, Uranus was natally peregrine (a highly anxious, rebellious, or different creature) and SA Uranus was coming to the Ascendant in Spring 1999, *at the same time as all of George's measurements.*

"George, is your sister one intense lady?"

"Wow! You can say that again! She's really, really . . . ."

"There's a classic suggestion here of lots of parental upset, unfinished business, from her point of view . . . ."

"Absolutely."

"Dare I say an obsession with those problems? Trying to make good with them (the parents)? *How is she tied to the parents still?*" (An assumptive question.)

---

70 His speech pitch dropped slightly; his speech slowed down. There were fewer words. The sinus resonance was richer, suggesting a relaxation of tension in the face.

"Oh my, yes. She's *'obsessed'* as you say, with that; our parents, they're in an extended care facility, can do nothing without her controlling it somehow."

"You know, I would venture that when they die, it would remove her from her purpose for living." (Think: she will hold on even afterward.) Here, I took another risk to invite inspiration.

There was a pause and a change of voice. "You can't say it better, Noel. You can't." (Whew! I was right!)

I then asked about the size of the estate (to learn how extensive execution of it would be) and learned also that the complications would be resolved by George *and* his sister working together as co-executors. George dreaded that.

Now, as you read this, are you thinking that, when the parents do die, George's time will be taken up considerably and nerve-wrackingly with work with his sister, who is on the scene where the parents live? What would happen to George's major business plans, which were focused across the country? *That* was what the call was about, wasn't it?

The consultation lasted about twenty minutes; George was relieved with the insight.

Going further with creativity, tests show that a sense of humor and a sense of playfulness are decidedly concomitant with creativity. We know that laughter has a cathartic value of its own, and we should be prepared in our creativity—our originality that grows throughout our work and career—to use humor and parody to defuse tension with a client. We can use humor to confront the client with difficult concerns in a less-threatening way, or to discuss taboo subjects that might be more difficult to approach from a more direct angle.[71]

In a recent consultation, it came out that the man was a recovering alcoholic. As our discussion went on, we came to a time of conspicuous difficulty in the recent past, something that could possibly have caused a relapse (a major Neptune transit was involved). I said, "Larry, what was going on that spring? It's a time when the ego can get wiped out."

"Right on! That's when I lost my job, when I was put out to pasture, so to speak. God, it was terrible . . . but then again it put me in the direction to get with the corporation I'm with now, and it worked out."

"Well, that took some time, about nine months I think. A long time."

"It was, It was. You're right on; nine, ten months."

"During that time were there any *binge benefits*?"

---

71 Kottler, 248–255.

Larry laughed, delighted, proud, stared me right in the eye and said, "No, absolutely not!"

I had to know. Earlier Neptune symbolisms had been handmaidens to his alcoholic fall. Were the effects used up, discarded through his convalescence? They were. Humor helped me get to different emotions and information, without the sense of inquisition.

Or, the female client who said over and over again in successive phone calls, "My marriage isn't improving, I can't stand it, can't you tell me when this is going to end?" The implication was very strong that astrology was not working (to make her life easier)!

Now, in the consultation discussion, we had agreed that the marriage was doomed. I suggested that the keenest suffering would be experienced over the Christmas holidays just ahead (when insincerity is the rule in cases like this, since the antagonists are forced by cultural pressures to be nice and loving), that depression would follow in January, and that she really should plan for release, get to a lawyer, aim for new growth in the Spring (note the dateline contrivance, in parallel with the measurements). She was procrastinating. There was nothing I could possibly do except get her to a lawyer. It would happen, I was sure, but unfortunately later rather than sooner, because of the lady's insecurity, fear of transient pain, etc.

I said, "Well, you *know* the astrology IS working, Helen! You *are* feeling more and more pain, getting more and more uncomfortable as we anticipated! Finally, it will force you to do what *you've told me you know you MUST do.*"

There is humor there, about a most difficult point of communication, and it had an impact. "Well, alright, I see what you mean."

Or, some serious, serious playfulness to make a point instantly under special circumstances just recently: I had just finished an intense, deep lecture to a group of astrologers and students dealing with many family development issues. I could see in many faces that the astrological observations were leading them to deep awareness of personal development issues.

After the lecture, a lady came up to me with tears in her eyes, a slight tremble about her. She thanked me for the talk and added, "All of that stuff fits me . . . it fits me . . . and I . . . ."

I interrupted her to seize her attention, to take charge of the moment strongly—just what she desperately wanted. I put my hand on her shoulder as a signal of that control and to help close the distance between us quickly. People were gathering around us. What was I to say? "Too bad! That's the way it goes." "Would you please make an appointment with me?" "I'm sorry. Next?"

I read her nametag, used her first name, and launched into the following imagery, playfully really, so as not to embarrass her in any way and, as well, to instruct others around us with similar concerns. I was creating a vivid image and making a major and very helpful point she could take home with her. I used a model for objectification that always works so very well, and it can be used more calmly during a consultation period.

"Mary, I appreciate what you are saying. (I'm speaking quickly, cleanly, and insistently). All of that is part of the process of your development, and you must get inside it and learn what it means. But you have *already done that* over the years, haven't you? (not pausing for a reply; trying to establish some distance from the pain.) And it's either getting to be a waste of time, boring, or just repetitively painful. You know. (Mary is nodding, with the slightest smile replacing the tremble of emotions). *"Sooner or later, Mary, you know you are going to have to put those troubles away."* (This is the key thought.)

I continued without any pause: "Now look at this box here. (I took my one hand off her shoulder and brought it to the space between us. With my other hand also there, I defined by pantomime a nifty box I was holding.) I looked at "the box." Mary looked at "the box." Everyone around us was looking at "the box"!

"Look what I'm doing: I'm opening this box up, carefully. See? (No pause for reply; rapid-fire imagery.) Now, Mary, sooner or later, you will have to put those awful pains away. *You could put them into this box!!!* So, let's try that and see how it *feels.*

"Put them in there. See! See! They are inside the box. We have PUT them in this box. All that STUFF that hurts. Who needs it for so long in life? THAT STUFF IS IN THE BOX. (I closed the lid.)

(And rapidly going on.) "AND look now (commanding everyone's attention in the circle gathered there), look what we will do. We will put the box up here on this shelf." (I actually took the "box" and put it up there on the "shelf," away from us both and above our heads, out of reach. Everyone was looking at the box up there!)

(Then I looked hard again into Mary's eyes): "Those pains are getting out of you. You can feel that. We just put them in the box!" (I looked and pointed to the box again, and there was gentle, relaxing laughter from Mary and the others.)

"And, one other thing, Mary, I'm going to take the box with me tonight and, tomorrow, when I'm on the plane . . . ."

Mary interrupted with a smile and lots of sparkle, ". . . and you'll throw it out the window! Right!"

I gave Mary a hug. She kept her smile. About forty seconds had flown by in concentration. A helpful image had been created, for sure.

On Perception

Perception and creativity go together; perception triggers creativity; together, they invite inspiration. We must work to be perceptive and creative. Regardless of our past education, we must work to improve ourselves in every way all the time. That we want more for our children than we had does not mean we have given up on ourselves and want nothing more for us!

We live in a society where everything unfortunately is thought out for us and told to us. Greeting card companies even tell us how to phrase our emotions. Schools push us out of the way even though we do little work and fail our examinations. The computer dial-up-and-get-it medium has made books shorter and shorter; attention spans have been conditioned by megahertz measurement. We are told not to ask openly for sympathy, to express upset, or to show complicated emotions.

When do we actually think on our own about the way we feel, about who and why we are? Is this why meaninglessness is one of the crucial existential problems for all of us? Shouldn't information help us fulfill our needs better, enrich us, rather than just explain how we expedite life? This is the focus of the therapeutic consultation, any therapeutic consultation, from the most extended psychoanalysis to Single Session Therapy (that may not even get past the making of the appointment!) to the explorative applications of astrology. The consultation, in any shape or form, is the gain of insight at a time *when we are ourselves*.

So many problems stem from attitudes that are founded on wrong information or not enough information. We must know that correct or additional information itself is often therapy! The man with a long history of all-day drowsiness and being overweight finally is led, with Venus conjunct Jupiter natally, to learn about his diabetes; his life is vastly improved with diagnosis and treatment. Couples, especially in their mid-sixties, with lower education levels and non-urban beginnings, who have lived with the male's impotence for years because of a lack of remedial information, have their lives together changed in many ways with the introduction of information leading to treatment. Parents informed about the Saturn retrograde concerns in their young children's horoscope, the potential of education being discontinued, the management of teen-age rebellion, the individual needs their children have that are pressing for form and fulfillment work constructively to improve family life and encouragement of the next generation.

Astrology is based upon perception and creativity. Astrology is a lofty calling. It is a field of great responsibility. We must be proud—and, indeed, how full we must become to do it well.

Let's cover some points of perception that show our brains the way to open up, to exercise themselves in taking astrological measurement guidelines deeply into clients' reality.

A lady has Saturn-retrograde (IMMEDIATELY, your mind registers this syndrome) opposed Venus in the 10th (IMMEDIATELY, your mind knows confirmation of the father syndrome and ties it to emotional/relational needs and expression potential; and you also know there is probably a tightness there, a frustration, a slowness to develop, a short circuit, a detour somehow . . . through the opposition).

Whooooooosh! It can be just that fast. Try it again: open your mind and react to this statement: "a lady has Saturn-retrograde opposed Venus in the 10th." Do you know it? Do you feel it? You *can* do it.

Now, this Saturn is also quindecile to the Sun in Aries (immediately, feel an obsessional, compulsive, heavy-duty link with the lady's ego-aggrandizement energy). As always, this typical set of developmental tensions is going to intrude severely on this lady's relationship development because of the lack of ego security taken on in the early homelife through her relationship, probably with the father, who was taken out of the picture early, was there and passive, or was so tyrannical—any combination of these—so as never to have given the guidance of authoritative love.

Additionally, this woman has *Neptune opposed the Aries Sun and square her Moon.* Just guess what house Neptune rules? THE SEVENTH! Everything here is going to complicate relationships. Think one more moment about that description: Neptune opposes the Aries Sun and squares her Moon. Neptune rules her 7th. WHAT HOUSE DOES THE MOON PROBABLY RULE? Automatically you know it is probably the 11th (Cancer is to Pisces on the 7th as the 11th is to the 7th; between signs of the same element, a trine; between the 11th and 7th, a trine).

It can be just that quickly surmised. The consultation, the art of astrology, uses that guideline information in conversation with the chart to discover the swirl of emotions, the feelings that are connected somehow to an event or a pattern in the past, and to make a connection with concerns in the present. We are studying this process over and over and over again in this book from many different angles.

Carol says, "Well, I don't quite understand; my father was really very involved with me."

"But he wasn't the authority figure in the early home."

"No my mother was."

"Alright."

"And I remember . . . yes, when I broke my back at fourteen, my father cared desperately." (Why did she use the word "desperately"?)

That was nice to hear. But, what about the tie we KNOW is there somehow; the tie between this father relationship and adult relationships which are chaotic and unreliable for this lady?

There are some creative, perceptive considerations for us to make in framing this analysis: perhaps the father came to the fore in desperate caring to overcompensate for not being attentive to his daughter for fourteen years before; it is possible he cared in order to take away some of the mother's place in the scheme of things in his tense relationship with her; maybe this desperate caring (why is this twenty-year-old memory so intense for Carol?), maybe it was *what Carol wanted it to be*, but it was not in reality! Remember there is a powerful Neptune dimension in this personality.

The objective here is not *to be right*, of course. We want an insight that is valid. The operational objective then is to take the analysis further through conversation into the client's reality. We want to risk deduction to forge creative links.

Would you believe that in asking about why she can not feel confident in relationships, Carol said, "I feel that any man who loves me is feeling sorry for me." Does that not suggest strongly that the father had been feeling sorry for her but *was not loving her the way her ego energy needed*? Carol's Moon ruled her 11th—remember?—and was squared by Neptune, ruler of the 7th, as we have seen. She did not feel loveable, *in spite of the fact* that her father had cared for her desperately!

Therapeutic discussion here would follow objectification, understanding, a bit of humored distance, and a careful reality check of her personal strengths, needs, proven attractiveness, etc. A desperate memory could be adjusted.

I recall Robert, who had a charmed life. His Sun-Moon blend of Cancer-Pisces simply manifested in a lovely, comfortable, sailboat way. He had a proud Leo Ascendant with Jupiter conjunct. He was quite a successful businessman, good-looking, and apparently relaxed and happy. He came to me for some business decisions (and we will be talking about them later in this book).

With his Mercury in Cancer exactly conjoined with the Nodal axis, I simply asked him about his mother: "Oh," he said with a great smile, "she was extremely supportive of me." And he stopped talking right there. Of course she was (Node, Mercury, mother, mind; for better or for worse), but there had to be more here.

The Sun was conjunct Venus, ruler of the 10th, another "nice" idealized reference to the early home. Easy to understand. Fine.

But Neptune was quindecile the Moon in the 8th and squared Saturn in the 11th (a gigantic need for love). What was all that tension? And here again, we can read the Moon as a maternal reference as well.

When Robert and I started to talk about his developmental years, he could literally remember nothing. Could this be selective amnesia?

Everything appeared to be just fine in his life development—and that is fine—but I was still preoccupied with the Neptune factor. Robert often mentioned his sister, very favorably, almost as if they were twins, of the same mind.

I asked Robert about his sixteenth year, hoping that the Saturn=Sun Arc shown in his horoscope would indeed have manifested and lodged in his memory somewhere!

Robert said, "I really don't remember, but just recently (Robert was now fifty-five) my sister and I were talking and realized that that was when my mother had her nervous breakdown."

There it was! Why were they discussing it? Why did the idyllic homelife situation have one recall only and that was the mother's nervous breakdown? What was blotted out? What was happening in the marriage that would have caused the breakdown? How was that affecting the two children who were clearly bonded by this? (It was not going to be shared with me; and it appeared it did not need to be.)

I realized easily that none of this was in the way of anything Robert was doing now. I just went on, and we got down to business with the plans immediately ahead (see page 134). It is the pattern of perception to help analysis that is important here in our study.

Recall Gayle's case (page 82), the lady with the private art world. When I asked her for permission to use her case in this book, she gave me a big smile and most enthusiastically said, "No; Go ahead!" There she was, between two worlds, but eager to start drawing herself out. It will take some time, and maybe astrology can help further.

And how often I have heard, "I really don't think about my childhood much anymore." When did you? Why? (Think about what "really" and "much" and "anymore" mean.)

We are talking about perception, creative listening in discussion, as a preparation for helpful analysis, as we pursue the process of disclosure, understanding, adjustment, change.

Visual perceptions are extraordinarily important, as well, to help us bring astrological measurements to life. We see without thinking, normally; we assume what we see, we overlook significance by not consciously seeing with purpose.

For example: a lady calls during the day for an appointment; she's relaxed, cheery, sixty years old; she arrives for her appointment on a weekday morning, and her appearance is a glorified and truly beautiful blend of a Barbie doll and a cheerleader; she has jewelry on, but you know the ring is not a wedding ring; her nickname is monogrammed on her sweater; her muscle tone is good. What do you know?

Life has been good to her; she does not work and probably never has; she spends money comfortably and well; she undoubtedly participates in the Country Club activities, and is *never* hurting for a date, probably with the best-off men around. This fills out perfectly her Sun-Moon blend in Scorpio-Taurus, the potential for life in the Grand Manner.

But there is Saturn retrograde in the 11th peregrine, on the Nodal Axis, ruling the 7th. Need we say more? We immediately sense the extreme overcompensation within her reality.

This truly lovely and beautiful lady was in tears (of recognition) as soon as I talked about the need for love, the father syndrome, materialism controls substituting for emotional lacks, linking everything together for our discussion. I learned of her "being kept by an older man" for an eight-year period; she said "And you know? He sort of raised me; taught me everything!"

I asked her about this word "raised," i.e., that which had not been done in the early home, etc. There were still more tears.

This lady had a Grand Trine defense mechanism (in water), a closed circuit of emotional self-sufficiency.[72] This was a marvelous protection for the hurts deeply imbedded within her, the haunting fears of being abandoned in every relationship, linked to the early times in relation to her needs. But this defense structure worked *against relationship*, that which she desperately needed!

Additionally, this Grand Trine did not include the Sun or Moon (a relatively infrequent occurrence; the Sun or the Moon is almost always included in any Grand Trine), so it operated as a *separate complex*, a private, solitary behavioral complex in parallel with the grand Sun-Moon blend. One would never, ever know that two worlds existed side by side within this woman, but they did and *still* do.

---

72 In Earth: practical self-sufficiency; in Air, social or intellectual self-sufficiency; in Fire, motivational self-sufficiency. See Tyl, *Synthesis & Counseling*, 284–301.

Perception immediately opened the door to the symbolisms in this woman's horo-scope, from the telephone call to her entrance into the office. In a flash, sociometric level was revealed, noted, and assimilated. We worked to understand all this, to bridge the space between the two realms; one of the key questions of our discussion, in relation to a marriage-under-consideration, was "What do you think you will have to sacrifice in this relationship, to keep it together with your way of life?" *That* was a serious question.

Another line of perception: you have a client seated across from you whose face muscles are apparently *totally lifeless*. This is hard to accomplish; even at rest, looking into a mirror, one can perceive the potential of the facial muscles to be expressive.

Where do we learn to activate those muscles?

From the person who picks us up the most, usually the mother who is supposed to "goo-goo, gah-gah, eenty-weenty" expressively at us to make us emote and delight her in return! What if the mother did *not* do that, and other neglectful, dis-tant, cold behaviors reinforced the barrenness? That would show as absence in the face of the baby. (Look at the faces of children with no parental contact, neglected orphans, etc.)

What does the complexion suggest about nutrition; what does grooming suggest about self-esteem (Did your client wash her hair or change his shirt especially to come see you?); are there evidences of nail biting, foot jiggling, defensive arm clasps, a way-ward gaze?

What about what I call the Neptune eye-flutter, when the eyelids flutter rapidly (for sometimes three seconds!) just about closed when a statement of opinion is called for? A man has Neptune conjunct Venus-retrograde in the 8th House, Venus ruling the mind-set 3rd : "Please let me share with you that I notice you flutter your eyelids like this . . . every time you state an opinion. Yes, really. I'll call your attention to it a few times, if I may. But what do you think of when you do this?"

Just think what other people—employers, personnel managers, loan officers, etc.—think when this man does this. The flutter manifests easily as preoccupation, not speaking directly, censorship. What is the filter protecting? How can this be adjusted to take advantage of the strengths of the horoscope, to communicate them *directly*?

There are clients whom we perceive as resisting the consultation process; they want the personal attention and possible enrichment it promises, but they can not cooper-ate with it. The reason might be that something about the astrologer—the setting or the personality or the communication style—has closed the door. It might be that the consultation is going too quickly, too deeply into things, far more than was expected (this is why the appointment-making discussion is so important; see page 64). It might be that there is a lifetime of communication protection (defensiveness) that is patterning behavior into its comfort zone.

Additionally, Kottler observes bluntly, "We live with such incredible dishonesty in client disclosures and reports—some of them unconscious omissions, others deliberate falsifications—that (clients) sometimes forget the rough fit between a childhood memory and its repetition years later after being squeezed through the mind's protective sieve."[73]

And then, understandably, emotions can get diluted or changed through translation into words, and the therapist (astrologer) adds to the focus problem (or even distorts it) by supplying "contextual assumptions to fill in gaps."

Our awareness of all these dimensions is part of our alert posture as consultants. Apparent resistance can be misinterpreted ("I'm doing a poor job here," arousing our personal insecurities) and diminish our empathy and respect for the client. We can become bored with the client and show it in many subtle ways through our own vocal nuance and body language. Value judgments can creep into our discussion and work to downgrade the client and elevate the astrologer. All these occurrences are all too human; they can happen in any relationship we have.[74]

I feel the single-session structure in which astrology mainly operates telescopes an enormous amount of information about human interaction dynamics into one hour, and this intensity must be regulated so as not to imbalance the session. Recall the image we used earlier of going to someone's home for dinner, the exchange of compliments and comfort-giving talk at the outset. Such perception and evaluation take place—indeed, are culturally required—in the very first minutes of arrival. How long does it take to feel comfortable? When are the "How do you feel about me" questions answered? *How* are they answered? The same light shines on the consultation moment, but the light is stronger, more is at stake, and there is professional expectation and exchange.

We can perceive that the client is tense, and that is understandable. That tension—knowing what to expect and not knowing what to expect—is caught up with the dreaded sense of "evaluation." Naturally the client is eager that he or she will be liked and will work instinctively to prevent hearing anything negative. This is why the client

---

73 Kottler, 182.

74 Freud found that transference and countertransference (how the client feels about the therapist and how the therapist feels about the client) were both the greatest tool in treatment and the greatest obstacle. See any overview of Freud's works with the "Dynamics of Transference;" see Kottler, 118.

normally tries to make the best appearance for the consultation; this is why the sense of trust must be created as quickly as possible between client and astrologer.

Here is how I used these dynamics with the client introduced above, the beautiful "Country Club" lady (page 114; with Saturn retrograde in the 11th, with Mars ruling the 11th and squared by Uranus; with Uranus conjunct the Moon also in the 11th; the Moon ruling the Ascendant: tremendous need for love, linked to some father-relationship pathology, residual anxiety about actually being lovable, all at the core of her identity concerns and tension, and defended by the closed circuit of emotional self-sufficiency):

During our brief time of small talk going into my office and sitting down at the desk, I said, "You are truly a beautiful woman, Mary. It's remarkable!"

"Thank you," she said a bit nervously, with an averted gaze—rather than matter-of-factly or wide-openly.

"And I'm sure you hear that a dozen times a day . . . throughout your life . . . ."

"Well, I don't know, I . . . ."

And as her voice trailed off just the tiniest bit, I noted that her eyes were filled with tears. I rescued the moment quickly and gently with, "and those are some of the things we must discuss today, Mary. It goes back to the relationship—or the lack of it, with your father who, it is suggested here . . . ."

I had pulled the probing statement-inquiry into the moment as I had done in similar situations many times before. The objective was not to get an answer, but to put the focus immediately on the situation behind her defenses (the closed circuit of emotional self-sufficiency). "Did your father ever say, 'Mary, I love you'?"

Of course, what followed in the drama of her development were manifestations of father surrogacy, fears of being abandoned, and a paradoxical (distrust) lack of desire for intimacy. And all that was being brought into the late-life concerns of finally settling into a marriage.

One might observe that Mary could very easily have said, "But of course! EVERYONE tells me that!" and flipped the compliment/observation back to me with high humor. But she didn't.

Chapter 4

Prediction: Timing, Common Sense, and Powers of Suggestion

WITH THE HUMANISTIC GROWTH AND SOPHISTICATION THAT have enriched astrology since World War II, the sensibility about astrological prediction has shifted from abject expectation of Fate to knowledgeable exploration of strategy. We now plan to "get with it," to improve life, not to submit to it. Since we know more about things, we can traffic better and improve our position. And, of course, in our explosive society in a smaller world, all of this must be done as quickly as possible.

But all of us slip back as we try to go forward. Our expressions of resignation still reflect the sense of fatalism: "all good things come to an end; into each life some rain must fall; when it's time to go, it's time to go; this was meant to be; etc." These thoughts somehow release us from duress, from things apparently out of *our* control. They announce an end and, at the same time, a hope for a new beginning. The present becomes a period of transition.[75]

---

75 In one sense, the present never exits, so inexorable is the advance of the future. In another sense, there is an *expanded present* that has a neat philosophical symmetry about it, including the developmental past and the projected future. Boundaries between past and future collapse; there is a *nunc fluens, the passing present* in Christian mysticism. Herein resides the cosmos, with all its time and the space in the world. See Wilber, chapter 5, 69.

How many times I have found myself observing during a consultation: "Well, we should appreciate that, if we can see these things so well guided by the horoscope, there must be a purpose for it all," hoping to give some strength of purpose to my client, to build confidence in the horoscope for the future—as my mind races to bring some learning significance out of the past into the present.

I do not like to hear myself making that particular observation, because it suggests I have lost my lead position in the consultation; that I am fishing for the movement of thought into the future. The answer that I am looking for as creatively as I can—in this instance and in any wrap-up of consultation discussion to introduce future planning—should ideally set up *adjustment, development, confidence, and activation of the future*. All of this is the *precondition* for prediction; it must ground the closing section of the consultation and spark the spirit of the client.

It is helpful to recognize and explore two major arenas of prediction in astrology: the time structures of development and the individual management of change.

Time Structures

There are certain predictive measurements in astrology that carry with them an enormous empirically substantiated reliability. The transit quadrature of Saturn, for example, reflects our social emergence into society.[76] We observe and understand the transitional periods around ages 7, 14, 28–30, 35, 42–45 especially, and 60. The transit cycles of Mars, Jupiter, Uranus, and Neptune seem to tie themselves as well to the Saturn time structure. These cycles define a formidably integrated complex of time.

We observe and understand the extreme importance of transits (Saturn through Pluto) in conjunction with and square to the *Angles* of the horoscope. For the young child, we see the angular transits as punctuation *in the life development of the parents* (the Ascendant is derivatively the fourth House of the Midheaven, the tenth House of the 4th; etc.).

We know with enormous probability that Uranian transits of the Angles (or squares to them; or often in relation to the Sun) correspond to dramatic, often separational change (relocation at the Ascendant, change of home at the 4th, of job at the 10th, or partnership at the 7th).[77] We know that Neptune transits of the Angles (or squares to

---

76 The research of Grant Lewi, *Astrology for the Millions* (Llewellyn Publications), is the indispensable ground base work on this Saturn subject.

77 In my life, tr. Uranus conjoined my Ascendant when my mother remarried (her 10th House in my horoscope); came to my fourth cusp, I began my opera career and astrology study; SA Uranus=Ascendant, left opera and entered astrology full-time as life work.

them; or often in relation to the Sun) suggest with high reliability a sense of ego wipe-out, a confusion, bewilderment, that is very difficult to manage for most people.[78] We know that Pluto transits of the Angles (or squares to them; or often in relation to the Sun) suggest milestones of development possible on every front of life, often with concomitant change among extended family or death matters of some nature.[79]

And in our work with transits of Angles we must remember that the transit that is conjunct the Ascendant, for example, is at the same time an *opposition to the Descendant*. This is the separatist sense of the Uranian transit of the Ascendant, a growth of individuation focus *away from* the relationship (partnership) routine. The Neptune transit of the 7th will invite disillusionment for the person in terms of the relationship, not just suggest a partner having a confusing, wipeout time. The point is that the reciprocal is always important; it takes two to tango, so to speak. One leaves a job to go on to something better: perhaps the person was fired but does not admit it; perhaps the former employer was glad to see the person go. Why? Has that happened before? Might it recur in the next position?

Similarly, we have the enormous guidelines of Solar Arcs[80] (with special awareness of the semisquare Arc accumulation at ages 44–47) and the swift, reliable movement of the Secondary Progressed Moon (which develops extraordinary affinity with the transit cycle of Saturn).

The reliability of these measurements does *not* suggest that the planets are doing things to us and that we are responding to them, that we have captured their supposed causal energies in our studies. The reliability has developed from *how we have interpreted the passage of these symbols in time in tandem with occurrences in life*. Planetary measurements and life realities both reflect structures of time. That there is a harmony one with the other is the miracle of creation with which we work.

The interpretation of the astrological measurements is subtly different every time we study a horoscope because we are adapting the measurements—harmonizing the measurements—with the reality being lived by the individual client (the process we are discussing throughout this book). *The client's experience* is what gives life to the measurements.

---

78 Basketball star Michael Jordan announced his retirement from basketball with tr. Neptune precisely upon his Midheaven. In February, 1998, when the Clinton scandal hit the news, tr. Neptune was exactly opposite Monica Lewinsky's Sun.

79 Jacqueline Kennedy-Onassis dies mid-1994 with tr. Pluto square Midheaven (SA Mars=Ascendant, SA Saturn=MC, 1-degree orb); TV star Arsenio Hall leaves his show with SA Pluto=MC.

80 See Review section, Tyl, *Astrological Timing of Critical Illness*, 79; see Tyl, *Synthesis & Counseling*, 204–215, 783–860.

Throughout the consultation, discussion is guided in time development through the major Arcs and transits. Gradually, we learn which needs and behaviors (planets as symbols) press the strongest and respond maximally in the client's horoscope and which do not. Gradually, in discussion, we discover, link, and evaluate occurrences, emotional attitudes, and routined behaviors in reaction to development.

Prediction and Projection

Prediction brings all of this forward into future time. Prediction becomes *projection*, less what is *"said"* ahead of time and more that is, literally, *"thrown forward"* out of the past. As we expand the present to include the future, we must recognize that *the client is making it happen*, is reflecting what is happening, is bringing more of his or her horoscope into the lifetime-structure ahead. He is throwing himself forward—his upbringing, learning, emotional attitude formations, relationship supports, hopes and dreams—into further development with the environment, and the individualized horoscope symbology is guiding us further.

The creative astrologer is investigating a plan in time. The absolutely crucial transitional passage into future talk is the question to the client, "What do you project for yourself in the next six months to a year?"

Management of Change

Throughout the consultation, we learn how the client has responded to developmental pressures in the past—the press of his or her needs for fulfillment, the reactions of the environment within the process. We learn about the events and development in the early home, including absorption of parental modeling-behavior. We learn how the client has found her way into society as an adult.

Not everything has been smooth and fulfilling. Frustration has backed up into the system, to one degree or another. Emotions have swirled together as attitudinal constructs and tied themselves to past events that are easily triggered by events present and future. There are accidents and serendipitous happenings (which still, for the most part, are beyond astrology's grasp) that enter the mix. And the capacities for self-projection, for dreaming, and for planning emerge. We learn *who* is going forward and *how* he or she sees themself getting there.

The major thread that is spun throughout the consultation is the thread of reality, and all the understanding—disclosure, objectification, reevaluation—and all the insight connected to that thread resourcefully by astrologer and client lead to *common sense*, the strategy that must be within the projection process. Given the client's development, responsiveness, and routines, WHAT IS PRACTICABLE for their further development? What adjustments need to be made to get them there? What weaknesses should be adjusted, what strengths augmented? How does this harmonize with measurements ahead that we presume reflect the process?

During this process, wish fulfillment is a danger. The astrologer desperately wants to please the client—to "grant" the wish, so to speak. While this reveals human sentiment, it is neither objective nor professional.

Expecting Relationship

How often do we hear, "When do you think I will meet someone?" or "Isn't there a soulmate for me out there?" We look for a measurement ahead that might classically make it reasonable to anticipate such a significant relationship (SA Sun-Venus or SA Venus-Sun, for example; SA Venus conjoining an angle; activity with the ruler of the 7th; the arcing Nodal Axis, which gives way to relationship concerns (meetings, contacts) as the client develops out of the home).

But we must remember, as well, that the client may have a fear of intimacy, a closed circuit of self-sufficiency that gets in the way of relationship, a defensive posture that protects a grievously debilitated self-worth profile, etc. All of that has surely emerged in the consultation, but lip service is "naturally" given to aspirations for the idyllic relationship.

The relationship itself—should it come along—will *not* be the answer to this client's yearning for change. And that is probably why there is no measurement in the near future that suggests relationship success. Recall Gayle, please (page 83): after the big loss of relationship potential four years earlier (SA Venus=Asc., with tr. Saturn opposed Moon-Pluto, 9/94), she had given up. Measurements had gone by unmatched, if you will, in her reality (e.g., SA=Jupiter, ruler of her 7th, with tr. Saturn conjunct the MC, 3/96; SA Sun=Venus and SA Mars=Venus, with tr. Jupiter opposed Sun-Mars, 6/98!). It was over, because of inner reasons far deeper than availability. This all reflected itself in her life routine and in her appearance: *charming but inaccessible.*

What is important with regard *to making relationship happen*, to attracting it, is most likely, first, *something else*: probably improvement of self-worth, grooming (they usually go together), dealing with specific routined habits of fear or patterns of avoidance behavior conditioned in the past; even tactical information about where to go to meet people, having something interesting to offer in conversations, etc. There must be *a remedial approach to the potentials of the future.* We will see shortly (page 160) the inspired techniques of hypnotist and psychiatrist Milton H. Erickson that will help the creative astrologer help with change.

It is interesting to note how often people who have lived busy, difficult lives feel they could write a best-selling book. All the client's friends tell him or her that "It would be great!" Indeed, the friends are offering this evaluation as an ultimate compliment to the gentleman or lady. Neither the friends nor the client knows how difficult it is to write a book, get an agent to promote it, and secure a publisher. And this is especially so if the client's horoscope shows nothing even remotely involved with writing (always pay attention to configurations involving the Mercury/Jupiter midpoint and the 3rd House).

"Have you ever written anything before? Published anything? We didn't come across that in our discussion of your past."

Or: "There is this flair here in the horoscope, sure, but let me ask you: what will happen to your work plan and income, if you dive right in to write a book about all this? How long do you think it would take, let alone really learning how to do it?"

Indeed, the client who wants to write his life story is probably exploring the therapy of journal-writing (see page 95). Perhaps the help in this case where the client is not a professional writer is to restructure the projected hope from "writing a book" to "keeping a journal and seeing what develops!"

When they are voiced, wish-fulfillment projections usually clash with the depth and significance of what has been accomplished by the astrologer and client up to that point in the consultation. The projections might just be a way to let off a little steam, enjoy a moment of self-aggrandizement, or indeed to give a bit of comfortable disclosure to the astrologer. The objective in the midst of all this is for the astrologer to elicit a projection, a plan, a *realistic* set of expectations from the client, to which the creative astrologer quickly ties measurements to come and begins a practical discussion.

Measurement preparation into the future ideally focuses on some angular occurrence, an Arc or transit (Saturn, Uranus, or Pluto) conjoining or squaring an angle, within, say the next year and a half (a practicable time reach, I have found). Such a "hit" is usually there(!); it is the dawning of that awareness that is somehow working within the client's system and actually brought the client to the astrologer. This is why we often note among groups of our clientele horoscopes the reflection of a major transit in the heavens, i.e., tr. Pluto at 7 Sagittarius will be touching an Angle, the Sun or the Moon, for example, in a whole string of horoscopes coming to our attention in a given period of time.

Recall how a mother explains her two-year-old's stubborn behavior: "He already has a mind of his own!" or "She will stop this when she has a mind to, not before!" That certainly applies to adults too. As uncomfortably close as it gets to predestation, I have to observe that, so much more often than not, the proper astrology has to be there in the horoscope for the projection of change to be tenable. AND, as well, there must be the focus within the client's mind that "I really think this is the best way for me; I feel fortified and clarified about these issues; it all sounds good; we've got to make it happen." Therapist Jeffrey Kottler says that when clients "are ready to change, they will do so. Our job is to help them get ready—on *their* schedule."[81]

The attitudinal substance of the consultation fortifies the client's self-awareness for more secure and efficient planning; realism and common sense come together; all of it is reasonable, including the planning. I repeat: the absolutely crucial transitional passage then, into future talk, is the question to the client, "What do you project for yourself in the next six months to a year?"

Prediction Technique

The entire consultation is built upon questioning, disclosure, creative listening, and making creative connections. Within that body of discussion, the analysis is helped by a question along these lines: "You have had this problem of relationships (self-worth, fearing intimacy, etc.) that we've been talking about, you say, for over a year and a half (or twenty years!). *What has changed about the problem* over that period of time?"

This is extremely important because it will indicate any alteration, of course, but *it will reveal if the client has worked on the problem her- or himself*. This presumes the client is aware of the problem, wants to change it, has gone to lengths to change it (gotten therapeutic help, for example; confronted the parents; divorced a husband; quit a job). In other words, *the client will have been engaged in change before this moment of consultation* when we expect the client to be seriously engaged with the future projections.

"How do you foresee *further* change, in the future, say, in four months (keying the time to a measurement)?" The answer will again suggest the inclination or the out-and-out determination to change or the disposition to continue with things as they are out of fear of transient insecurity within change, out of seriously deeply routined patterns of behaviors anchored in fear.

The creative astrologer can approach the future projection section of the consultation with the sense of: "Now, with your understanding, we can solve some of these habits (anxieties) that have brought you such upset; you can STOP marrying your mother over and over again!!!" (as an example); or saying it this way, "you can find a

---

81 Kottler, 141.

way in your mind to divorce your mother and break the bond,[82] now that we understand just what has been happening over the years. It will take a little time but, *as long as you are ready to start doing what you know is necessary* . . . ."[83]

Now, note these words: "as long as you are ready"; there is a *condition* being set up by the astrologer, placing pivotal responsibility within the client where we know change must originate; if the client is ready, the project is a "GO."

Then, note the phrase, "doing what you know is necessary," which is recognizing the values of the consultation discussion, obviously, reinforcing them, but *the phrase is also triggering the client's unconscious to keep the answers that have emerged during the consultation and* **to add to them in the time ahead.**

This is very subtle talk emerging from very natural conversation. The astrologer is letting the client know that change and development are *in his or her hands,* that *he or she* is expected to be an active participant in the process. The planets do not do anything; people do.

Let us study some actual prediction strategy and technique in three generic areas: Circumstance and Strategy; New Discovery; Remediation and Growth. Elements of any one area can be found and explored in the others, but each brings with it a defined mindset and technique-focus for the creative astrologer. The approach to and management of prediction are not always the same in application to astrological cases. The process does not come out of a rule book; *it is thoroughly permeated with the sense of reasonability and respect for probability*.

Circumstance and Strategy

I think we can group into this area of circumstance and strategy the planning for the sale of a house, getting a new job, obtaining a legal resolution, being out of a marriage, etc. These concerns depend enormously on the client's involvement with the process, i.e., actively selling the house or planning to, actively looking for a job position, involved with a court proceeding, seeing a lawyer (or just about to) about a divorce. They seem to have time-frames that are clearer than, say, attitudinal changes or long range change. In short, *the circumstance and strategy arena is more event-oriented than the others.*

---

82 Recall, the "graveside farewell" suggestion, page 90.

83 Key phrases like this one should be said aloud in different tones of voice ten or fifteen times a day for several days so that the sense and the words become the astrologer's own, so that they flow easily within consultation conversation. The same goes for the Saturn retrograde paragraph (Tyl, *Synthesis & Counseling,* page 40) and other special conceptual and motivational phrases.

These concerns also often have a sense of Horary or Electional Astrology about them, but they *are* different: they are ensconced within the client's developmental path from earliest days as it has been developed and illuminated in the consultation; the time ahead is bringing the Self and its whole life developmental scheme forward. And indeed, had these questions been brought forward as Horary issues, free and clear of personal in-depth involvement, the birth horoscope would almost certainly show measurement development relevant to the issue(s).[84]

Case Study: Miriam

So this first example addresses the strategic projection of a house sale. "Miriam" has been a client of mine for some fifteen years. We have worked through a lot of concerns, including a divorce, the growth and maturation of her son, several job changes for herself, and finally a terrific new start in her life, free of so many old concerns. We had worked these things out, and she had done her part: her written update report began, "Noel, you told me my life was changing dramatically and for the better."

When we had had our last consultation on October 10, 1995, I had tied her determination and activities to the measurements listed below, suggesting with the first set of measurements that there quite possibly could be a new job at the end of the next month (November). She was *indeed* looking for a new job and was having a hard time with the hunt:

- SA Saturn square MC ("major change in the profession, etc.")—*November 23, 1995*[85]

- Tr. Pluto semisquare MC—*November 23* (same day as Arc partile!)

- Tr. Mars conjunct MC— *November 25*

Miriam continued her report, "He (senior company officer) had a position available and interviewed me on November 21. The position was offered on November 22. I started on November 27."

---

84 According to astrologer Lee Lehman, an expert with Horary astrology, if the Horary chart does show the move, for example, and it is not clearly corroborated in the natal chart, the move is not negated, but changes or ramifications to the move will usually occur, i.e., the move takes place not as expected.

85 While this is the date of computer exactness for mathematical fulfillment of this Arc, we must remember that one Arc degree applying to partile is equal to one year in real-time development. This reflects the gradualism of major-event development that is most often the norm in life progress. Major transits could have tied themselves to this Arc earlier than partile and called attention to a specifically strategic time earlier than partile, triggering the significances.

My next observations that I presented to Miriam on October 10 went beyond her high probability of getting a new job late in November, they were as follows:

- Tr. Saturn conjunct her Ascendant (for the last time; the earlier touches being part of her grand life change just before our latest consultation)—*February 12, 1996*. Miriam had followed our ahead-of-time plan to start a major weight-loss program (Saturn) at this time.

- Tr. Jupiter conjunct the Sun *March 27, June 11*, and once again in *November 1996*. (Miriam became so involved with the weight-loss program that the reward period in business that we anticipated—her Sun is in the 10th, with Jupiter ruling the 10th—was partly her becoming a distributor for the company conducting the weight-loss program that was going so well for her. "I actually signed the papers on March 24 and took a business loan to start on March 25.")

- Tr. Pluto Stationary-Direct precisely conjunct her Venus, ruler of her 2nd and 7th—*August 10–September 19, 1996* (Still within the contemporaneous Jupiter tie with her Sun, to hit a last time in November, this strong punctuation of her Venus reference to her 2nd House reflected two raises at her new job: the first one in the first week of June [see Jupiter position in the preceding paragraph] and the first week of August!) I had projected an extremely positive and rewarding time for her "six to eight months" after her probable employment in November 1995.

- And finally, the last Jupiter transit of her Sun on November 16. Miriam continued: ". . . my life was changing dramatically and for the better. This is a huge understatement. I don't feel like the same person I was six months ago. My son and I are getting along very very well these past two and a half months, and [my ex-husband] and I, too. I love what I do for a living. I'm finding social situations more desirable. I have health, energy, and a positive attitude that I never even dreamed of. And did I happen to mention that I'M THIN!!!!!"

All of these developments for Miriam gave her more and more confidence in her new life, with her son now on his own, with her being free to found a new life for herself. But she now had to sell her home.

I began this follow-up consultation with the question, "*When* do you think you will put your house up for sale?"

Miriam said that it would probably be listed in mid-April 1998. In mid-April, Miriam would have tr. Jupiter square her Uranus, tr. Mars square her Pluto. As we know, Jupiter rules her 10th and had correlated very well with her successes earlier. Additionally, Jupiter *and* Uranus are both peregrine in her natal horoscope: these planets will dominate her attitude and help enormously in her new-life transition. It is reasonable, then, *that this transit contact between the two would accompany the placement of her house on the market*; Jupiter-Uranus suggests "the big break, success or going one's independent way; optimism."[86]

Looking ahead, I realized that there was no significant contact with the ruler of Miriam's 4th House (for the sale of the house) within a "comfortable" period of time. Normally, that would be a key anchor of projection about selling a house. However, Miriam's Moon in Cancer was in the 4th; this reference *could* key the 4th House.

I looked ahead for "Moon action." I noted that the SP Moon would oppose her "responsive" Jupiter *June 9, 1998*,[87] and then tr. Jupiter would square the Midheaven on *June 17*.

Next, I noted that tr. Jupiter conjoined her Ascendant on *September 13, 1998*.

I was able to suggest, "Miriam, I think we can anticipate that the house will be sold between the first week of June and the third week of September, outside date, say, the 16th of September. I know that's a pretty broad period, but I can't pin it down more specifically. I think the stronger times are at the beginning and end of this period. So, this can help a bit in planning your advertising, etc."

In addition to listing the house with a broker, Miriam was also thinking of promoting the sale of the home herself, right in line with her Jupiter-Uranus contact (and natal predisposition).

Indeed, we had several discussions during this period, and there was some sense of futility in the long summer period of little interest or response to the sale of the house.

But things did pick up, and the house *was sold*, on *September 18, 1998*.

Then our attention shifted to her leaving the area: *why, to do what, at what sacrifice, for what potential gain?* All of this was timed by the SA Uranus=MC!! in February 1999, along with many supportive measurements.

---

86 I make little differentiation between so-called "hard" aspects (square, opposition, some conjunctions) and "soft" aspects (sextile and trine). The objective in development is to make things happen, not to keep things as they are. We *need* the developmental tension of the more driving aspects. In the end, aspect *contact* is what is significant, not the nature of the contact.

87 Again, the computer-exact date should not take us away from the efficacy of the SP Moon contact here *throughout* the month, some time ahead and some time afterward. This is the consideration of what I call "Time Orb."

For sure, it had not been difficult to see this whole three-year period ahead of time in our consultations. I had spotted the Uranus Arc and worked backwards, noting other strong contact periods noted above. That was my preparation for our "circumstance and strategy" discussions. As experience accumulated, as the plan unfolded, the "schedule," if you will, gained strength and conviction; and so did Miriam!

Case Study: Linda

"Linda's" horoscope shows a Sun-Moon blend of Libra-Leo, the positions of the "noble romantic: the king or queen needing to do good work to enjoy the love of the people." This is what we should expect to emerge through development. There would be a social idealism expressed emphatically, dramatically, and/or artistically. These expectations are reinforced by the Neptune conjunction with the Sun at the Midheaven. Pluto is in the 8th—a reliable reference to psychotherapy to help establish values (semisquare Venus, ruler of the Midheaven). Interestingly, Linda is herself a successful psychologist.

The developmental tension in the horoscope is high, but not immediately obvious. Note that the Ascendant ruler, Saturn, is exactly conjunct Mercury. It is the *only* Ptolemaic aspect these two planets make; the conjunction is a *peregrine island*; the severe thinking process, the didactic thrust of the mind will do the queen's bidding for sure and dominate the developmental process. This is reinforced by Mars in Sagittarius (the need to apply energy in a decidedly arch-opinionated way) trine to the Moon, sextile the Sun, etc. Linda needs to and does speak her mind forcefully, insistently; there is little doubt about this.

Here we have our first glimpse of deeper developmental tensions that must be discussed and understood, i.e., *there must be some reason for such forceful focus of personal views*, wrapped up in a noble, socially aware idealism (note also AP=Mercury/Venus). Whenever we see something in life behavior that is so pronounced, we can assume that *it is overcompensatory for something else*. In other words, a pronounced behavioral trait or attitude *issues from a formidable cause*.

When we check the significators of the parental axis, we see little classic developmental tension, yet the Venus and Mars, the Neptune and the Sun all do have much to do with the parental axis and are "the players" in our first assessment of the horoscope organization.

The Southern hemisphere grouping promises that Linda will somehow be swept away by events, victimized, no matter how hard her thinking tries to anchor her position. This may not be the case throughout her life, but it will undoubtedly begin that

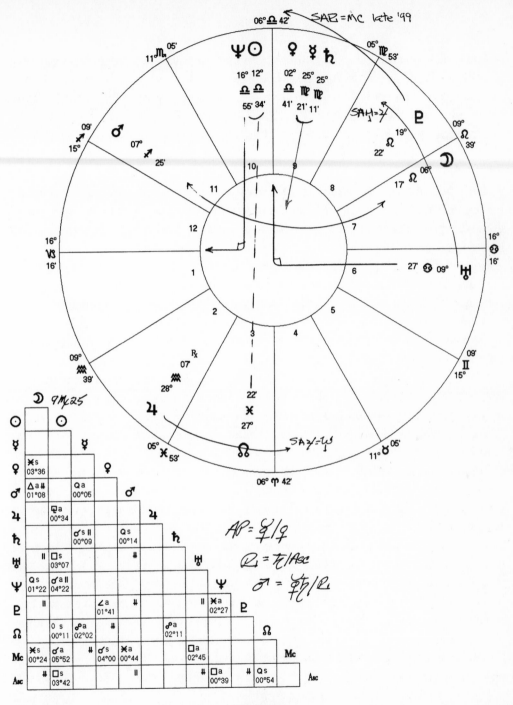

Figure 13
Linda

way in early development. As our first impression expands, we start to feel overcompensation, even defense, all the more strongly.

The tension tip-off is signified by Neptune conjunct the Sun in the 10th and ruling the mindset 3rd, *exactly square to the Ascendant*. Here is tension with one of the parents leading to identity confusion in the early home. Then, Uranus, ruling the self-worth 2nd, is *square the Midheaven* and the Sun-Neptune conjunction; yet another statement of early homelife upset, idiosyncratic development.

Two midpoints are quite telling: Pluto=Saturn/Asc, "Violent upset; deep anguish; being put down by others" and Mars=Mercury-Saturn/Pluto, "fighting battles to keep life going; enormous undercurrents of frustration; a gun with a cork in its barrel." We know a great deal.

And finally, we have the major analytical key of an exact quindecile between the Sun and the *Node* (an obsessive mother situation) and the congruence of Mercury-Saturn and the Nodal axis, the residual focus of the mind's severe assimilation of the developmental tensions.

Linda was prepared, naturally and impressively, to commandeer the progress of the consultation herself. The client can not be allowed to do that, except in very rare and special strategic instances. The authority of the astrologer must be established, one way or another, immediately, and sometimes confrontation is a viable technique. This is pointedly so in the scope and spirit of Single Session Therapy.

Vocally, I stopped Linda in her tracks: "Thank you for coming to see me, for having faith in the discussion we are going to share, but I want you to know that I am going to conduct this consultation, not you. I am well prepared; you see all the work I've done. I know what will help us best in our discussion. And until you get used to this, I want you to hold your theories and answer my questions. That is the only way we can proceed, *and you know it*. Fine."[88]

I delivered this paragraph with very strong impact, without threatening in any way through body movement or posture, but using my voice and eyes sternly. But note that I purposefully put security statements among the control statements: "thank you . . . for having faith in the discussion . . . until you get used to this (i.e., this one-sided style will end soon) . . . we are going to share . . . I am well prepared . . . the work I've done . . . to help us best . . . the discussion (not further tirade) . . . and *you know it* (we are of the same mind and this is the security of the moment)."

---

88 Confrontation is a psychotherapeutic technique that can be used carefully for considerable effect. Most therapy texts will cover the considerations and techniques.

Additionally, showing authority strongly suggested that I was not afraid to speak my mind, to make my points free and clear of censorship or intimidation. Therefore, *I was distinctly credible*, and this would be/is important at the end segment of the consultation, the projection into the future.

I then delivered a cascade of deductions along the lines written above, and only THEN did I ask for her comment, specifically about all I said to the relationship with her parents, especially with regard to the mother role. Linda spun quite a tale about a father who was non-communicative, whom she idolized (this is so often the case: the idolization is the yearning for his attention, love, and leadership, the beginning symptom of unfinished business), who *"put me into the mother role at eight."*

Immediately my eyes searched for a rapport Arc of 8 degrees: there was Uranus=Asc at 7 and Saturn-Mercury=MC at 11, along with MC=Sun/Neptune. The birthtime may be slightly off, and I took that into consideration to check as the consultation continued, using arcs to match up with her life development.

Basically, Linda's tale revealed a strange situation: the father told her clearly and strongly that *she* must take over the mother's role (was this some kind of displaced sexual-abuse energy?) because "mother is weak." The tale revealed that her parents (and we can imagine the mother's view of all of this, the jealousy) developed severe resentment of her. "Now that I am everything they would never become, when I got my Ph.D., *my father introduced me as his wife*! I was never his daughter. I was *the other woman*!"

Our discussion worked well. Creative connections led up to discussion of her marriage: "My husband is everything they (her parents) are . . . ," which surprised me since the Moon (ruler of the 7th in the 7th) is well situated. There is much more here, but for our purposes with prediction technique we must now appreciate how this very intelligent, insightful therapist had begun to rescue herself and build her development to a target in the future, to embrace a nobly romantic ideal of helping others live more fulfilled lives.

Linda had written her parents quite a letter (at their fiftieth wedding anniversary) calling for a cessation of their behaviors toward her. She did much the same with her husband, summarily cutting him out of her emotional life, although they lived together still with their younger children.

Throughout all of 1999, Linda would face tr. Pluto squaring *the Sun/Moon midpoint* at 9 Virgo 25. Any contact by transit or by Arc with the Sun/Moon midpoint throughout life will be very important in any horoscope; as an adult, it usually focuses most strongly *on relationship* (male and female). There was little doubt within Linda's reality that her marriage will come to an end formally in the months immediately ahead after the consultation. At the same time, and certainly the dominant measure of all (with perhaps the slightest adjustment of the Midheaven to accommodate it), is SA Pluto=MC, an enormous change of life spread over the year ahead as well.

"What do you project for yourself now, Linda, in the next six months or so, now that you are freeing yourself from the past? There is every indication of a final closure in your marriage."

Linda had important professional plans with a book she had written, with speaking engagements, and grand, national public-image development as a psychotherapist. Everything looked so very good: there was Uranus=Jupiter ("the big break, boundless optimism") and Jupiter=Neptune ("idealism; grand spirit; feeling quietly special; looking ahead to nice times").

Transits punctuated these background arcs very strongly: tr. Pluto conjunct Mars (opinionation giving way to *publishing*; perhaps a new home, since Mars rules the 4th); success and appreciation through tr. Uranus opposed Pluto, ruler of the 11th, and finally, tr. Saturn square the Moon (ambition) in the Spring along with SA Moon= Mercury/Saturn in the 9th, Mercury ruling the 9th, publishing.

Personal freedom, rebirth, new image, and success were finally going to come to this queenly lady, and we are most grateful that she has allowed us to share and learn from part of her story.

New Discovery

Case Study: Robert

We met Robert first on pages 112–113, dealing with his selective amnesia (if that indeed is the case) about his childhood. This became very important to me in the consultation because I was led there in the first place through strong attention to the Moon in the 8th House; there is also the Uranus square with the Moon and, very importantly, the Neptune quindecile with the Moon. I noted that the Moon is in the 8th and rules the 12th; and, very dramatically positioned in the 12th, we see Mercury in almost precise conjunction with the Nodal Axis. Discussion about the mother should be very important.

The defensiveness of the Eastern hemisphere orientation is simply not to be felt in meeting Robert. He is charming, attractive, accessible, well-spoken, and very successful. His only comment about his maternal relationship is that she was "extremely supportive."

But then, there was the fascinating answer to my question led by the Saturn-Sun arc just before his sixteenth birthday: Robert couldn't remember anything, except that it

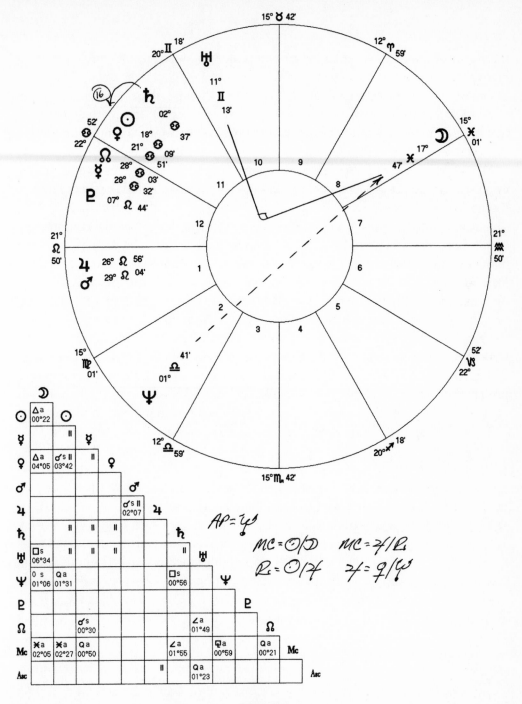

Figure 14
Robert

was the time he and his sister had just been speaking about in relation *to their mother's nervous breakdown(!)*.

The Moon is a singleton, reactively powerful in Pisces, alone, highly charged in terms of sensitivity. Perhaps there was a hurt that was so great that Robert needed to blot it out. I do not know, of course; neither does Robert; and, all things considered, there was no need to go into it. Robert is apparently in splendid balance in his life.

BUT my experience told me that the Neptune-Moon quindecile, etc. had to "speak" in Robert's life somehow. Neptune was within orb consideration of the Aries Point; it should "come out."

Robert is a big businessman (*MC=Sun/Moon*; Venus, ruler of the MC conjunct the Sun in Cancer; Mercury, *ruler of the 2nd is peregrine*; Mars in Leo (getting away with murder, so to speak) conjunct Regulus, rising; Leo Ascendant (nascent king complex); *Pluto=Sun/Jupiter; MC=Jupiter/Pluto*). He is wealthy and secure, long divorced, proud of his children, socially popular, at peace. But what about this Moon and the developmental tensions attached to it? I could not get away from this.

I noted as well that Robert has the midpoint picture Jupiter=Venus/Neptune—the Neptune once again—quite often suggesting *an idealism, a romantic swoon, a spirituality*. Here was an echo of the Pisces dimension wrapped around the Moon; here was a push into my understanding the Moon in Pisces, in the 8th, ruling the 12th. And suddenly I heard myself asking Robert, "Let me ask you a research question please: what is the possible spiritual dimension here in your makeup that we should discuss?"[89]

There it was! Robert beamed and said something like "Decidedly so!"

So quickly, we were then talking about a businessman friend of his who *has* "followed the spiritual path" and is extremely active in helping others live a better life. "In fact, I was talking with him about this just the other day!"

Here is why this was important, at the conclusion of our consultation on *November 17, 1998*: Robert would have ahead of him an *SP Moon conjunct his Pisces Moon* in mid-April, 1999. This would refocus the reigning need of the personality; in this case in Pisces, the need to be agreeable, pleasant, highly intuitive, and sensitive to the needs of others. At the same time, tr. Jupiter would square the Sun, ruler of his Ascendant), and, again at the same time, *the very challenging tr. Saturn square Pluto ruler of his 4th* (a loss threatened; real estate holdings?).

---

89 I note with humor this very effective device: whenever you do not feel quite so sure about a deduction you are risking, a potentially important deduction, say to your client, "May I ask you a research question, please?" This protects the credibility of all you have already established in the consultation. If you are inaccurate with the question, no harm done! It was a research question anyway! *But if you are right*, the research element of the question is forgotten, and it's full steam ahead!

You see in the inset that follows (page 138–139), exactly what I was looking at in the prediction phase of the consultation. Look further into July: there is the first of three transit "hits" (there are usually three hits by the outer planets to any given point due to retrogradation; the first and third are usually the most demonstrable; significance and expedition accumulate over the time period) by *tr. Saturn to the Midheaven,* a time of culmination. This will be extremely important to this businessman, of course. And at the same time, there are tr. Uranus square the MC and SA Mars=Venus, ruler of the Midheaven.[90]

Then in late October, there is a SA Sun=Uranus. With Uranus ruling the 7th that *could* suggest marriage.

We are seeing a tremendous set of developments brewing in Robert's life. So, working *backward* from that Sun=Uranus Arc, we see the second Saturn transit of the MC, we see the Arc of Pluto=MC late in September (sesquiquadrate, but extremely significant), the Mars Arc to Venus in July along with the first Saturn transit to the Midheaven, and then the beginning of it all, the SP Moon conjunct the Moon.

How was this development to occur? At what level? More business as usual? An increase in business outreach? Or something entirely new?

This discussion was issuing out of the disclosure discovery of the significance of the Neptune-Moon quindecile, the Moon's significance, etc. Many fresh dimensions were forming around the surprise development possible in Robert's life: leaving his business track and pursuing the spiritual path to help others live fulfillingly.

To open the door to major change, i.e., leaving his present business, I asked about financial security, and Robert answered that he did not have to work further for a living.

We know of his strong interest in the "discovery." The circumstances of our discussion had riveted his attention to what was developing.

"Robert, *what would need to happen for you to change paths?*" This is the same kind of question as "What do you project for yourself in the next six months? Notice how strategically it is worded. It got Robert conceptualizing and projecting himself into the future. (The word "need" is a very powerful catalyst for thought.) What he would say would be what could be reasonable to a high degree.

"I think my partner and I would have to get free of some 15,000 apartments. And, you know? I think he *needs* to be free of that." What I was hearing was that his partner would be open to divesting the apartment holdings.

---

90 Additionally, earlier in the consultation, Robert mentioned he had just met a "new lady," a foreign woman (Mars rules the 9th). The measurement had been SP Moon square Uranus, ruler of his 7th.

	DATE	TIME	EX	JOB	#	P1 POS.	HS	P2 POS.	HS
Asc ∠ ♂	21DEC98	Ø8:Ø8 AM	X	AR-NA	Ø4	14♎Ø4	Ø3	29♌Ø4	Ø1
♂ ∠ ♂	23DEC98	1Ø:53 AM	X	TR-NA	Ø1	14♎Ø4	Ø3	29♌Ø4	Ø1
♄ SD	29DEC98	Ø3:36 PM	X	TR-NA	Ø2	26♈46	Ø9	26♈46	Ø9
♂ □ ☉	31DEC98	12:52 PM	X	TR-NA	Ø1	18♎Ø9	Ø3	18♋Ø9	11
☽ ⚻ ☿	Ø3JAN99	Ø5:4Ø AM	X	PR-NA	Ø3	13♓32	Ø7	28♋32	12
♃ ⚻ ♇	Ø6JAN99	Ø5:Ø6 AM	X	TR-NA	Ø1	22♓44	Ø8	Ø7♌44	12
♂ □ ♀	Ø8JAN99	Ø3:47 AM	X	TR-NA	Ø1	21♎51	Ø3	21♋51	11
♂ ⚻ ♅	17JAN99	Ø3:Ø8 PM	X	TR-NA	Ø1	26♎13	Ø3	11♊13	1Ø
♂ □ ☿	22JAN99	11:36 PM	X	TR-NA	Ø1	28♎32	Ø3	28♋32	12
♂ ⚻ ☽	Ø2FEB99	Ø2:27 PM	X	TR-NA	Ø1	Ø2♏47	Ø3	17♓47	Ø8
♄ □ ☿	12FEB99	Ø6:17 AM	X	TR-NA	Ø1	28♈32	Ø9	28♋32	12
♃ ∠ Mc	16FEB99	Ø5:33 AM	X	TR-NA	Ø1	ØØ♈42	Ø8	15♉42	1Ø
♆ ∠ ☽		Ø8:Ø5 AM	X	TR-NA	Ø1	Ø2♒47	Ø6	17♓47	Ø8
♂ □ ♇	17FEB99	Ø1:34 PM	X	TR-NA	Ø1	Ø7♏44	Ø3	Ø7♌44	12
♃ ☍ ♆	2ØFEB99	Ø2:11 PM	X	TR-NA	Ø1	Ø1♈41	Ø8	Ø1♎41	Ø2
♃ □ ♄	24FEB99	Ø5:2Ø PM	X	TR-NA	Ø1	Ø2♈37	Ø8	Ø2♋37	11
♇ SR	13MAR99	Ø5:27 PM	X	TR-NA	Ø2	1Ø♐3Ø	Ø4	1Ø♐3Ø	Ø4
♃ ⚻ Asc	14MAR99	Ø3:36 PM	X	TR-NA	Ø1	Ø6♈5Ø	Ø8	21♌5Ø	Ø1
♂ SR	18MAR99	Ø1:49 PM	X	TR-NA	Ø2	12♏12	Ø3	12♏12	Ø3
♄ ∠ ☽	26MAR99	Ø3:Ø9 PM	X	TR-NA	Ø1	Ø2♉47	Ø9	17♓47	Ø8
♅ □ Mc	3ØMAR99	12:5Ø PM	X	TR-NA	Ø1	15♒42	Ø6	15♉42	1Ø
♃ ⚻ ♃	Ø4APR99	Ø7:58 PM	X	TR-NA	Ø1	11♈56	Ø8	26♌56	Ø1
♃ ⚻ ♂	13APR99	Ø3:Ø4 PM	X	TR-NA	Ø1	14♈Ø4	Ø9	29♌Ø4	Ø1
♂ □ ♇	14APR99	Ø9:18 AM	X	TR-NA	Ø1	Ø7♏44R	Ø3	Ø7♌44	12
☽ ☌ ☽		Ø3:27 PM	X	PR-NA	Ø3	17♓47	Ø8	17♓47	Ø8
♂ ⚻ ☽	28APR99	Ø6:Ø7 AM	X	TR-NA	Ø1	Ø2♏47R	Ø3	17♓47	Ø8
♃ □ ☉	3ØAPR99	Ø9:19 PM	X	TR-NA	Ø1	18♈Ø9	Ø9	18♋Ø9	11
♅ ⚻ ♆	Ø5MAY99	Ø2:18 AM	X	TR-NA	Ø1	16♒41	Ø6	Ø1♎41	Ø2
♄ □ ♇		Ø3:34 AM	X	TR-NA	Ø1	Ø7♉44	Ø9	Ø7♌44	12
♆ SR	Ø6MAY99	Ø7:41 PM	X	TR-NA	Ø2	Ø4♒22	Ø6	Ø4♒22	Ø6
♂ □ ☿	1ØMAY99	Ø7:42 AM	X	TR-NA	Ø1	28♎32R	Ø3	28♋32	12
♃ □ ♀	17MAY99	Ø5:28 AM	X	TR-NA	Ø1	21♈51	Ø9	21♋51	11
♂ ⚻ ♅	19MAY99	Ø1:24 AM	X	TR-NA	Ø1	26♎13R	Ø3	11♊13	1Ø
♅ SR	21MAY99	Ø8:38 PM	X	TR-NA	Ø2	16♒48	Ø6	16♒48	Ø6
♂ SD	Ø4JUN99	Ø6:Ø7 AM	X	TR-NA	Ø2	24♎27	Ø3	24♎27	Ø3
♃ ∠ ♅	Ø7JUN99	Ø3:36 AM	X	TR-NA	Ø1	26♈13	Ø9	11♊13	1Ø
♅ ⚻ ♆	Ø8JUN99	ØØ:37 AM	X	TR-NA	Ø1	16♒41R	Ø6	Ø1♎41	Ø2
♃ □ ☿	19JUN99	Ø3:59 PM	X	TR-NA	Ø1	28♈32	Ø9	28♋32	12
♂ ⚻ ♅	21JUN99	Ø3:37 AM	X	TR-NA	Ø1	26♎13	Ø3	11♊13	1Ø
♂ □ ☿	3ØJUN99	11:39 AM	X	TR-NA	Ø1	28♎32	Ø3	28♋32	12
♂ ⚻ ☽	12JUL99	Ø9:Ø7 PM	X	TR-NA	Ø1	Ø2♏47	Ø3	17♓47	Ø8
♅ □ Mc	15JUL99	Ø7:3Ø PM	X	TR-NA	Ø1	15♒42R	Ø6	15♉42	1Ø
♃ ∠ ☽	18JUL99	Ø4:59 PM	X	TR-NA	Ø1	Ø2♉47	Ø9	17♓47	Ø8
♄ ☌ Mc	19JUL99	Ø9:19 AM	X	TR-NA	Ø1	15♉42	1Ø	15♉42	1Ø
♂ □ ♀	21JUL99	12:29 PM	X	AR-NA	Ø4	21♎51	Ø3	21♋51	11
♂ □ ♇	24JUL99	11:32 AM	X	TR-NA	Ø1	Ø7♏44	Ø3	Ø7♌44	12
♆ ∠ ☽	Ø2AUG99	Ø1:29 PM	X	TR-NA	Ø1	Ø2♒47R	Ø6	17♓47	Ø8
♄ ⚻ ♆	Ø6AUG99	Ø1:25 AM	X	TR-NA	Ø1	16♉41	1Ø	Ø1♎41	Ø2
♂ ☍ Mc	Ø9AUG99	Ø8:2Ø AM	X	TR-NA	Ø1	15♏42	Ø4	15♉42	1Ø
☽ ⚻ ♇	11AUG99	ØØ:Ø8 AM	X	PR-NA	Ø3	22♓44	Ø8	Ø7♌44	12

Robert's Data (Dec. 98–Aug. 99)

	DATE	TIME	EX	JOB	#	P1 POS.	HS	P2 POS.	HS
♂ ∠ ♆	11AUG99	03:33 AM	X	TR-NA	01	16 ♏ 41	04	01 ♎ 41	02
♂ ⚼ ♄	12AUG99	08:36 PM	X	TR-NA	01	17 ♏ 37	04	02 ♋ 37	11
♇ SD	18AUG99	09:42 PM	X	TR-NA	02	07 ♐ 44	04	07 ♐ 44	04
♂ □ Asc	20AUG99	06:41 AM	X	TR-NA	01	21 ♏ 50	04	21 ♌ 50	01
♃ SR	25AUG99	02:07 AM	X	TR-NA	02	04 ♉ 59	09	04 ♉ 59	09
♂ □ ♃	28AUG99	08:32 PM	X	TR-NA	01	26 ♏ 56	04	26 ♌ 56	01
♄ SR	30AUG99	00:39 AM	X	TR-NA	02	17 ♉ 11	10	17 ♉ 11	10
♂ □ ♂	01SEP99	07:17 AM	X	TR-NA	01	29 ♏ 04	04	29 ♌ 04	01
♂ ⚼ ☉	07SEP99	07:11 PM	X	TR-NA	01	03 ♐ 09	04	18 ♋ 09	11
♂ ⚼ ♀	13SEP99	12:44 PM	X	TR-NA	01	06 ♐ 51	04	21 ♋ 51	11
♂ ☍ ♅	20SEP99	02:50 AM	X	TR-NA	01	11 ♐ 13	04	11 ♊ 13	10
♇ ⚼ Mc	23SEP99	01:36 AM	X	AR-NA	04	00 ♎ 42	02	15 ♉ 42	10
♄ ⚼ ♆		02:10 AM	X	TR-NA	01	16 ♉ 41R	10	01 ♎ 41	02
♂ ⚼ ☿		01:35 PM	X	TR-NA	01	13 ♐ 32	04	28 ♋ 32	12
♂ □ ☽	29SEP99	06:28 PM	X	TR-NA	01	17 ♐ 47	04	17 ♓ 47	08
♃ ∠ ☽	01OCT99	08:30 AM	X	TR-NA	01	02 ♉ 47R	09	17 ♓ 47	08
♂ ⚼ ♇	06OCT99	08:55 PM	X	TR-NA	01	22 ♐ 44	05	07 ♌ 44	12
→ ♄ 2nd TIME ☌ Mc	11OCT99	03:27 AM	X	TR-NA	01	15 ♉ 42R	10	15 ♉ 42	10
♆ SD	13OCT99	09:34 PM	X	TR-NA	02	01 ♒ 35	06	01 ♒ 35	06
♂ ⚼ Mc	18OCT99	00:50 AM	X	TR-NA	01	00 ♑ 42	05	15 ♉ 42	10
♂ □ ♆	19OCT99	09:14 AM	X	TR-NA	01	01 ♑ 41	05	01 ♎ 41	02
♂ ☍ ♄	20OCT99	04:21 PM	X	TR-NA	01	02 ♑ 37	05	02 ♋ 37	11
♅ SD	23OCT99	02:24 AM	X	TR-NA	02	12 ♒ 52	06	12 ♒ 52	06
♂ ⚼ Asc	26OCT99	10:44 AM	X	TR-NA	01	06 ♑ 50	05	21 ♌ 50	01
→ ☉ □ ♅	30OCT99	08:25 PM	X	AR-NA	04	11 ♍ 13	01	11 ♊ 13	10
♂ ⚼ ♃	02NOV99	08:49 AM	X	TR-NA	01	11 ♑ 56	05	26 ♌ 56	01
♃ □ ☿	03NOV99	03:59 AM	X	TR-NA	01	28 ♈ 32R	09	28 ♋ 32	12
♂ ⚼ ♂	05NOV99	05:12 AM	X	TR-NA	01	14 ♑ 04	05	29 ♌ 04	01
♂ ☍ ☉	10NOV99	04:14 PM	X	TR-NA	01	18 ♑ 09	05	18 ♋ 09	11
♂ ☍ ♀	15NOV99	02:06 PM	X	TR-NA	01	21 ♑ 51	05	21 ♋ 51	11
♂ ⚼ ♅	21NOV99	07:58 AM	X	TR-NA	01	26 ♑ 13	06	11 ♊ 13	10
♃ ∠ ♅	23NOV99	11:18 PM	X	TR-NA	01	26 ♈ 13R	09	11 ♊ 13	10
♂ ☍ ☿	24NOV99	09:04 AM	X	TR-NA	01	28 ♑ 32	06	28 ♋ 32	12
♂ ∠ ☽	29NOV99	10:09 PM	X	TR-NA	01	02 ♒ 47	06	17 ♓ 47	08
♂ ☍ ♇	06DEC99	08:47 AM	X	TR-NA	01	07 ♒ 44	06	07 ♌ 44	12
♂ □ Mc	16DEC99	04:17 PM	X	TR-NA	01	15 ♒ 42	06	15 ♉ 42	10
♂ ⚼ ♆	17DEC99	10:33 PM	X	TR-NA	01	16 ♒ 41	06	01 ♎ 41	02
♂ ⚼ ♄	19DEC99	03:42 AM	X	TR-NA	01	17 ♒ 37	06	02 ♋ 37	11
♆ ∠ ☽	20DEC99	11:04 AM	X	TR-NA	01	02 ♒ 47	06	17 ♓ 47	08
♃ SD		02:41 PM	X	TR-NA	02	25 ♈ 01	09	25 ♈ 01	09

Robert's Data (Aug. 99–Dec. 99)

Bang! THAT explains the ominous tr. of *Saturn square Pluto*, ruler of Robert's 4th: this was not loss, loss, loss; this was *creative divestiture*, a tactic. I shared this with Robert, and he not only agreed, he lit up!

We have since met once more on this issue specifically. "I'm really thinking about this a lot, Noel."

Now, the feel of "new discovery" here is not a feel of something "out of the blue" or of impractical wish projection. It is an exciting sense of finding something *that has been there since he was born*, inside Robert, waiting for this time to emerge! The power and, dare I say, insistence of the Neptune-Moon quindecile came to the surface at this time.

Confidence in the discovery and its projection is now reinforced in Robert by the fact that someone outside himself, the person unknown to him called an astrologer, discovered this dimension, unlocked it, and talked about it sensibly. Authority had been established throughout the consultation and was crowned by this last suggestion, deduction, vision.

Illness Potential

Another kind of surprise discovery through an astrology consultation is illness, especially critical illness. Toward understanding this frontier of astrology a bit more, I hope astrologers will share my research and findings presented in *Astrological Timing of Critical Illness* (Llewellyn, 1998).

The objective for the astrologer who is not a medical doctor is to assess and have corroborated the weak points of the client's body and systems, note pointed aggravation of those areas in the present or near future, and recommend a physical check-up by a medical expert well enough ahead of time to ward off danger. Of course, the older the client is, the more pressing this responsibility is.

In Robert's horoscope, we are keying the approaching accentuation of Pluto activity (a proved concomitant for critical illness) in the development of the astrological symbolism: there is the SA Uranus=*Pluto* (in the 12th), promising the buildup of "overturning the status quo, creating a whole new perspective for ego-recognition" (accumulating to partile in 2003) and tr. Uranus opposed that *Pluto* (for the third time) in January 1998, ten months before our consultation (could that have been the beginning of something debilitating systemically?).

Then, there is the ominous loss-for-renewal transit of Saturn square Pluto in May 1999, which we have interpreted as strategic divestiture of home holdings (Pluto ruling his 4th) but which *we must also consider within the whole scheme of things as a challenge to the health system.*

Natally, Robert's Pluto is conspicuously peregrine and, while it may dominate as a corroboration within his big-business profile (MC=Jupiter/Pluto, Pluto=Sun/Jupiter), *it is also his prostate gland*, and Robert is fifty-five years old.

I asked him, "Robert, the horoscope has ways of suggesting the places in the body that can weaken conspicuously during the aging process. I'm not a medical doctor, but, please, let me ask you, have you had a physical examination lately?"

"Yes, just recently."

"Did the doctor take blood for a PSA examination (Prostate Specific Antigen)?"

"Funny that you should mention that . . . ."

"What was the number, Robert?"

Robert's score was high, perhaps *twice as high* as is normal for a man of his age. This was a real alarm, in my opinion. We discussed this very calmly.

Robert's doctor had taken the course of "watchful waiting." But I explained much about the condition to Robert and asked him to get another reading, a second opinion, if you will. The point was to protect Robert with a warning (represented by the PSA score) in the light of the major life changes ahead, i.e., the extra challenge to the system and the personal perspectives of development (Pluto).

Robert was very grateful, went for a second PSA reading, and this time obtained a score twenty-three percent lower than the first reading, but still high. While gaining reassurance, Robert planned yet a third test in thirty days. Through warning and checking, astrology was doing further service.

Bad News

Another surprise discovery is *bad news*. I feel that the creative astrologer feels good about life, feels that there is a purpose for developmental tension. This is our spirit of humanism. While clients may sometimes bring into the consultation the vestigial sense of "bad news a'comin'" (because of early identification of arcane astrology with doomsday fatalism), astrologers must prevail with recognition of life as a press with purpose: there are things to do to help us help ourselves to reach the sun.

But each of us has had extraordinary down-times in life. I recall the period, when, in unrelenting order, transiting Neptune, Saturn, and then Uranus crossed my Sun over and over again for three years; it was my "mid-life crisis." I learned a great deal; I had thought myself above the process; I had tried to ignore it; but the suffering and learning were inexorable and, at times, painful.

If an astrologer had suggested to me earlier that this was coming into my life, I would have done everything I could *not* to heed the observation; I would have probably demeaned the astrologer (to discredit the source of the observations), and gone my merry way. In reality, my business and personal life were in a shambles, and the planetary movements reflected that.

But, I do believe—and perhaps this is part of what I learned during my mid-life crisis—if the astrologer had been able to discuss the pending period with me in terms of empirical evidence (*to prove and dramatize what **could** happen in my life*) as well as in emotional terms (*to recognize my feelings and how they might fare*), things would have been different. The pain and bewilderment would have been much less. It would have been helpful to hear what was *beyond* that down-time; what was *on the other side of that time*; what could I project for myself through such a time and then *expect again to be full-steam ahead*. Hope and plan.

I would have listened more. I would have learned more earlier. Discovery and communication of bad news are difficult; ask any doctor. (I have, and I learned a lot.)

Case Study: Bonnie

"Bonnie's" horoscope should focus itself easily for you. Let me guide you: there's an obvious stellium accent of the 11th House, suggesting the need for love psycho-dynamically. This is intensified clearly by Saturn's presence in the 11th and its exact conjunction with the Sun and Venus (a severe idealism involved defensively). Additionally, the Eastern orientation suggests lots of protectionism around the lovable-ness issues.

The Sun-Moon blend (Aquarius-Leo) suggests quite a self-dramatizing romantic; in the light of the 11th House issues under stress, we have a princess-queen complex that has much trouble getting off the ground.

As our first impression grows, we work to fit all other observations into that impression, establishing a portrait and scenario of development that hold together in reason. We see Mars, ruler of the Ascendant, is peregrine in the strategy-orientated Capricorn 10th: Bonnie will strategize her way through some defense plan to establish herself strongly as lovable, important, etc.

And finally, within the first look at the horoscope, we see that the burning Saturn-Sun conjunction is quindecile the Node. The mother relationship has got to be at the core of these issues. Saturn rules the parental 10th; the Moon, ruler of the parental 4th, is conjunct Uranus.

Venus rules the 7th and is with the Sun in conjunction with Saturn: all of the developmental tensions about being lovable will be played out strategically somehow

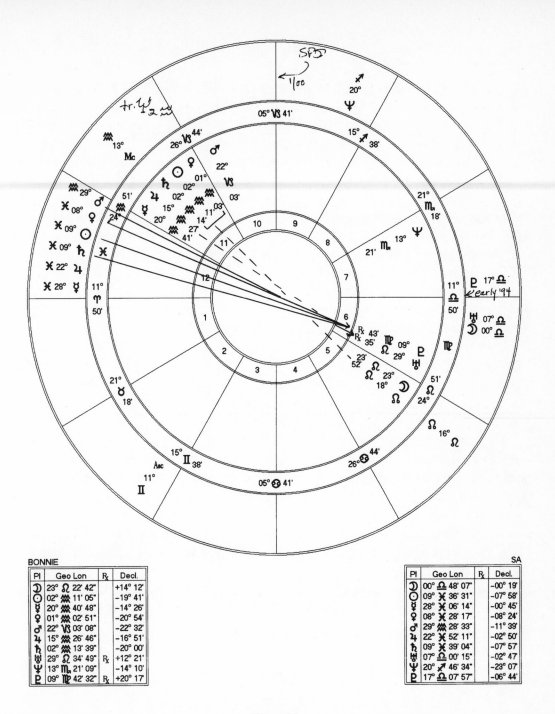

Figure 15
Bonnie
Inner Chart: Natal, Outer Chart-SA: Legal Case

in relationships. *We can expect overcompensatory activity in that direction, to prove that she is lovable.*

As soon as I mentioned this complex at the beginning of our telephone consultation, Bonnie replied with easy disclosure: "My mother always made me feel very insignificant. It was a total putdown, but then she would tell me, 'But you must be successful.'"

Bonnie said that her mother was totally removed from her emotionally. "I would ask her, 'How do I look?' and she would say, '*Nobody's* looking at *you*.'"

I suggested that this could well have been a projection on her mother's part, putting onto Bonnie an evaluation or description that the mother felt keenly about *herself*.

Clearly Bonnie took forward into her life an enormous weight: *having to prove herself lovable*, building her self-worth profile (note that Venus rules the 2nd as well as the 7th and is in the conjunction with Saturn). She would work her way into relationship and look for the confirmation there in an imbalanced, perhaps even self-sacrificing way (the Southern Hemisphere and Eastern emphases).

During the consultation, when I was tracking her development in relation to the SA Pluto=Ascendant (Pluto 32 degree/years to the horizon; early 1994), I learned that a major relationship suffered "many breakups." Two children had been born in this period of three years, and I suggested they had been conceived as a security for her within the live-in relationship, to keep the man, the success.

The relationship ended finally in the Spring of 1996 with tr. Uranus conjoining Venus-Sun-Saturn. The next year, tr. Saturn came to her Ascendant, April 1997. An enormous legal battle had been created as Bonnie cried out for support and identity affirmation, establishing yet further that she was indeed valuable. The legal case is very, very complicated since her mate is extremely wealthy and his business holdings are complicated. Lawyers were demanding huge sums of money. At thirty-six, Bonnie was under siege again with security concerns of the present framed within value pains from the past.

Look at the Solar Arc positions for January 1999. The tension is enormous. Additionally, other key measurements appear only to add to this difficult picture:

- SA Saturn=Pluto *February 1999* "Threat of loss; potential self-destruction"
  SA Sun=Pluto "New perspectives confirmed; power needs"
  SA Mars=Uranus "Test of nerves; urge to action"

- Tr. Saturn square Sun-Saturn *March 1999* (more of the same)
  Tr. Uranus conjunct Jupiter, ruler of the 9th "Excitation of legalisms"
  SA MC=Neptune *April 1999* "Being pushed around; disruption, losing it"

- Tr Pluto square Pluto *May 1999* "Changing the way of doing things in life"

What an uncomfortable line-up of measurements ahead for Bonnie. One can feel the estranged mate (who had avoided marriage for so long) really putting it to Bonnie in an ugly battle. If the battle continues past May, it will go to mid-July 1999, when Bonnie will have tr. Saturn square her *Jupiter*, ruler of the legal 9th and, at the same time, tr. Uranus conjunct *Jupiter*.

Bonnie is in the film production business. The measurement of tr. Neptune conjoining Sun and Saturn, ruling her Midheaven, seems to speak of freedom for her, on her own feet again professionally in November-December 1999. Because of the nature of her fledgling business, the symbolism of Neptune can speak supportively here. And in January 2000, *the SP Moon conjoins her Midheaven!* Finally.

Bonnie and I went through much in the fifty-minute telephone consultation. We revived the past, the thorough devaluation from her mother. Discovering this helped Bonnie see it clearly; she needed to relate it to the acceptance of several consecutive relationships, without marriage but with great emotional investment. The final relationship now had the assets of two children; Bonnie's insecurity was now on the threshold of being transferred *into her children's lives*. She would be free of this siege in approximately four months, and then finally on her own feet seven months later.

This is how I presented it. "It's the culmination of lots of bad times, Bonnie. This is tough. It is not a statement that you're worthless or unimportant. *You know better now*. You've got *your own future already beginning!* This is it, though; an ugly, unfortunate emotional/financial crunch. *And then you should be free of it all*. The courts have to be fair, with the children involved. Keep me posted, please. I'll stick with you."

On my notes as a summary of the consultation, I wrote "documentation of human value issues," not without resentment of Bonnie's mother's problems long ago.

Very often, with the hearing of bad news, the client will very quickly start to re-explain things to assimilate the news, *to make it acceptable*. This occurs often when a person does not necessarily have priorities straight: a "first things first" dictum is often extremely helpful, "The way we've been discussing this, it is absolutely clear, isn't it, that your job comes first, the changes and rise we know that have a high probability of coming to bloom three months from now? We don't see any way clear for the 'romance of your dreams' as you put it! This is not bad news; this is delayed news, if you will. (Now the positive lift.) Just think what this new job situation is going to do for you: *you will be giving off a different vibe; you'll be circulating with different people*. THEN, then we can look again; but let's *let this fine work-improvement situation sink in first*. Fair?"

"Of course, I see that. Interesting. And, you know, I sort of felt that too. I've got a lot on my plate right now, and with my job if I did have a romance, it could very well end up being a distraction."

Case Study: Lilly

Yet another discovery of discomfort in astrology is meeting with the client who has given up his or her life's way (usually a female), rationalized or indeed caused by caring for an aged parent. Usually the woman and the mother or father, in their late eighties or early nineties, are sitting around doing nothing, waiting for death. But, then what?

"Lilly's" horoscope (not shown here; see it in your mind's eye as I describe it)—she is her early sixties—shows a distinct orientation to the West, *giving oneself away to others*. This is echoed by the observation that Neptune is square to the Nodal Axis, *confusion in identity development*. The root concerns for this are certainly the mother (the Nodal axis conjunct the horizon) and the father situation (the Saturn retrograde phenomenon). The father is probably quite passive, in default to the mother who clearly is centrally so strong (exactly on the horizon). Saturn retrograde rules the self-worth 2nd House.

Additionally, Venus, ruler of the 10th, is exactly on the Aries Point and squared by Saturn retrograde. While there is an artistic dimension possible within the career choice (Venus rules the MC), there is a tightness of the emotional need complexes involving relationships.

The mindset is rattled: Uranus, ruler of the 3rd, is quindecile with Mars, and there is probably a lot of anger about it. Uranus squares the Sun, ruler of the 9th: the education was almost surely interrupted, yet it means an enormous amount to her (Mercury is final dispositor, co-ruler of the 9th, and is in the 9th).

The midpoint pictures Sun=Moon/Mercury and Jupiter/Mercury (the writer's portrait) are very interesting and must be explained.

In her introduction to me for making her appointment, Lilly had explained that she was living with and taking care of her father who is in his early nineties.

Of key interest in my preparation was the obvious confluence of arcs at age fourteen and fifteen: Neptune=Midheaven, Mars=Ascendant; Uranus=Mars; and Pluto=Sun. This is extraordinary. I looked just before this time in 1951–52[91] and saw that in the Summer of 1947 *tr. Saturn and Pluto were conjunct Lilly's Sun*. It was dramatically clear that this period in the early family life would be extremely important for explanation of the difficulties I knew she had.

---

91 Very easily in the "Quick Glance Transit Tables" (100 years) in the appendix of *Synthesis & Counseling in Astrology*.

Here are some key verbatim excerpts of our telephone consultation:

N: [After some small talk on the phone.] Do you work?

L: I did, but now I take care of a ninety-two-year-old father for the past five years, since my mother died . . . I had to give up my job . . . [note: she did not say "My father"; how much emotion was left here?].

N: And what was that job?

L: In the decorative arts, making jewelry, selling estate jewelry . . . that was my main situation. I'm an artist, I'm a poet. [The Venus=Aries Point square MC measurements.]

N: Ah! The writing is something I was just going to ask you about. Have you ever published anything? [Sun=Mercury/Jupiter.]

L: No. Everything I write is very personal.

N: Well, you have the signature here of writing, conspicuously, and I'm curious why you never shared that with anyone.

L: Because I felt that my poetry was very personal; it only comes in spurts. I can't sit down and write, *unless I go through some kind of trauma.* [Quite a statement of the Saturn retrograde square with Venus conjunct the Aries point, in the 7th. These two sole angular planets would surely return to the discussion.]

N: Ah! I'm sure many poets would agree with you. [In other words, everybody suffers, even sensitive people who write poetry.] We've come a long way to this state here, the development shown in your horoscope. There are a lot of short-circuits and difficulties shown in it.

L: [Nervous laughter.] I'm living it!

N: And I need to talk about them with you a little bit, Lilly, so that I can get a grip on the level of frustrations and the kind of things you are going to be able to take with you into the near future. [Showing her I am already thinking ahead for her.]

L: Go ahead, ask me anything.

N: There's a double dose here in the parental department, if I may say it that way, so objectively [talking with her as unemotionally as she was presenting to me].

There's a legacy of difficulty and inferiority feelings taken on in the early homelife here through the relationship or lack of it with your father.

L: With my father? Because I always had problems with my mother.

N: Well, we're going to get to that. The point is that either the father was passive or not there . . . .

L: That's exactly right.

N: And this deprives you of an enormous amount of reference, modeling, encouragement, support from the authority figure our culture ordains, in your home.

L: Which was my mother . . . .

N: We're going to get to that; you see how she is dominating everything right now!?

L: Yes.

N: But I have to point that out to you. Did your father and you have any kind of relationship? [I should not have asked a yes/no question here; but I was not worried about Lilly's responses; she was very talkative, and she has Mercury in Virgo peregrine!]

L: I always thought that whenever he was around, it was a good one [relationship], but like you said, it was passive, I mean, you know, if I would argue with my mother, she would say "go ask your father." He always gave in . . . .

N: *Does* your father ever say to you . . . *did* your father ever say to you, "Lilly, baby, I love you"? [I juxtaposed tenses here, because I knew where I was going with the consultation: was she ever appreciated, even now, having sacrificed so much, caring for the father still, day in and day out?]

L: *Nobody* ever said, "I love you." That was the story of my life. Looking for somebody to put their arms around me and say "I love you," put their arms around me and say "You're good at this," or "you're good at that." I had so much talent in me . . . .

N: I know.

L: I mean artistic talent . . . .

N: Yes.

L: . . . that was crying to be let out, and a very, very strict, domineering mother . . .

N: Now [interrupting her], we are going to get to the mother. She has come into the conversation so many times already! She is so dominant. She comes into our conversation once every fifteen seconds [objectifying my point]. There is an imbalance here, and this is a short circuit to which I was referring earlier.

The question about your mother being an extremely dominant force in your development is so clear in this horoscope [Nodal axis conjunct horizon]. The relationship with her is almost by default because of the passive father situation. Can you appreciate that?

L: He gave in to the family situation; he let it be known that she was the boss of the house.

N: And how did that really affect you, do you think? Why didn't she care about you? Why didn't she support you? Was she competing with you [testing the wide orb of Moon-Pluto]?

L: [After some background details of her mother's problems from her family brought into the marriage with Lilly's father.] My own personal take on it, looking back on it, I always thought that she was jealous of the relationship that I had with my father. I don't know why. I had a feeling that she resented me, that she didn't want to have children so soon [reaching for explanation; there was hardly a father relationship for the mother to be jealous of].

N: Tell me please, is there a brother or sister who is conspicuously involved here? [Uranus, ruler of the 3rd square the Sun.]

L: Yes, he died two years ago; she gave all her attention to my brother who came along three years after me; who had very bad asthma [his reaction to the tension-wracked homelife]. I wanted her love, and I never got it.

N: [Abruptly diving into concrete experiences.] At age ten in 1947, around August, was there any major shake-up in your family? [Tr. Pluto conjunct sun, tr. Saturn conjunct Sun.]

L: [Replying immediately.] Yes, yes, big time! Yes, it was in the summer!

Lilly told the story of how the father's brother had caused a scandal for everyone. The problem was in the newspaper for all to see. The father, an attorney, was mortified (he developed bleeding ulcers). The children at school taunted and ridiculed Lilly. She didn't want to go to school to face the daily trauma.

N: Sorry I had to zoom right in on that . . . it was very clear.

Lilly disclosed that at fourteen or fifteen she met the man who would become her husband. The parents objected strongly to the relationship, and this added so much extra hurt to the problems that already had besieged the family. Lilly went to college for one year and left. The next year, to get away from it all, she married, with tr. Saturn conjunct her Ascendant with tr. Uranus conjunct her Sun.

The marriage had enormous problems with tr. Pluto conjunct the Midheaven (1972), and then a reconciliation, children were born, and then finally divorce with tr. Uranus conjunct the Ascendant and tr. Saturn square the Sun (1984). The Ascendant and Sun appeared extremely responsive throughout her development.

The measurements immediately ahead for Lilly were *tr. Uranus opposed the Sun in January 1999* (final time), the time of consultation, a bid to recognize individuality; *SA Node=Sun in April* (with tr. Pluto sesquiquadrate Uranus and tr. Mars square the Sun; and SA Saturn (semisquare)=Moon); *SP Moon square Pluto in September*; and the application of the ominous Arc of *Mars=Pluto to partile in November 1999* in the 8th House with the Sun and Moon. Shortly thereafter, in *February–June 2000, tr. Pluto would conjoin the Ascendant and tr. Saturn would square the Sun.*

There is little doubt the matter of her father's death would finally have to be addressed later in 1999. Then there was a time of conspicuous new start, new perspective, and freedom, if I may, early in 2000. How would Lilly be able to prepare in the months ahead, through the imminent death of her father, and be ready to be on her own, finally, shortly thereafter?

The conclusion of our consultation is presented here:

N: For your peace of mind, let me suggest that around July and then in November, we have important times of challenge to your father's system, according to your horoscope. Now, it's important to understand that, when he leaves, you have to go on. And it's about time that you go on with some *sense of style.* [Trying to put the spotlight on her.]

L: I would hope so!

N: Are you in line for an inheritance when he dies? [Will she have resources to build a new life?]

L: Yes. Yes. It will be quite substantial.

N: Now then, now, I would start to think about all of THAT, because I think it will make you feel better, show you a light at the end of this very dark tunnel, and I think that, if you start to plan, *and not feel guilty about it*—what you can do in your life in its next chapter—that you would be very, very well off [consciously using a financial term for feeling disposition]. Now, are you having any social life at all?

L: None. None. I've become very reclusive.

N: You can not go out at night and leave him alone. You do not belong to any clubs; no friends?

L: No, and I used to [something to work with]. I don't know what's happened to me. I've become very, very . . . . [I did not want reiteration of the negative status quo; I interrupted her.]

N: There's *an opportunity to resume this* in April, and when it comes, I want you take every *opportunity* possible to make it happen in your life and start rebuilding. I think you will find that in the early part of April—that's in about sixty or seventy days. There must be somebody on your horizon or knocking on your door or phoning . . . . [SA Node=Sun is due ("new contacts come into the life").]

L: I did get a phone call, unexpectedly, just recently from an old friend of mine, an invitation to go on a cruise . . . .

N: In mid-April [getting us back on the track], there should be an improvement in your social outreach. Doesn't necessarily mean a male friend; it means social activity. You have got to get back on the track or you're going to be a hermit. [The tone of my voice made the contrasting alternative quite vivid.]

L: I know it's up to me. I know that. [Finally, client involvement with change!]

N: And I think we have a concern here, leading into July, that if your father is weakened considerably, that this could be the time of his passing. [The companion Arc Saturn=Moon] And the next time that is suggested, and even stronger, is in *November*. As I look at this as carefully as I can, November really looms large, and there seems to be a trigger for that just after Labor Day in the first week of *September* [SP Moon square Pluto]. And I'd like you to contact me when this starts to happen, and then I can help you with the strategy, the patience and calmness and strength you have to have for that.

L: Well, if anything happens, when it does happen to him, I'd have to take him back to Connecticut for burial.

N: These are the logistics we would have to talk about. There are just these two things. And I think a positive state of mind being resumed by you now [said very deliberately] is very important to your health later [my concern about the Mars=Pluto arc, with Pluto ruling her 12th, holding Mars].

L. I don't feel well—all the time.

N: This should tell you: if you start projecting yourself into a new healthful direction, while attending to your father caringly before his death, *this is going to change things in your body. There is simply no doubt about it.*

L: I have been getting acupuncture and herbs for the past two years! [There *is* a self-help spirit alive.]

N: Good. These things will help. *But it's a psychological attitude that has to start to improve.* You have to start getting out of yourself, getting brighter, and cheerier, and you can only do this when you are out of the home. And gradually, this should come into your experience, and when he does die, *what you will have been doing will make you stronger*.

   Now, it's a very real concern here, Lilly, that, if you don't start to improve your life quality, when he goes, you're downtrodden to such a degree that you are going to get very ill yourself [recognizing the alternative head-on].

L: Uh-huh [very thoughtfully in agreement; formulating what is being discussed].

N: You understand how that works. The aches and pains, these health concerns now are already part of this picture, coming out of despondency and upset. It's a kind of tension, it really is. *It's amazing how you can see in people's bodies, the change of their frame of mind.* [Lilly was listening raptly; I could feel that on the telephone. I slowed down my speech. I measured my words for maximum impact, especially that last phrase.]

L: [A long pause.] I . . . I fell into this . . . this . . . .

N: . . . routine . . . .

L: . . . routine and lack of anything; it's like getting into a hole and trying to climb your way out of it; in fact, I have dreams about it sometimes. I'm in a hole, and I see the blue sky and I'm trying to climb up, and I can't get my mother out of my head. When I was out in the West, I had a breakdown, I had a freaky image of my mother watching me . . . .

N: *What was she watching you for?* [A powerful question indeed.]

L: I don't know. [I trusted that her mind was still working out the answer; I jotted myself a quick note on a pad in front of me to return to this—if she didn't beat me to it!]

N: Where is your mother buried? [Sharp "sentence shock" to get through the idea threatening to back-slide the discussion.]

L: In Connecticut.

N: Well, Lilly, when you take your father up there for his burial, why don't you go and say "goodbye" to her and get rid of it all?

L: When she died, we never had a chance to say goodbye; she was sick with lymphoma and in a week she was gone. I feel like there's unfinished business.

N: Yes, there is. *And how would you classify that unfinished business?*

L: I would classify it as . . . as . . . as . . . asking her . . . why . . . maybe . . . why she treated me the way that she did or . . . or . . . why didn't she ever kiss me or hug me or . . . and . . . and then finally say goodbye . . . and . . . and, because I was with her in the emergency room . . . . [Her speech was sensitive, halting; deep significance here, clearly.]

N: Let me say, Lilly: [speaking slowly] this is all very natural, strong, honest, deep, and poignant, what you are saying. Now, what if I ask you a kind of bizarre question, *"Why is it important to ask her why she never hugged, kissed, and loved you?"* [Getting back to why her mother was "watching her."]

L: [Plaintively, almost childlike.] It's important because maybe there's something wrong . . . *with me,* that she didn't *want* to do it! I want to know if there's something wrong with me. [She had found the answer.]

N: *Don't you think other people would have told you there's something wrong with you, if there were?*

L: [Very gently, slowly.] Well . . . I never looked at it that way. I guess, I guess, I guess . . . . *Yeah,* I guess you're right: people would've! [Resuming with surprising energy.] People always complimented me about how I looked, how I acted, and how I held myself, and how I . . . I . . . .

N: . . . how well you communicate . . . .

L: . . . and communicate, and I never had any negativity coming from other people, except from my husband.

N: [Very quickly.] Well, we know that's because he had problems—you know that. So let's not even count that.

L: OK.

N: [Very gently.] *Look at the blessings that you've been able to enjoy.* I think that your poetry is a terrific opportunity for you to start to relate to other groups of poets [exploring her pervasive Venus at 00 Cancer, the Aries Point]. They would welcome you, and *you will learn* [notice the emphatic change of tense] to share some of *those private beauties* that you have created, and *you will see* how really special you are!

L: That's interesting. I never thought of that; my poetry. It was always so private and personal, but I did make a tremendous success with my jewelry. I made over a thousand original pieces of jewelry [the Venus=Aries Point again; her sleeping pride, Sun in Leo, is awakened now] . . . .

N: . . . and people loved them!

L: LOVED them! I had a terrific business!

N: Alright! We have had some very positive points of recognition at the end of this call!

L: Yes! And something just came to me [with much enthusiasm]: you asked me after my father goes on, what's going to become of me. I recall a conversation with my father—because he asked me the same thing. I said, I'm going to go back to school to learn to make more jewelry [with great enthusiasm], *to work with gold!*

N: Good. What you want to do is *you want to shine!* [Reinforcing the Sun in Leo, the gold.]

L: Yes, I want to shine, but I've always been very shy about shining. My children used to holler at me about never putting my name on the jewelry I made! I never wanted recognition for it.

N: What we have been talking about are *indirect* ways to get recognition; ways to appreciate *indirectly* that there is nothing wrong with you, that people *have* enjoyed you; *indirect* [always protecting her shyness and inexperience] ways through your poetry, *being accepted for your emotions.* And you've got to think about this now, and in about mid-April I think that you are going to get some glimmers of ways for that to come out. I'd like to hear from you then. [By being asked to report back to me, she will be watchful for opportunity to evaluate progress.]

L: Alright. And the only way I have to worry about serious illness is [she is reviewing what we have discussed] . . . in the event of my father's death, if I don't come out of this . . . start to come out *now.* [Lilly is working out a relationship between attitude improvement and avoiding illness. This will be the thought that will stay with her, that will lead to social outreach, and bring more meaning back to her life.]

N: I'm not a medical doctor, but *you know as well as I do* [persuasion] that what I am saying here is really and truly on the track, and the track is, if you're feeling really bad, and death is all around you, sickness is going to start to show in your body as well.

L: It has already.

N: *We want that to change*. We want to change our mental attitude, our outreach to people [helping her not to feel alone, "our"]; do it indirectly, cautiously at first, and you will see that you will shine. You will shine gradually again, and people *will* tell you how they appreciate it. I appreciate you. I'm intrigued with your potentials, and [in humor] I think that should mean something to you, if I dare say so myself!!!

L: [Laughingly.] You know, what I wanted to say to you?

N: What?

L: The letters of your name spell *Tylenol!* [Her offer of levity in return! She is secure with what we have covered in the consultation. Time to go.]

N: Yes, I know! I give some people a headache, for sure!

L: I saw it right away!

N: Thank you, my dear!

L: I've got the picture. I guess it's something I really knew inside myself already anyway [self-congratulations; very healthy and empowering].

N: That's what it's always like, and that's what we have to deal with: to remove the covers.

L: But I . . . I . . . was afraid that something serious was going to . . . [a short repeat about health concerns].

N: It could be, but there is something seriously beckoning you to [intentional pause] . . . .

L: . . . *to change* . . . . [She supplied the key word!]

N: Yes, to change. To put the lights on.

L: OK.

When the astrologer discovers that there is minimal interaction with the environment, when there is no obvious dream or plan, when a pervasive labor of self-sacrifice and routine dominates, the work of astrology is never easy. With Lilly, everything in her life now had triggered swirls of feelings that had tied themselves to unfinished business in the early home. The creative astrologer must rely on ultra-sensitive listening within disclosure to measure the record of response *and* the potential of astrological patterns. Then, *language must be adapted to a course of helpfulness* normally within the single session, explaining possibility, facilitating understanding, involving the client with change, and leaving the client with "homework," with *something to think about to keep change and development going.*

Case Study: Doris

A final illustration of bad news management is the case of Doris, a female in her mid-sixties. Her horoscope is dominated by a few clearly delineated measurement clusters:

- Four quintiles and AP=Venus (as you read here, make shorthand notes about what these measurement capsules suggest to you!)

- Saturn opposed Neptune-Moon (I-VII) with that axis squared by Mercury in Gemini, ruling the 4th, on the fourth cusp, opposing the Midheaven

- Saturn in the Ascendant, rules the 11th and the 12th

- Pluto conjoined the Nodal Axis

- Uranus ruling the Ascendant is peregrine

I greeted Doris on the telephone, and after three sentences or so of comforting small-talk, I said, "Doris, two questions please at the outset of our time together: [the quintiles] what is the creative outlet in your life . . . there is such potential here for creative expression!" Doris replied, "Oh, yes, I've danced, taught ballet, played the piano, been an artist, run a gallery . . . but it really was all stifled."

"And my second question, please," interrupting Doris so that she wouldn't tell me too much before I spotted the focal points of tension development [Mercury=Saturn, Neptune-Moon], "is have you been treated for clinically diagnosed depression? (see page 44)." Doris talked about having visited psychiatrists, but did not say a word about depression. I asked the question pointedly again: "Doris, your mind is everything here (Mercury in Gemini, on the fourth; Moon in Virgo), have you been treated for clinically diagnosed depression?" Doris, resignedly said, "Yes."

We know there are problems: being squashed in creative expression and being clinically depressed. "When we see something so clearly as we see this, we have to be able to find a probable cause, and that cause here for us to discuss could well be a tremendous anxiety *about not being lovable* (Saturn rules the 11th and 12th), and that is further linked, I think, *to the mother specifically* (Pluto conjunct the Nodal axis; the involvement of the Moon in the T-Square; the tension of Mercury at the fourth cusp)."

I heard a gasp on the phone, and I said, "I think I have hit a nerve here."

"Yes you have."

"And what is that nerve, Doris?"

Doris trusted me enough to disclose that "I" was right, that her mother had savagely abused her, "she never touched me except to hurt me." Her mother had beaten her to perform on the piano, to study painting, to dance. The mother had been obsessed with sex and had scrubbed Doris' genitals until they were raw and hurting. She would also get Doris' father to beat her.

Now, four minutes had elapsed in the consultation. I pointed that out to Doris to show her how much we would be able to do in our much longer time together. We both settled in to some keen sharing.

At the time of consultation, transiting Pluto was at 8 Sagittarius, precisely square, for the first time, to her focal point natal Saturn in 8 Pisces in her Ascendant. In other words, tr. Pluto (very reliably a significator component in profiles of critical illness[92]) was dramatically within the natal Grand Cross, with Saturn ruling the 12th (another component of the critical illness profile). I brought this potential to her attention, and she corroborated in detail, with my diagnostic leads, her systemic and somatic breakdowns that were beginning "with a vengeance." Doris was besieged with illness from her teeth (root canal poisoning through mercury [Saturn-Neptune], gynecology [Uranus quindecile Jupiter in Scorpio], and much more). Successive operations were scheduled well into the future, and Pluto would not abandon this complex until some two years into the future.

What were the problems here? Body breakdown, being taken care of at very fine medical facilities; and aloneness during the process. The bad news corroboration about the former was taken care of common sensically: "We've had a tremendous amount of accumulated developmental deficit uncovered in our discussion, Doris, and that's a lot of roads with lots of bumps. The car's going in for repairs; they're going to get fixed, and we've got to see it through. You know that."

---

92 Tyl, *Astrological Timing of Critical Illness.*

"Yes, I do. We're going to get it done."

"But it's hard to see something like this through *alone*.

"Yes, it is. But all my relationships . . . well, I feel that they will let me down. I feel I have to buy them, somehow . . . ."

"And that's what we've been talking about so much: your anxiety about being love-able, the struggle to get some love—which you never got—from your mother, from your father." Then, with strong authority, I added, "I think it unnecessary now, at your age, to continue such anxieties; under these conditions. You must KNOW that people will want to be helpful . . . you are a fascinating lady!"

"Well, I do have two men who call me and who really seem like they want to help and to be with me."

"Which one are you going to call first, when we are finished with our discussion and our planning?" (A kind of double-bind statement; see section below.)

Bad news was recognized, assimilated, and ancillary concerns were adjusted to empower and support the client as much as possible.

In the section below, we will explore more about listening and creative management of motivation through language, and persuasion.

Remediation and Growth

Milton H. Erickson (1901–1980)[93] was a psychiatrist, director of psychiatric research, and professor of psychiatry at several universities and in private practice over a long career. He was also perhaps the most creative, inspired medical therapeutic hypnotist the world has ever known, and he was founding president of the American Society for Clinical Hypnosis. He is a recognized genius in "strategic therapy," and his collected papers fill four large volumes, in addition to several books of technique.

Erickson approached hypnosis not as a performance ritual but as a way of commu-nication between people. In his work, we meet yet again the finding cited several times in this book, that therapy—regardless of technique—is mainly based upon the interpersonal impact of the therapist "outside the patient's awareness of anything that has gone on before." Erickson did not deal with helping people to understand how or why they behaved the way they did, attracting this kind of life or another; he went *beyond causes* directly into the remediation of behavior, the substitutions of behavior.

---

93 Erickson was born December 5, 1901: Sun in Sagittarius conjunct Uranus, both opposed by Pluto; Mars-Jupiter-Saturn conjunction in Capricorn; Moon in Libra, with Neptune peregrine.

Through his communication and relationship with his patients, he magically prodded the mind to rearrange things and create change. Indeed, Erickson did work with disclosure, past history, and enormously sensitive listening in order to fortify his therapeutic directives, but change was conceived and implemented *through suggestive language and persuasive command*, not formalized psychoanalytical understanding.

Erickson did not always use the hypnotic trance medium for this communication. His remarkable techniques were easily deployed in client discussion without the benefit of hypnosis; in other words, Erickson could *reach the unconscious directly through the conscious mind*. And, I would like to add, he did so in sublime fashion.

The creative astrologer is encouraged to study Erickson's works, to appreciate his technique and power. We can learn the skills of meticulous observation and complex and subtle communication; we can see time and time again how to communicate with persuasion and enduring value.

For example, when a doctor gives you a prescription slip—especially in person, with direct personal contact—or the actual pills, and says "Take this medicine right away. You will feel better in thirty-six hours," he is combining a voluntary act (taking the pills) with an involuntary change (feeling better). The linking of the two strengthens both persuasively. The patient is responding voluntarily, participating in the process, and knows he will respond accordingly.[94]

That is exactly what is behind the "grave visit" prescription (page 90); the client can go to the grave voluntarily and say farewell, and, as I would have suggested strongly, THAT will free him, i.e., the hitherto tie-up with the father. The break with that parent is involuntary (or it would have been done earlier), but in connection with the grave visit, it would be accomplished by adjusted intent and will.

The ritual meditation ahead of time for prescribed periods reinforces that suggested eventuation *ahead of time*, involving the unconscious with working out all the mechanics and details of attitude change. Outside the meditation time periods, the client's mind is consumingly busy with this process all day and all night for several days. This is the client's personal involvement with the self-help process.

Then, there is the much-anticipated taking of the medicine, the grave visit itself. Imagine the anticipation (the energy investment, the involvement)! Everything that has been built up ahead of time is now triggered into discharge. It is done.

---

94 Recall this feeling in your own experience: leaving the doctor's office *with confidence*; getting to the pharmacy as soon as possible, eager to commence the cure. The motivation changes priorities in your life. And, at the same time, to recognize that energy most clearly, let us appreciate that the doctor could well have given you or prescribed for you a *placebo*.

As Professor Robyn Dawes writes, "Much of the success of all therapy may be influenced by the fact that the client is taking action and no longer feels helpless in the face of disruptive emotional pain."[95]

The Double-Bind

Here is a brief case study of Erickson in action, drawn verbatim from his *Collected Papers*.[96] As you read it carefully, think constantly of why Erickson is saying what he does. Think what is being accomplished in the boy's mind in response to the doctor's words:

> *A father and mother brought their 12-year-old son in to me and said: "This boy has wet the bed every night of his life since he was an infant. We've rubbed his face in it; we've made him wash his things; we've whipped him; we've made him go without food and water; we've given him every kind of punishment and he is still wetting the bed.*
>
> *I [Erickson] told them, "Now he is my patient. I don't want you interfering with any therapy that I do on your son. You let your son alone, and you let me make all my arrangements with your son. Keep your mouths shut and be courteous to my patient."*
>
> *Well, the parents were absolutely desperate, so they agreed to that. I told Joe how I had instructed his parents and he felt very pleased about it. Then I said, "you know Joe, your father is 6'1", he is a great big powerful husky man. You are only a twelve-year-old kid. What does your father weigh? Two hundred twenty, and he isn't fat in the least. How much do you weigh? One hundred seventy."*
>
> *Joe couldn't quite see what I was driving at. I said, "Do you suppose it is taking a deuce of a lot of energy and strength to build that great big beautiful chassis on a 12-year-old kid? Think of the muscle you've got. Think of the height you've got, the strength you've got. You have been putting an awful lot of energy in building that in 12 short years. What do you think you'll be when you are as old as your father? A shrimpy six foot two weighing only 220 pounds, or do you think you will be taller than your father and heavier than your father?"*

Now, we can see clearly how Erickson is identifying the boy with his father's manliness, hinting that in the future Joe could pass all that by normally. At the same time, Erickson is distracting Joe from the embarrassing issue at hand. Joe was listening

---

95 Dawes, 75.

96 Erickson/Ed. Rossi, Volume I, 416–417.

attentively and with respect *because Erickson had sided with Joe and had put the parents in their place*, instructing them to respect the child (after what they had done in desperation).

> [Erickson continued] *You could see Joe's mind turning handsprings in all directions, getting a new body image of himself as a man.* Then I said [and here is a classic Ericksonian technique of binding suggestion], *"As for your bed-wetting you have had that habit for a long time and this is Monday* [what a juxtaposition of time concepts; riveting!]. *Do you think you can stop wetting the bed, have a permanent dry bed by tomorrow night? I don't think so, and you don't think so, and nobody with any brains at all will think that sort of thing. Do you think you will have a dry bed permanently by Wednesday? I don't. You don't. Nobody does. In fact, I don't expect you to have a dry bed at all this week. Why should you? You have a lifelong habit, and I just simply don't expect you to have a dry bed this week. I expect it to be wet every night this week and you expect it. We're in agreement* [note the phrase], *but I also expect it to be wet next Monday, too, but you know there is one thing that really puzzles me and I really am absolutely thoroughly puzzled—**will you have a dry bed by accident on Wednesday or will it be on Thursday, and you'll have to wait until Friday morning to find out?"***

Erickson strings sentences out for long spans of time. It is part of his technique for commanding attention; the patient is being drawn in to the process, to listen as attentively as possible and think constantly about what is being said, how to decipher it all. This is *involvement*, without which no change can be expected. And note the phrase "by accident" in the key last phrase: this sets up with Joe the *fact* that *he need not be the agent to stop the bed wetting*; he's not going to do anything; *it's going to happen.* You will get well Wednesday or will it be on Thursday. Pick one, body!

> *Well, Joe had been listening to me, and he wasn't looking at the walls, the carpet, or the ceiling or the light on my desk or anything else. He was in the common everyday trance* [intense concentration, immobile] *listening to all these new ideas, things he had never thought of before. Joe didn't know I was putting him in a double bind because the question wasn't, "Will I have a dry bed?" The question really was, "which night?"* [The dry bed was assumed!] *He was in a mental frame of reference to find out which night he would have the dry bed. I continued, **"You come in next Friday afternoon and tell me whether it was Wednesday or Thursday, because I don't know; you don't know. Your unconscious mind doesn't know. The back of your mind doesn't know, the front of your mind doesn't know. Nobody knows. We will have to wait until Friday afternoon."***

So, "we" both waited until Friday afternoon, and Joe came in beaming and he told me the most delightful thing, "Doctor, you were mistaken, it wasn't Wednesday or Thursday, it was both Wednesday and Thursday."

I said, "Just two dry beds in succession doesn't mean that you are going to have a permanent dry bed. [Here, Erickson introduces the dimension potential of permanency; it must be demonstrated somehow for Joe to believe.] *By next week half of the month of January is gone, and certainly in the last half you can't learn to have a permanent dry bed, and February is a short month. I don't know whether your permanent dry bed will begin on March 17, which is St. Patrick's Day, or will it begin on April Fools Day. I don't know. You don't know either, but there is one thing I DO want you to know, that when it begins it is none of my business. Not ever, ever, ever is it going to be any of my business."*

Now why should it be any of my business when his permanent dry bed began? That was actually a posthypnotic suggestion that would go with him for the rest of his life. Now that is what you call a double bind. Little Joe couldn't understand what a double bind was. **You use double binds and triple binds always as a part of the strategy of psychotherapy. You present new ideas and new understandings and you relate them in some undisputable way to the remote future.**

It is important to present therapeutic ideas and posthypnotic suggestions in a way that makes them contingent on something that will happen in the future. Joe would get older and taller. He would go on to high school and college. I never mentioned high school to him. I mentioned college, the remote future, and the idea of being a football player. I didn't want him thinking about a wet bed. I wanted him thinking about the remote future and the things he could do instead of thinking: what am I going to do tonight—wet the bed.[97]

There are two keys to proper use of the double-bind technique. First, it must fit an appropriate need or frame of reference *within the patient* (not, say, between the therapist and the patient, but only for the client's gain). Second, something new to the situation that is related to the client's central motivations must be explored, to fascinate the patient, to involve the patient strongly. (Recall my conversation with Lilly, especially pages 154–155. Note the light trance rhythm of my suggestions and her responses, how they slowly developed into that stillness and absorption.)

---

97 We must note that *planets* did not stop Joe from bedwetting specifically, but indeed, planetary development in his horoscope surely paralleled his being brought to a therapist, absorbing major change, and perhaps precociously conceiving a plan for his future.

As well, this is precisely what occurred with Robert (page 134). He was fascinated by astrology's discovery within him of the spiritual way and was wide open to exploration. The motivational directive I gave him in our second discussion was actually a double-bind, "Will you be calling your friend back about further information of his spiritual work *first* or will you be talking to your partner about divestiture?"

Remember: this technique is giving your client a suggestion to action that is dependent upon a choice between two courses, neither one of which had probably ever occurred to him. The suggestion is given within the understanding you have created in the consultation; the client's involvement with the process ahead, the projection out of his reality in the present into the reasonable developments in the future.

Here are some simple double binds for practice, used to empower someone into action with regard to something that is reasonable and in their benefit: to your child, "You know as well as I do that it's right for you to clean up your room this afternoon or tomorrow afternoon, whichever you prefer; I'll leave that to you. Which is it?" To a client, knowing full well that, say, tr. Saturn is squaring or conjoining the Ascendant soon, "Do you want to start losing weight this week or next? But, then again, that may seem too soon. Perhaps you would like to wait a longer period of time, *ideally* like three or four weeks. Which is it?" To a client insecure about taking action for the clear-as-the-nose-on-your-face divorce: "Do you want to call a male or female lawyer for advice? Which do you think would be better? Or do you want to contact the lawyer who's been doing your family business for so long?" And finally, to a client reluctant to ask for a promotion when you know the time is right and everything checks out for high-probability success: "If your inner conviction about how important you are in your work wants you to 'go for the gold,' then you will make an appointment with your boss to discuss all this next Thursday; otherwise choose the following Tuesday."[98]

Building Anticipation/Impact

In parallel with commanding involvement, Erickson used the technique of building anticipation, with extraordinary artistry. His patients waited through their sessions—which on occasion were very long and may have seemed interminable—to get the promised reward, *the indisputable statement that would help them*, promised by Erickson at the outset of the consultation and delivered at the end.

---

98 This manipulation of language can become very subtle, and astrologers are urged to study Erickson's works for quite an eye-opening glimpse of the use of motivational language.

Sex Problem Case

An extremely prudish couple, both college professors, came to Erickson about a sex problem. They spoke alternately about the problem—strung out *to great length* by Erickson's listening and prodding. Shortly into the clients' presentations, however, Erickson seemed aware of what he was going to do: he interrupted them and said that he would accept them as patients IF they would accept the one statement he would give them at the end of the session. He *warned* them that the statement would be jarring, shocking, startling. But IF they wanted his help, they would *have to promise to accept what he said at the end of the consultation* and *obey every instruction he gave them in connection with the statement.*

Erickson repeated this over and over and over and over again during the couple's presentation. They kept agreeing (preconditioning to acceptance, as every salesperson recognizes). Erickson kept increasing the promise of "shock": "You will have to hold onto your chairs when I tell you what to do, and you have promised to abide by what I will tell you." Then, he began to add the instruction that, when they heard what he had to say, they WOULD NOT SAY ONE WORD; that they would immediately leave his office and drive home WITHOUT SPEAKING ONE WORD TO EACH OTHER; and only after entering their home and closing the door behind them, *"would they be able to react."*

Well, we can imagine the extraordinary build-up of THAT tension!

The ultra-conservative, prudish couple were presenting their sexual concerns about conceiving a child. They spoke in a style that was polysyllabic, technical, academic, and clinical. Obviously the sex act had become icily technical and of no more interest to them. The mindsets were surely working against conception. Other problems were arising between them because of this "procreative chore." Erickson listened and listened and listened and listened and listened. The couple must have been exhausted with all this. And the only thing Erickson contributed frequently was the promise-threat of the solution that he would deliver under very, very shocking and strict conditions at the end of the consultation, all of which they had promised to accept.

Finally, the moment came: "Remember, you will maintain silence until after you have entered the house and closed the door. *You will then be free!*" Here, Erickson was simply but powerfully *tying freedom to compliance with his instructions.*

> *Now hang tightly to the bottom of your chairs, because I am now going to give you the psychological shock. It is this: For three long years you have engaged in the marital union with full physiological concomitants for procreative purposes* [here he was mimicking their technical language] *at least twice a day and sometimes as much*

as four times in twenty-four hours, and you have met with defeat of your "philoprog-enitive desires." **Now why in hell don't you fuck for fun and pray to the devil that she isn't knocked up for at least three months. Now please leave.**[99]

The forty-mile drive to their home, in absolute silence, had allowed a riot of repressed thinking to run free in their minds. This resulted in enormous sexual anxiety and desire quite distinct from the clinical, stultifying practice into which they had fallen. The mindset had been changed. They *were* free. Erickson reports that the couple engaged in sex immediately upon their return home—immediately, on the floor, not even in the bedroom—and their child was born nine months later.

I often use an echo of this technique with my clients, when I am sure to the highest probability that circumstantial change is due. This is usually promised by a powerful angular transit or Arc, such as Uranus conjunct the Ascendant or Pluto conjoining the Midheaven or fourth cusp. From the outset of the consultation I promise terrific resolution: "I'm so glad to see you; thank you for coming! Please sit here and be comfortable. I've worked hard on your horoscope, as you can see. And I am delighted to look forward to the things we are going to discuss. *At the end of our time together*, the situation you are in is *going to be resolved.* I promise you: *you will have a plan of action that can't be denied.* But first, let me tell you generally what the horoscope suggests about . . . ."

I deliver this statement with enthusiasm, in a dose that is not unreasonable from a stranger and definitely welcome from an involved professional. The statement is loaded with cues about authority, positivism, and confidence. The client takes on the mindset to cooperate, to believe in her or his potential, and to become involved with what is coming. I repeat it reasonably often in different ways throughout the consultation.

Enthusiasm, conviction, and authority are all very important in persuasion about helpfulness. The simplicity of the treatment regimen for mild depression presented on page 42 is imbalancing: how can something so simple work? The astrologer suggesting this plan must add authority to it, to kindle the client's faith in its potential, to involve the client with potential.

I must repeat again and again *how important client involvement is with development and change.* Just recall how Erickson involved this academic, prudish couple for almost two hours and then dramatically forced their involvement after they left the consultation. He put their minds to work in spite of all their conventional preconditioning.

---

99 Haley, 164–166. And it should be added here that this took place in the early 1940s, when societal repression of sexual matters and sexual language was yet very strong. Imagine the shock of these words from the famous doctor.

The consultation with the astrologer should be fascinating, interesting, and as captivating as possible. This is accomplished through depth of discussion and the speed with which significance is developed, word choice, questioning freshness, creative deductions, tones of voice. *The client should leave the consultation with the birth of a plan*, not in a passive posture to await what the planets might bring! The creative astrologer *arranges the thoughts* with which the client goes forth to experience what is projected. (Please recall the significant final statement I made to David (page 39) that "I think your grandfather would have approved of these things." I know David still lies in bed some nights and thinks that through.)

Moshe Talmon in *Single-Session Therapy* says that the art of therapy depends largely on the practitioner's ability to mobilize clients' resources to improve (heal) themselves (involvement). We involve our clients with the process during the consultation; we convey messages of hope and empowerment. Talmon even found that, with such involvement, patients reported following suggestions *that he could not remember having made!* The patients had created their own interpretations of the consultation's discussion and benefited mightily![100]

Going with the Flow

Another extraordinary technique used continuously by Erickson in his work is to accept the client's way of behaving, going with the flow, accepting the difficult, the dysfunctional, *while simultaneously introducing ideas and acts that lead to change.*

If a client has an acknowledged fear of intimacy, after the discussion dealing with whatever creative connections can be made to anxieties developed earlier, we can suggest, "Well that's what it's all about, probably, *and we know it's really got a hold on you. But quite apart from this* what if I suggested, for fun, that you learn dancing or photography?" What is happening here is we are trusting that, over the time ahead, understanding will help to relax the problem; we are acknowledging the problem and letting it flow on; *and* we are offering activities that *eventually* will be the doorways to free the tensions and help with relationship anxiety, the fear of intimacy.

> *What if you started some dancing classes yourself! You say your friend George has done this and is meeting some neat people! We* [note "we"] **don't necessarily want to meet people,** *but you could be with George and enjoy one hell of a physical workout. Let me tell you, square dancing is nothing to be sneezed at! You're looking*

---

100 Talmon, 58, 60.

for an exercise program. There it is! And you can watch George score a few, or even make a fool of himself a time or two!

Here I'm going with my male client's anxieties, giving him a reason to go dancing, that is other than the obvious, and I have him with a friend at the same time. In fact, I even went so far as to put my client in a position to evaluate George in the relationship gambit! All of this is better than being alone very night of the week.

Or:

> *What if you went to the museum and took up some photography lessons. They have a course there. Did you know that?* [Sudden involvement of the client.] *You have this art appreciation indication in your horoscope, and we've talked about how you love beautiful things, collecting prints, etc. Now, let me tell you, photography is an extraordinarily fascinating hobby. The techniques will intrigue you, and what you can do with them! And then, of course, y***ou can look from behind the camera and see all sorts of things in the people you're photographing.*** *They'll love it when you give them a gift of the pictures. . . . now, look here, let me show you my camera . . . .*

Here again, there is nothing threatening. My client (in this case a woman) could be behind the camera, but she could give copies of the photos to people as ingratiating gifts! People would appreciate her for that. She can learn a lot about people (and they can learn about her at the same time!), take her camera to parties, hide behind it, etc.

The creative astrologer can do so much with observations and discussion points that emerge during consultation. It requires deliberate thought into the directions presented in this book and then instinct can take over with idea after idea after idea.

For instance, remember that behind the self-worth anxiety syndrome there is usually the concomitant concern about body image, appearance. There are many ways to address that, the body image, that then work back in tandem with the understandings discussed therapeutically to create improvement and change.

"I really do have a dreadful self-worth profile. Just as you say. I really do."

"Well, I would have to agree with you. You know why?"

"What? No. Why?"

"Because you look it!"

"I look it?"

"Well, you're paying me to be direct and as helpful as I can be—and that's what we're doing, right? But I can ask you a question now, and you won't easily be able to answer me accurately." (Note the Ericksonian style.)

"What is it?"

"When is the last time you went to a dentist to get fixed up?"

Notice the planned phrase "to be direct and as helpful as I can be—and that's what we're doing, right?" You see that I am convincing her and acknowledging for us both that the consultation is proceeding successfully. I wait for the client to nod her head or acknowledge the opinion verbally. Therefore, what I will *then* say will be accepted *within the approval mind-set.* I delay it a bit by the ostensibly imbalancing, possibly off-the-track statement "but I can ask you a question now, and you won't easily be able to answer me accurately." Then, when she can not answer it easily, *I am again proved correct!* Authority grows and so does the impact of suggestions we derive out of the consultation discussion.

Of course, the specific thrust of your question should be to something noticeable like dirty fingernails ("When did you purposefully last clean your fingernails?"), a frayed shirt ("When was the last time you bought yourself a new, crisp shirt?"). There is a reasonable presumption here that someone coming to see you for a consultation will want to look his best. A self-worth problem works against that, with you and the others with whom your client deals.

Many therapists in protracted courses of therapy are reluctant to tell people what to do. Jay Haley observes that this may be because the therapists fear that the person will not do it.[101]

I suggest that that is changing with the popularity of Single Session Therapy. More and more, people coming to see me *want* a program to follow into the future. They want it to be fast and reliable. This is so pronounced in my practice that I often have to make very clear before the consultation the areas in which I have no skill, e.g., financial concerns, investments, the law. And always I remember that so very often the problem that may be stated at the outset of a consultation is actually *not* the real concern; that it changes by the end of the consultation when perspectives of development have been clarified. "I want to divorce my wife" might very well change to "these damn problems I've been having with my business partner." Or, "I'm at odds with my husband about selling the house; it's blowing our marriage apart, actually" might very well change to "I've got to find a way to help him with his enormous job insecurity; it's been going on for so long and I guess I'm not giving it proper consideration." Think it through: the astrology is very similar for *both* problems in each set.

---

101 Haley, 70.

Indirection

Another technique we can learn from the masterful Erickson is how to approach a problem indirectly, obliquely, and help the client achieve the desired results. It is actually easy and creatively forceful to think out such an approach during horoscope preparation and it is distinctly gratifying to implement it effectively.

Case Study: Laurie

The horoscope here belongs to "Laurie," a lady in her sixties. Laurie is conservative, modest, slightly slow in her speech rhythm (born in the rural far West), attractive, but with two looks in her face: one is a resigned, heavy, "every day is like every other day look," and the other, when she smiles, is a radiant, delighted, openly-sharing, self-confident spirit. The two looks alternatively capture the Sun-Saturn conjunction in Pisces rising, opposed by Neptune, and the radiant Moon in Leo squared by Uranus.

Quite quickly, we see the primary organization of the horoscope:

- Probable father-husband syndrome (Saturn-Sun, Sun ruling the 7th)

- Mother influence from a power position, affecting self-worth development (Moon conjunct Pluto, Pluto quindecile Node, Mars square Node, Mars rules the 2nd)

- Highly nervous predisposition about cooperating with others' expectations (6th House significances) working defensively (Eastern orientation of the horoscope)

- Dominating need to be appreciated, significant, loved, recognized doing something helpful of social significance (Moon in Leo, Jupiter peregrine as co-final dispositor, ruling the 11th, tie-in with the Aquarian Ascendant through Uranus square with the Moon)

- A very strong social idealism (Mercury-Venus conjunction in Aquarius at the Ascendant

- An interruption of education (the Pluto rulership of the 9th, being retrograde involved with the Node; the sociology of her region fifty years ago that women did not go on to further education; her way of speaking)

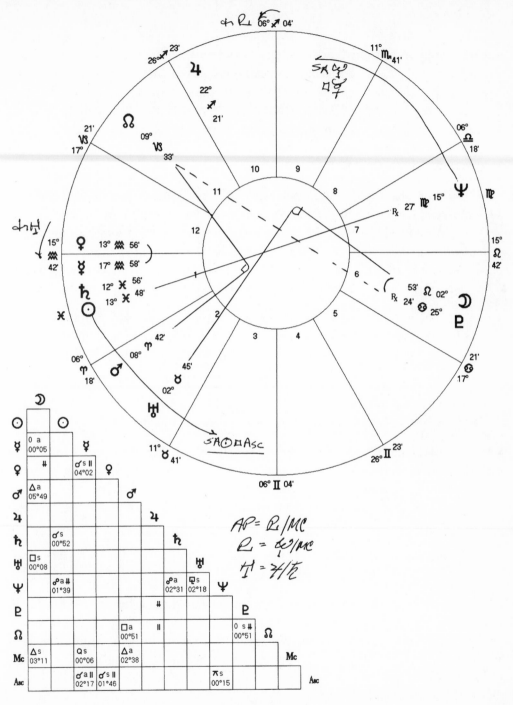

Figure 16
Laurie

Laurie easily corroborated these deductions and we went immediately into the classic development scenario we see so often, in this book and in everyday practice: the father had been out of the picture working very hard, the mother was all-powerful, education was never given a thought, "I went right out of high school onto a tractor in the field" (at age eighteen, tr. Neptune square and tr. Uranus *conjunct Pluto, ruler of the 9th*).

Four more observations were to be very important in the analysis, a second level of preparation, going deeper after the initial assumptions of development were clarified:

- The Sun ruled the 7th; Mercury ruled Virgo intercepted in the 7th; Neptune opposed the Sun-Saturn conjunction and itself was in the 7th, retrograde (quincunx with the Ascendant); the husband was a key here somehow to help Laurie "do her thing" (since her father had *not* done it long ago, setting up the routined normal life for this special lady), to get the Pisces-Leo Sun-Moon blend out into the open . . . the beaming grand spirit she showed any time she smiled

- Neptune usually carries with it the sense of "something is other than it seems"; placed in the 7th House, it reliably suggests a mate one must help, uplift, support; and this dynamic justifies the relationship, makes the person feel needed and important and strong, helping the mate

- The idealistic conjunction of Mercury-Venus at the Ascendant also linked together the rulers of the 2nd and 8th Houses, the sexual profile

- The midpoint pictures were telling: AP=Pluto/MC, recognition, power with the public (perfect complement to the Moon in Leo reigning need, clearly); and Pluto=Neptune/MC, again the contact between Pluto and Neptune, "the supernatural as a profession"; Uranus=Jupiter/Saturn, "needing to prove a point, upset with the ways of the world"

- At the time of consultation in January 1999, tr. Pluto was at her Midheaven, and tr. Uranus was very close to her Ascendant!

Clearly, this was Laurie's time, perhaps the biggest time of her life, a new birth. What was it? She was a lady of senior age, a former secretary at her peak long ago; her husband was retired from a career in real estate. What was the theme here now exposing itself so strongly in the preparation analysis? Was she just a humanitarian helper, perhaps organizing volunteer services at a hospital? Was she active in her church? Was she all these things and more?

"Noel, I am deeply involved with perfecting my skills as a medium." Laurie was gifted with "special sight" and was deeply involved with this spiritual endeavor. She needed to fulfill a calling to public service in this way. Her sincerity and deep explanations were beautifully compelling.

Immediately, everything I had prepared whooshed into order: with the link between the father-situation and husband (Saturn to Sun, Sun through rulership to the 7th), Laurie needed all the support possible now at the new biggest time of her life development. She could not just be left alone "to do her thing." Her husband had to (should) participate with her, support her, express love for her, share the bloom of this special lady, not be on the sidelines or in the background as her father had been. Explaining to him what she was doing, etc. would not be enough. Already, it had not been. This was a big change, and it needed *all the support and focus of resources possible in the relationship.*

Now, we have to look at some reality in terms of relationship (especially with the Neptune factor calling attention so strongly to the 7th House): statistics tell us that 30–40% of men over fifty years of age develop erectile problems and impotence. The probability was very high that this was the case with Laurie's husband.

This would be very important to determine because of the emphasis of the sex profile in Laurie's horoscope (the rulers of the 5th and 8th conjoined at the Ascendant in Aquarius). We know that the nervous system (here very strong with Uranus square the Moon) is linked to sexual arousal and release, or frustration, as well as with creativity, etc.

Sexuality could be the way to (re)bring husband and wife closer together at this powerful time of development in Laurie's life. Sex could lead the way to a beautiful, mature closeness.

"Laurie, with your permission, may I please ask you some questions about private things?"

With a beaming smile, extending her arms wide apart, "You may ask me anything you want to, of course!"

"How does your husband need you? And what does he resent about that?"

First here, I was exploring the Neptune-in-the-7th symbolism, asking an open-ended question followed by an assumptive question; a very powerful probe that would bring a lot to the analysis. How did he depend on her?

Very carefully and precisely, Laurie began, "He resents my strength . . . ."

We talked about this. It was clear that Laurie's husband, because of his own developmental anxieties, background modeling, etc., found Laurie a bit intimidating when it came to her resourcefulness (when the queen complex emerged!).

"The sexual profile here in the horoscope is quite pronounced. (Laurie smiled affirmation.) How *is* your sex life?"

Laurie said that there had been no sex with her husband for some eight or nine years (I looked at my notes and saw that this time period was corroborated by the transit of Saturn over her Ascendant and the sexual profile focus there). This was my opportunity within my plan to improve the relationship for mutual support.

"You *are* alert still, sexually, yourself, in private?" This is a yes/no question for the obvious sensitivity of the question, giving the probable answer in the question and making it brief.

Immediately Laurie answered, comfortably, matter-of-factly, "Yes, I *have* to." This unusual answer discloses the importance of the sexual energy in her life.

"Well, Laurie, " I answered, quite happily and quickly (showing confidence) and surprising her, "*this is no longer a problem!* Let me explain what can be remedied with Viagra,[102] or with a simple vacuum pump that can bring about erections quite easily. Tests are showing that sometimes the body even starts to remember its own way, and everything goes back to AOK, naturally! But the point is, *the problem can be solved* right away!"

Laurie beamed once again and showed much enthusiasm, "I'd love that!"

"Here is the name and phone number of an absolutely superb urologist. Please take your husband to see Dr. _____ (from my file of physicians and therapists). This will all be fixed *very quickly, I promise you*. You've already wasted too much time!" We laughed easily; Laurie was thrilled.

This was a case of not understanding earlier (not having full information, of doctors accepting things as the way they are), of embarrassment, avoidance, suppression, denial, abstinence. Now with new drugs, understanding, openness, it could all be reversed.

"Are you thinking of building a new home?" This abrupt change of subject was designed to depart from the emotional focus and signal completeness of the previous exchange. The directive had been given, *with authority, objective demeanor, and emotional impact.* The abrupt shift now actually reinforced the earlier directive to see the urologist.

The question about the home was keyed by the transit of Uranus over the Ascendant (the high, high probability of relocation; "build a house" rather than "move" because of the couple's age and their obvious permanence in the area; the husband retired from real estate). Many measurements backed this up, as they also backed up her rise in the world of spiritual mediumship (SA *Neptune* square *Mercury*, SA Moon=*Neptune/Pluto*,

---

102 The trademark name of the erectile dysfunction drug marketed by Pfizer Laboratories.

for example, and more.) Key to all perhaps, for the lovely lady's immediate future—all of these factors coming together at once—was *Solar Arc Sun square her Ascendant:* recognition—from the public and anew from her husband as well!

What had been accomplished in this high-focus section of the consultation is that indirectly we had worked to get Laurie support for her rise in her field. She would not be just benignly "left to do her thing." We were assuming the rise and we were working on the husband-wife relationship for the ideal support.

While the planetary symbolisms guided us to the concerns and, at the same time, defined the needs and energies of potential, in the consultation and thereafter, human beings took over.

Another short example of indirection at work is presented by Jay Haley in his book about Ericksonian therapy: a woman complained strongly about not getting along on her job. Erickson noticed that her hair was very, very poorly combed. The woman saw Erickson noting her hair and said, "Don't do what my boss does; he keeps telling me to comb my hair, and I do my level best."

Erickson replied, "You want to get along better in your job, and you do your level best with your hair, *but I wonder how afraid you are of looking your best?*" We can note that this is akin to the technique we studied earlier, the radical probe (page 116): "What would happen *if you did not do* this behavior, did *not* ignore your appearance?"

The lady later reported that she went home, showered, dried off, and stood in front of a mirror, with hand mirrors as well, studying not only her hair but her body as well. She was "[Erickson:] Examining it against the background of her boss finding fault with the way she combed her hair. And she resented her boss criticizing her. The more she scrutinized herself, with the background of her resentment toward her boss, *the more she approved of her body.*"[103]

Here the initial tension was attacked to achieve something productive at the core, *beyond* the initial tension: it was not her hair that was the problem, but the self-image, the self-worth.

Image Persuasion

Therapists, astrologers, doctors, priests—everyone must be persuasive. We have to be able to sell: we sell insight, self-empowerment, and a future. Why else do people come to an astrologer? To find out what the planets are doing?

---

103 Haley, 105.

If we are expert and trustworthy, we are influential. Our trustworthiness and effectiveness are increased if we present a position that has little to do with our own self-interest. Our attractiveness reinforces the desirability others feel for our message.[104]

These are primary concerns in being persuasive. The creative astrologer—just as she or he must be concerned about appearance, work place atmosphere, exhibiting intelligence, etc. (see page 101)—must pay attention to these particular concomitants of persuasion. We must show our expertise, use self-disclosure to suggest trustworthiness, behave selflessly, and make as fine a personal presentation as we can, accentuating whatever there is about us that is most attractive (voice, eyes, figure, accuracy of speech, kindness, strength, empathy, etc.).

The prestige of the astrologer in the community is also important to establishing expertise and trustworthiness, and building a clientele.

The creative astrologer should pursue such avenues of public involvement, lecturing to clubs, business and fraternal groups, the local radio station, etc., projecting the image of specialist information and expertise in sharing that information.

Another concern related to expertise is age. The young professional in her twenties or thirties is not going to attract a clientele of people over forty-five, for example. There is a *generation gap* that defines disparate levels of experience, learning, knowing, and communication comfort. The older astrologer will *not* have the difficulty attracting the young client for the very same reasons; the comparatively greater scope of experience, learning, and knowing are at a premium. While much of this is being relaxed today as the older get younger and the young learn more more quickly—the Information Age—we have to know that: "Somebody will turn forty-nine every thirteen seconds for the next fifteen years."[105]

While the field of astrology itself is top-heavy with older practitioners and it needs the energy and inspiration of the young, all astrologers must recognize the responsibility to understand and be conversant with issues of maturity, strategy, health, and planning involved with being over fifty years of age.

The younger astrologer must listen to news, read books, and observe life with older senses. Wisdom and additional business are the rewards.

---

104 Aronson, chapter 3.
105 *TIME* magazine, Oct. 26, 1998, page 86.

Why Predictions May Fail

Why predictions sometimes do fail has nothing to do with planets and almost every-thing to do with the astrologer and the client. We can not presume to say simply that our astrology is incomplete, even though we do not yet know all there is and we are still constantly learning about what we *do* have in our grasp. Instead, since the planets are symbols that guide humans to the understanding of what can happen in life, we must inspect our management of the symbols in terms of *living that life*. We look for insight about becoming and we create strategy within time.

For the most part, we want what we see in the horoscope to *be that way in life*. This is how we confirm our skill with astrology, establish our importance, and express our humanness in our desire to help others. But it is impossible, except in the most super-ficial way, to see accurately, significantly, and strategically *unless we seek understanding in terms of the specific reality of the client. We must bring the horoscope to life in terms of the life being lived by our client*, or we dangerously indulge *our* wish fulfillment on behalf of the client or myopically focus only on what we know about astrology.

This bringing the horoscope to life requires disclosure on the part of the client, and we facilitate that disclosure through careful, creative questioning, about which so much has been said so far in this book.

Development in life falls into patterns that are culturally dictated and individualis-tically altered (distorted). Growth is fueled by needs pressing for fulfillment and is identified by emotional reactions to success and failure. The capacity to dream, to hope, and to project works to establish the perspective of fulfillment.

Within this overview, I think that predictions fail because of reasons among the fol-lowing seven observations. Normally a list of insights like this is shorter than seven points and it is designed as a clear-cut checklist for remedial adjustments. This list is different: while it *is* a checklist for profitable study, it is an acknowledgement of how difficult prediction is, not only in astrology but in any discipline. Prediction strains all the dimensions of the discipline; in astrology, these dimensions are related to records of past events in the external environment *and* developmental change throughout time in the internal environment. Since we are so humanistically involved with this process in astrology, short-fall or failure of predictions is more painful than missing a call on a weather forecast—except, indeed, if the event is a tornado!

In the balance of this chapter we will look at several pitfalls that can lead to unsuc-cessful consultations.

Not Finding the Astrology

It bears repeating that, in the main, significant occurrences in life reflect major Transit and Arc activity (Saturn through Pluto by transit; Mars through Pluto, by arcs, including development of the Angles themselves) involving the Angles or the Sun or Moon in the natal horoscope. The Secondary Progressed Moon is also helpful.[106]

Other methods of horoscope projection such as the Solar Return, while not having been conclusively tested and thoroughly understood in application, certainly serve astrologers who have a demonstratedly sensitive personal tie to that particular developmental ordering of symbols and time.[107]

If the astrologer misses (overlooks) an extremely important contact in the near future, projection of horoscope development will not be as viable as it could be. This is not the forum for the study of rectification, but we need to be aware of inaccurate birthtimes, rounded off birthtimes, misremembered birthtimes, etc., at the outset of the consultation process, the data submission when the appointment is made. We must question the knowledge of the reported birthtime.

Overlooking Past Responses

Much can be said for the adage that people *never* change. This conventional wisdom refers to the development of personality and character, not initially to behavior patterns or choices, which can indeed be modified. Of course, personality development does involve the establishment and sustaining of behavioral patterns, but they can be adjusted. Any such adjustment works closely with choices that are made in life.

The creative astrologer learns about the client's personality and behavioral patterns (and the emotions connected with them) by learning about the client's development, especially during the years of the early homelife. Guided by generalized Solar Arc measurements to begin with (abbreviated by the "one degree equals one year" method of

---

106 Secondary Progressions pale in comparison with Solar Arc theory and practice, because of the intrinsic slowness of development of the planets SP Jupiter through SP Pluto. The Moon is very useful because of its speed (one month per degree in progression). The SA Sun is the same as the SP Sun. Any argument then comes down to the efficacy of reflecting ever more complicated living through the Progressed movements of Mercury, Venus, and Mars. In Solar Arcs, there are some 1,014 new aspect relationships possible within any horoscope development, an overwhelming measurement advantage.

107 There are many variables to be worked through in Solar Return technique: birthplace, residence, locale; including the precessional increment or not; using the Angles of the Return chart or the Angles of the natal horoscope. The fascination of the Solar Return technique is with the concept of the Sun returning to its exact birth position (longitudinally) once a year and the fact that the transits of that moment are captured in an interpretive *gestalt* that is applicable to the life-year ahead.

rapport arcs) and coincidental transit measurements, we learn how the horoscope has grown and responded within the client's individual reality.

This patterning is what is projected into the future. In the developmental sense, the future has already happened, it has been mapped out, and it is up to the astrologer and client to discover what is probable within this time stream.

Not testing past developmental responses is to overlook learning the client's history; who the client is.

And not testing the past does not allow the tests of the birth time for security within analysis.[108]

No Client Involvement

The client must become involved with the process of analysis and projection. The client defines and fills out his or her reality. Client involvement is perhaps the dimension above all that improves the probability of a successful prediction.

For the client who does nothing, who is not involved, *nothing happens* except perhaps an Act of God, an accident in time, or systemic breakdown from gross boredom and accumulated frustration. So many people stop living long, long before death! They wait for the miracle that never comes.

When astrology is brought into this stagnant mix, astrology and astrologer are often blamed for not delivering the miracle of change. Measurements do not seem to manifest, "to work." Finding the cause of the dulled life behavior does no good. Resignation prevails. Routine protects. Charade persuades others of contentment.

Just as people in therapy sometimes substitute their relationship with the therapist for peer relationships outside therapy, so a person in the grip of inexorable routine can use the astrologer as entertainment and diversion, as a substitute for and harbinger of new experiences: "I wanna know what's gonna happen to me."

The answer for these people, of course, is not in the astrologer or in astrology, but within themselves. The creative astrologer must find a way to excite interest in and appreciation for what could be possible; in short, with grace and perhaps a bit of sermonizing, going with the flow, observing it, explaining it, saying finally, "I would be very happy to hear how you think your life can get moving again (or develop further). Please share that with me." There are adult education courses, exercise programs (to improve self-esteem), clubs to join, trips to take (and study for ahead of time, for

---

108 For rectification technique and adventure, please see Tyl, *Astrology of the Famed*, rectification of the birthdates and times for Cleopatra, St. Francis of Assisi, Dracula, Leonardo, and Beethoven.

greater involved enjoyment), reviving the secret wish from long ago that now may be approached for fulfillment, re-invigoration of sexual expression and closeness, helping others, planning gifts to give, etc.

Often, the hardest pressure upon an astrologer is to tell the client what she wants to hear. In situations like this, I keep telling myself (self-talk) that this person knows inside how dismal the life routine has become, but maybe I can show what *can be*, on the outside. I use less celestial astrology and more community resourcefulness. And then, when the consultation is finished, I realize that I carry for a while the desultory feelings that have just been deposited with me. Part of the job.

We must do all we can to awaken clients to and fascinate them with the consultation. They must be involved with the words and the directions of analysis. Then the consultation time is not long enough; the eagerness to go on is palpable; the feelings of empowerment abound for astrologer and client alike.

Impracticality

As we have seen dramatized strongly in our case examples, *projected life development must be attached sensibly to astrologically developing patterns*. No person will experience change *until the time is right*, and that time might be later rather than sooner, it might be just past and the now is catch-up time, or the time might be immediate, with the extraordinary energies of discovery and corroboration at their highest.

"Is this reasonable, possible, probable?" are the questions I ask myself continuously as I listen to the client make her projections. "What is the tightest focus I can put on this? How would it probably work? Does the astrology coming up fit that scenario? Is it soon or later? *If I looked back on this period, say, two years from now,* **what would I see, how would I interpret the astrology**?"

Practicality increases the probability that a prediction will be fulfilled.

Weak Personal Projection

What will be your impact upon the client, nine times out of ten, through your personality and where you do your work? Is your client pleased to be with you?

Just as your mind might wander during the consultation, while your client is talking to you (you're distracted or bored, or you do not like the client), so your client's mind may be wandering when you are talking to him or her (for the same reasons)! Is each of you finding a point of interest in the other? Your client desperately *wants to feel close with you as quickly as possible*, to feel accepted, secure, to get as much as possible out of the consultation that is developing.

How are you working to impress the client with insight, empowerment, confidence, and planning? Are you inviting disclosure by disclosing facts about yourself in moderation (but remember, it is *not* your life you are talking about in the consultation!)?

Projection of your personality to the client through the consultation process, along with securing client involvement, are together the key essentials within the consultation that work toward prediction fulfillment. They are the essentials of empathy.

Not Acknowledging Other Key Horoscopes

We must understand that the client's will, his or her horoscope, is not always *the* prevailing dimension within change. For example, think of the scores of millions of family moves that have taken place in the United States *that were longed for by the wife* (or were not wanted) but were *effected by the husband*, due to his authority, his job, his money, his courage, his needs for adventure and change, his escaping from something, etc.

While the wife may have wanted the move and was in full accord with it, the move was seen more strongly *not* in her horoscope *but in her husband's*. In consultation with the wife, in this case, the creative astrologer would have tempered the prediction to fulfill the projection made by the wife: "How does your husband feel about your desire to move this summer?"

Indeed, the wife, in her projection, may have offered that: "My husband is getting this promotion, we think, and it will carry a relocation with it. We're so eager for this to happen!" It is an easy task now, with our computers, to get a glimpse of her husband's horoscope quickly, or, if the time is unknown, just to check the ephemeris dateline and apply transit development to the natal positions. An enormous amount can be deduced: you have the husband's whole Sun-Moon blend and need complex lying open before you; keys such as Saturn retrograde, Nodal axis involvement, aspects to Sun or Moon, etc.

Think of the thrill in seeing a pending Jupiter transit of the husband's Sun. "Twelve years ago (the Jupiter cycle), in June, did your husband have a great reward then as well—a promotion, a raise, a fine new job?" You would be testing the past responsiveness. The wife might reply, "Why yes! He did. That's remarkable! In fact that's when Tommy was born and we were able to afford to move into the house we're in right now!"

The point is that *other* lives may be key to the projections your client is making. For my businessman client Robert (page 134), with the discovery about his spiritual change in life development, while he is his own boss, he does have a business partner, and that becomes an important issue for strategy, for practicality. The tension about this was relieved when he said, out of the blue, that he thought his partner "needed to be free" of the 15,000 apartments. So, the projection for Robert was gathering steam quickly.

But if the wife were to say, "No, my husband is quite against it. He really is. He's so happy with his job here, and really, a move across town is not what I'm talking about. I desperately want to get out of this city, for the kids' sake. I had vowed quietly to myself that I would do everything possible to bring them up, in those junior high years, in Florida. Gosh, you know, the sun, the swimming, the laid-back attitude."

Now, this might sound frivolous, but if you are sitting say in Scranton, Pennsylvania, Florida takes on much more importance and significance than, say, if you were living in Atlanta. For the mother, this is a very, very important issue. She is talking about a major change of life (a clear angular Arc or transit). Just realize that the tension about this projection at home is probably diluted for presentation to you, the astrologer.

"Might your husband see that it would be possible, maybe not this Summer, but *next* year?" As you look at his astrology cursorily, you see some help for a date fifteen months off, plenty of time to seek out a new job, trying to relocate within his present corporation if the corporation reaches that far afield. *Or is the move to Florida a way for the wife to say something else?* Does she have those high probability angular measurements? There probably is another discussion to be started here.

Another example is the Clinton scandal in the White House. The scandal is presaged *not* in Bill Clinton's horoscope but in the horoscope for his second inauguration.[109] Here is an "outside" horoscope that truly interacts with Bill Clinton's horoscope. The inauguration chart presents Neptune upon the Midheaven (ruling the 12th), seven minutes of arc from precise conjunction! Additionally, the Moon is Void of Course, Venus (ruler of the Ascendant) is quindecile the Moon, ruler of the 4th (the party out of power; obsession with Venus concerns by the Republicans) and Mars and Saturn both square the Moon as well.

There is much more to this inauguration chart, but the point here is that it colors the astrology of Clinton's development as president in the term signified by the inauguration. Clinton's SA MC coming to his Sun and his SP Moon coming to his seventh cusp in January 1998 normally signify enormous public exposure and popularity. In this case, the exposure of the suspicions of scandal were forming, but Clinton's popularity with the people was beginning an historic rise at the same time. However, we start looking at the measurements with suspicion.

---

109 Inauguration: January 20, 1997 at 12:05:45 EST at the Capitol, 38N54 077W02. Clinton: August 19, 1946 at 8:51 A.M., CST in Hope, Arkansas.

The transit of Uranus (natally in Gemini in the 9th) square to his Mercury (ruler of his 9th) at the same time starts to leave international tension reference and decision making behind in order to accommodate legalisms. The Mars-Saturn transit conjunction opposed his Jupiter in April 1998 takes on different nuance as well. The negative outlook gains credibility and probability!

And finally, in August 1998, with SA Uranus precisely conjunct his Pluto we expect "overturning the status quo; creating a whole new perspective for ego recognition." This image offers no value judgment, but it is the influence of the Inauguration horoscope and the accumulating record that give it values that deal with scandal. One chart is fulfilling the promise of another. From mid-August into September, transiting Saturn was square Clinton's natal Saturn, *ruler of his fourth cusp* (the party not in power). While this aspect is absorbed into the lives of millions of people one way or another every day, in *this* particular case, the dynamism of horoscopes interacting with each other, reflecting the unfolding of complex reality, specify the story this particular way.

Vice President Al Gore's horoscope[110] absorbed the transiting Mars-Saturn conjunction of April 1998 exactly on his Midheaven (i.e., Gore's Midheaven is opposed Clinton's Jupiter)! This is normally a time of being at the top of one's powers, but the scandal diluted this time of his life; i.e., his work environment (Saturn rules his 6th) forced him back, suppressed him, threatened his prominence. Was this period in April the time that reflected upon Gore's father (Midheaven), who died nine months later, in December 1998?

With Gore, still in echo of the inauguration chart for Clinton, we have to be wary of our interpretation of the transit of Neptune over his seventh cusp Spring-Summer 1999 and then again at election time late in 2000.

We must be aware of this extraordinary complexity, and learn, learn, learn with every experience. A recent client was facing a legal case at the end of January. She wanted a prognosis. The time of the trying of the case was covered by tr. Mars conjunct Saturn, ruler of her 7th, tr. Jupiter semisquare Jupiter, and tr Pluto square *Mars in her 9th*. Immediately thereafter, i.e., applying during the case, was tr. Mars opposed Saturn. These measurements are on the down-side indeed.

How difficult it is in such a case: the client has invested time, money, faith in lawyers; the case is nearing its climax; and the astrologer is to stand up to all of the investment, the interaction of the judge, the opposing attorney, the defendant, etc. It is

---

110 Al Gore born March 31, 1948 at 12:53 P.M., EST in Washington, D.C.

awesome, and all we have to go on normally in the court case is not our personal judgment of the issues but our evaluation of the symbols within the client's reality. We search inside for a "feeling" that will help us. We fight against wish fulfillment on behalf of our client. This is not easy, but with each trial, we learn more and more how to phrase a "take" on the situation, and with experience we grow in poise as well as skill. "There is no good news here; I'm sorry. But, may we look now at what follows thereafter."

My client lost the court case.

A closing note: I have learned that many questions (all?) have their answer within them. I listen for the intangible; I open the door to some other dimension and I hope it reveals itself and helps me. Listen oh so carefully!

What We Do Not Know

My study of the Popes of Rome since the Vatican became fully independent from Italy on June 27, 1929 (at 11:00 A.M.)[111] reveals an extraordinarily clear profile of papal death and new coronation. Pope John Paul II's horoscope responds to past activity extraordinarily reliably (to the day for his installation), but he has transcended the time within the established cycle that promised the end of his reign. Indeed, the Pope has suffered falls, illnesses, and physical debilitation to an extreme, one could say, but he endures beyond what we can measure, know, or project.

Based upon the horoscope of the kingdom of Iraq, I was able to predict the Gulf War—to the day—nine months before it happened (before the name Desert Storm was created), as well as its duration, its tactics, and its close.[112] Yet, follow-up predictions regarding the fall of Saddam Hussein failed,[113] though they were based upon the most exact and reliable measurements. Indeed, six covert uprisings were organized (and begun) and then aborted in Iraq at the time when the predictions were pressing for manifestation, but overthrow did not occur. But what has kept the predictions from fulfillment? Why have they failed?

The horoscopes of King Hussein of Jordan[114] and of Jordan itself are well timed and tested throughout the past. The King's critical illness with cancer is clearly suggested.

---

111 Please see Tyl, *Synthesis & Counseling*, 532–540.

112 Tyl, *Prediction in Astrology*, chapter 5.

113 Tyl, *Predictions for a New Millennium*, 124–128.

114 See Tyl, "Astrological Timing of Illness," *Dell Horoscope* magazine, January 1999, page 42. King Hussein born November 14, 1935 at 10:35 A.M., EET in Amman, Jordan (high probability birth time).

The key time for transferral of power is focused on May 2000. Why has the king died in February 1999? This is more than a death of a person, it is a change in history. The astrology should be more reliable. Why isn't it?

Further considerations: I was able to predict the fall of the Soviet Union; and the new regime in Israel and its strategy to make a peace treaty with the PLO, the former exact to the month and the latter exact to the week, *nineteen months ahead of time*.[115] Similarly, the impeachment scandal of Bill Clinton: almost two years ahead of time, exact to the month.[116] But why was my prediction of "a death in the family that jars everyone" for Prince Charles and Prince Harry, especially, three months early and not specifically, clearly "wife, mother, or Princess Di"?[117]

What is the variable, the elusive part of prediction, beyond the measurement and interpretative discipline we can bring to the task? Indeed, with an individual cooperating in the process we have more input, we have a partner working toward an outcome. And in Mundane work, we have individuals whose lives are publicly exposed and we have detailed historical record for checking the past, all to help buttress the precarious birth data of nations. But our work on the one hand can be astoundingly accurate and on the other so easily (and too often) undercut by incompleteness and small inaccuracies that loom very large indeed within the spotlight of news coverage and history.

We do not know the answer. Ours is an imperfect art, as art is. Knowing that gives us caution. Knowing what we do not know is part of wisdom indeed.

As we have discussed, prediction best becomes projection in order to provide greater tenability to what we see in the past and create for the future. In private practice the projections become strategies with probabilities attached to them. "Chances are that," "I think it's safe to say that," "Our experience suggests that, in such a case, next spring, April particularly, we will see," are ways to present predictions/projections that are more reasonable than out-and-out pronouncements along the lines of "On March 5, a tall dark stranger will come out of the shadows and . . . ."

When I am working with a confluence of measurements over, say, a two or three months-long period, I try to "average them," recognizing the time-orb each measurement carries with it, in overlap with the other measurements. I do the averaging in

---

115 For the Soviet Union: Llewellyn Publications, *1992 Moon Sign Book,* prepared in March 1991, published in the Fall of 1991; for Israel: 1993 Moon Sign Book, prepared in March 1992, published in the Fall of 1992.

116 *Llewellyn's 1998 Astrological Calendar*, text written in March 1997.

117 Tyl, *Predictions for a New Millennium*, 222–223.

terms of calendar dates and then by the use of Tertiary Progression,[118] watching for the TP Moon's movement into sharp aspect and/or movement over an Angle (as well as other aspects by other planets to the natal configuration, using only hard aspects and 1-degree orbs). The TP Moon moves approximately one degree every four days of real time. Many people seem "to live" in TP time management (I, for one). Through the Tertiary Horoscope a single day of focus for all active Arcs, transits, and the Secondary Progressed Moon aspects can be established. It can be presented as a research reference point in time, but it grounds the strategy of the projection, and it is startling (and gratifying) how often that day-specific dimension does find corroboration in real happening.

So, we simply must continue through failure, buoyed by success, being careful with how we phrase projections, and rarely profess with total confidence the 100 percent reliability of predictions. "The probability is very, very high—from our experience and within your job situation that we've talked about (discussing, say, a Jupiter transit of the Sun; or SA Jupiter=MC)—that you will get that raise, become head of the department. Lord knows, you deserve it, and the time looks right. Let's work to make that happen!"

---

118 One Lunar Month after birth equals one year of life, symbolically.

Chapter 5

Analytical Guidelines and Creative Connections

AS WE RELATE THE HOROSCOPE TO THE LIFE BEING LIVED BY the client, we must be thinking constantly. We can not simply spot measurements and then describe traits. We have to know the potential of the measurements, link them together, and conceive a scenario of human development. Then, in discussion with the client, *we adapt all of our preparation to the reality at hand,* to the client's station of life, assimilating the detours, the short circuits, and the smooth avenues of development the person has experienced to get there. With this respect for and inclusion of the client, we are bringing the horoscope literally, figuratively—and significantly—*to life.*

It is astounding how the brain learns to organize myriad measurements and nuances of potential into a cogent, interpretation-rich whole. We live in a message-dense and decision-rich environment. We see some seven million advertisements in our lifetime; we read and hear scores of thousands of words every day; we make decisions all the time, awake or asleep, some important, some trivial. It is the same with our astrology work, with the innumerable connections possible among symbols. It is impossible to think deeply about *every* scrap of information or *every* stimulus. *We learn to take shortcuts, to establish patterns and links among all the data.*

Social psychologists say we forever try "to conserve our cognitive energy." Given that we have a limited capacity to process information, we attempt to adopt strategies that simplify complex problems. We learn to ignore some information and overuse other information. Indeed, this can lead to serious omissions and biases, but this is our way of thinking; shortcuts and patterns, assumptions and hypotheses drive our learning.[119]

Our judgment is relative. How we evaluate and perceive information and potential are highly dependent on the nature of the modifiers and alternatives around the information and its promise. When we see Saturn in the 11th House, for example, we are immediately alerted to a *tremendous need for love:* some focus of controls necessary to development is placed in the area of our developmental experience that we call "love received, hoped for, earned, expected." Of course, we can say that *everyone* needs love, but *this* Saturn situation is a particularly intensified concept framed within the inner environment of the particular person; a great deal of the life will be driven by this particular need. Ask people who have Saturn in the 11th about this, and they will acknowledge unequivocally *the special depth of the need.*

At the same time, we search for context; we think *how intense* is this need? *How has it been managed?* The behavioral patterns that are inspired and developed to fulfill the need, *are they successful, disruptive, debilitating, self-sacrificing, saddening?* How do they change during life development? Have they spilled over into other areas of life experience, like making it difficult to give love (5th House) and/or undermining self-worth security (2nd House)? Have other areas of anxiety compounded the nature of this need: lack of education, for example, job underachievement, relationship disappointment? Have defense mechanisms been created and routinely triggered—like idealism (Sun-Mercury-Venus, sometimes Jupiter and/or Neptune involvement) or self-isolation (Grand Trines)—to protect the sensitivity?

As the mind rushes to judgment, it does so *holistically*. The part reaches for the whole, and the whole establishes identity.

Studying Creative Connections

Please let me share with you thoughts that can come to your mind helpfully about astrological measurements as they are distributed throughout the twelve Houses of the horoscope; thoughts that are dynamic, holistic, that reach out to make creative connections with other thoughts arising from other measurements. *Everything that is presented here is from case experience, not from theory.*

---

119 Aronson, 122–123.

I want to begin with the 12th House because, while it is a difficult place symboli-cally for astrologers, it dramatically represents, as an ending of sorts, the beginning of life, the harbinger support of what is to be born or reborn and developed. My objec-tive is not to be cookbook complete but, rather, to stimulate your creativity further in analysis, to give our minds some practice!

These paragraphs are for careful study—a little bit at a time—and expansion into your own observations, application, and style. They are not necessarily intended to be read in continuity.

The 12th House

- The 12th House has the sense of getting prepared, perhaps of making corrections, especially when observing the buildup of a major transit to the Ascendant. **Pluto in transit** through *any* House can activate the generic significances of the particular House it is in, as background for development. It stirs into background consideration the field of experience depicted within the particular House. While in the 12th for quite a few years, Pluto will underscore the gathering of sensitivity, of other-dimensioned knowledge, spiritual or religious teaching in order to inspire a new birth at an inner level when crossing the Ascendant. "You surely feel a sense of preparedness now for this time next Summer (when Pluto will transit the Ascendant); how does it feel and where is it going with you?"

- **Pluto natally in the 12th** suggests that, under pressure, the defensive attitude can be that "the world doesn't understand me." This is often a cry from a position of not being able to control life one's own way, especially in the realms and tactics of the emotions. Might that enduring attitude—or some other attitude that clearly defines the person's self-perspective—have been established at the time of major change in the early home? Check the Arc projection of Pluto=Ascendant. Check for any major transit activity at about the same time (it is almost *always* there!). Remember the Ascendant is derivatively a parental fourth cusp or Midheaven.

  When **Mars is in the 12th** natally, we are keyed immediately to expect fight, rebellion, inner anger, especially within 8 degrees (see page 29). The 8-degree margin is arbitrarily set to keep our attention on early-life formative development, i.e., within the first eight years, as Mars arcs to conjunction with the Ascendant. It can be later (higher in the 12th), of course. This developmental measurement is key, I believe, to appreciating the Gauquelin research that high-lights the 12th and 9th House areas, i.e., the arc potentials in development *will characterize the life expression thereafter*, seeding the system when the Arc crosses the Angle.

What House does Mars rule? Is that tension there the source of the anger? How might that have been keyed into developmental experience at the time of the Arc Mars=Ascendant? Are there other Arcs that time out to the same age? How might they work together? What were the major transit triggers then? How will I ask the client about this?

- With **Neptune arcing down to the Ascendant** from within the 12th House, what kind of suppression might occur? Because of what in the family? What House does Neptune rule? Might that be the root of the wiped-out feeling that will register after, say, five years of age (an arc of more than 5 degrees)?

- **Uranus arcing to the Ascendant** (or the transit of Uranus to the Ascendant) is going to suggest horoscope responsiveness in terms of self-assertion (that which usually challenges relationship). What did the early move, if there was one, do for personality development? Did it open up new opportunities or uproot something that was going along very smoothly? What about peer-group ties at this time? If this thinking starts to reveal an extended pattern of uprooting, of breaks (a military-family child, for example), are there links through aspects to the 7th House? Could there be a complex forming about abandonment, about nonpermanence? All of this is reasonable out of growth patterns from the early conditioning.

- Early-life tensions, especially before clear self-consciousness and verbal abilities, will often be focused in illness. The **tighter the conjunction** to the Ascendant, the more reliable an early health crisis is. Extreme closeness seems to correlate often with adoption, i.e., the dissolution of the mother-father relationship before or at birth, or enormous family tension at the time of birth. Remember: the natal horoscope is a transit record in the lives of the parents.

- **Quindecile measurements into the 12th House** or with the ruler of the 12th House, regardless of the planets involved, can often suggest the avenues of illness-buildup later in life. What are the Houses ruled by the planets making such an aspect? If Uranus is involved, the fight for individuation seems to be highlighted. What makes this happen developmentally? Why might there be such a struggle? Is there competition from the mother (in a female horoscope, Pluto square, conjunct, or opposed the Moon)? Is there smothering from the mother (in a male horoscope, Pluto square, conjunct, or opposed the Moon)? Is there a blanket over the potential individual bloom? (Pluto square, conjunct, or opposed the Sun)? Is the Nodal axis on the horizon or configured strongly elsewhere, suggesting the maternal influence?

- **Venus in the 12th:** "What is this 'private sense of beauty' I see here in the horoscope? How does it get in the way of easy enjoyment, more frequent fulfillment? Why do you think you are so very hard to please? How do you explain that to others? What if it were NOT that way?" With Mercury and/or the Sun involved nearby, it is idealism. What does the idealism defend against? What is the condition of the 2nd House, the planet ruling the cusp, especially?

- Look for a **square aspect from a planet in the 12th** to the Midheaven, not only to link up a parent with problematic concerns but, as well, to link a need-fulfillment press in the 12th to an outlet in the profession.

- With the **Moon in the 12th**, we can expect a behind-the-scenes nature, a consultant posture, someone most comfortable once-removed from the line of action. Why is that probably so? Why is the sensitivity so "dark blue"?

- **In critical illness**, there is simply no doubt that the 12th House is key. The 12th House and the Ascendant, as the health center, are clearly involved (along with Pluto, natal, transit, or arc), in critical illness more so than any other House or planets. Critical illness begins with developmental deficits accumulated from earliest life.[120]

The Ascendant

- The Ascendant is the **health center** of the horoscope. It works with the 12th in profiling critical illness (through significator transits and arcs).

- The **ruler of the Ascendant being retrograde** suggests a difficulty in shaping identity, a possible second agenda at work compensatorily. If the ruling planet is Mercury, note the other House it rules; it will probably be on the parental

---

120 Please see Tyl, *Astrological Timing of Critical Illness.*

axis. What is the condition of the other parental significators,[121] Saturn, the Node, etc.? If the ruling planet is Venus, note that it probably also rules the 8th or the 6th, questions of values in relationship, cooperation with others. What is the difficulty here, relating Venus retrograde to those experiential concepts of the other House(s) ruled by Venus?

- When the **ruler of the Ascendant is under high developmental tension,** there will be difficulty in identity development. What do the parental significators have to say about this high probability? Self-worth? How might it be transferred into (played out in) relationship experience (note the significator(s) of the 7th)? *Was this the way it was modeled by the parents in the early home?*

- With the **Nodal Axis conjunct the horizon**, the maternal influence upon identity development will be extraordinary. Why is the situation so out of balance? Is it a default from Saturn retrograde (or Saturn in aspect with the Sun)? Was the father also victimized by this power influence? Was the child left with any support anywhere?

- **Leo on the Ascendant** is going to suggest a nascent king/queen complex, something bright and grand, a yearning to get free and out from under suppressing tensions, should they exist. It is a way to salvage a poor situation: "What will it take to bring out the 'king complex' (queen; prince, princess) that's been kept in the cellar too long? The way I look at it, and the way we've been discussing your strengths, they are just about ready to pop! *What will finally make you proud of all that?* How do we make *that* happen?"

- **Pisces on the Ascendant** with Aries intercepted in the 1st House (*or the Moon in Pisces with an Aries Sun*) is going to suggest a hot soldering iron plunged into cool water: *steam.* The client will recognize this image easily. *What* is steaming? "How can we get the vapor out of the way?" Where does the smokescreen come from? What do we need to do to balance the sensitivity (possibly lack of confidence) with the bravura just begging to be recognized? Who *never* recognized it early on?" What supports this hypothesis in the horoscope? How can we let all that go and recognize it now . . . and believe it? Maybe the astrologer is the first person to see it all and encourage it!

---

121 Significator: the planet ruling the cusp sign, possibly the planet ruling the intercepted sign, possibly a major planetary placement in the House that commands attention. Pick the one that presents itself most strongly through aspect configuration.

Another observation here is the possibility of martyrdom to others or to an ideal, to ennoble the Self.

- With the **Moon in the Ascendant**, we immediately anticipate a do-your-own-thing kind of self-extrication from any developmental snags. A break-away from the norm IS possible. The person *needs* this, or there is frustration, the feeling of being hemmed in. Does the person have the educational back-up to take such a stand (check the significator of the 9th)? If not, how does she or he overcompensate for that? Does idiosyncrasy substitute for skill?

- When a **planet in the Ascendant aspects the Midheaven** tightly (close aspect of any quality, including quincunx or sesquiquadrate), this planet as part of the personal projection of identity *will usually also figure strongly in the profile of the profession.*

- The **quindecile to the Ascendant** from the 7th or 6th will intensify possibly to the point of obsession the drive to individuate, to be recognized for who one is (especially from Mars, Uranus, Jupiter, Pluto). Why is the fight so difficult? Why is this necessary? What tends to block the recognition? If the quindecile is from Saturn or Neptune, there may be much excess baggage weighing down the train, suggesting a depressing state of affairs that requires a lot of discussion, disclosure, and understanding.

- **Neptune rising** seems to correlate with dreaming in color, which suggests a high emotional content in the dreams. If this is so, what does the dream life say about the drama of personality development? How does this Neptune relate to the significator of the mindset 3rd and to the condition of Mercury by Sign and aspect? Is there perhaps a mutual reception with some other planet that will give Neptune more focus here?

The 2nd House

- If the **significator of the 2nd is under high developmental tension**, there is a difficulty with self-worth development that must be discussed. How is this condition related to the parental axis, to keys like Saturn and the Nodal axis, with regard to the parents? How are the significators of the 5th and 11th, especially, configured; self-worth must be secure before love can be given and before love can be expected *and believed!* How are you going to approach this with the client? What words? How are you prepared to work gradual adjustments to the self-worth profile throughout the consultation?

- **Money matters**, normally connected with the 2nd House, can often be a major substitution for the psychodynamics of self-worth; there is a thin (and sometimes *no*) line between money and love (some people buy love). Pluto in the 2nd often seems to suggest income from several sources. Does a double-bodied sign on the Midheaven (Pisces, Gemini, Sagittarius) corroborate this? On the material/money level, what role does the 11th House play, as second of the 10th, i.e., income and recognition from the job, in relation to the 2nd? If the 2nd House is highly developed, is there jealousy from a sibling (2nd is the twelfth of the 3rd), a sense of separation, the money factor having been substituted for something else between the two family members?

- Is the **significator of the 2nd tied to Uranus** by aspect? This intensifies the sense of insecurity, brings it very strongly into the nervous system; **with Neptune**, a cloudiness tries to hide it; **with Pluto**, it acutely defines personal perspective; **with Saturn**, there is usually a demoralization connected with the planet.

The 3rd House

- The **Moon in the 3rd Hous**e almost always suggests *communication* needs and power; the *sales person*, the middle-person; the persuader. How does this strong suggestion work with the aspects there may be with the Midheaven to build up a professional profile? When this Moon position is supported by the Mercury/Jupiter midpoint picture, involving the Moon or another planet,*writing* is powerfully indicated. Even without the Moon being in the 3rd House, the Mercury/Jupiter midpoint picture keys the sense of writing professionally.

  A man has Mercury *on the Ascendant*, ruling the 3rd and the 7th (public communication at his core). That Mercury is opposed the Moon in *Virgo* in the 7th (enormous communication emphasis out to the public). The Moon is square the Midheaven (the public communication power is a profession).

  Jupiter in *Gemini* is in the 3rd House, ruling the 9th (publishing, long distance) and itself is *quindecile the Midheaven*, a tremendous reiteration of the core synthesis . . . for Alexander Graham Bell, who was a teacher of the deaf, was married to a deaf lady, and who invented the telephone. (The inventiveness of the horoscope was Mars square Uranus, Mars quintile Mercury.)[122]

- The concept of **"Brothers and Sisters"** has fallen away from astrological prominence in the last forty years because the family unit has changed so much throughout this century, especially since World War II. Individuals in the family scatter, relocate, or break up so much more than ever before; their influence (interdependence) one upon the other is much less that it used to be, but, we must ever be aware that we may be in consultation with the exception. A sharp aspect from the ruler of the 3rd to the ruler of the 9th, especially in a female horoscope, suggests that the brother was given the education she should have had, that she was overlooked in the brother's favor. How has she assimilated this devaluation, then and now? "I think it's fair to ask why this estrangement between the two of you continues. He had nothing to do with your parents' preference of him over you. Talk to me about that, please."

- **The mindset** is often seen very clearly in the 3rd House. This is what's behind the accentuation of the 3rd that supports communication and writing (a fulfillment of Gemini's affinity with the 3rd in the natural distribution of the Signs, of course). Venus or Mercury ruling the 3rd or being in the third and in touch with each other or with Jupiter or Neptune is going to suggest an idealistic mindset (see page 44). Saturn signifying the 3rd or aspecting its significator will suggest a weightier mindset and less humor; possibly even a first glimpse of depression, should Mercury be involved (see page 40). Uranus suggests the nervous system similarly (see pages 40, 65); Neptune a secrecy, subtlety, imagination, or smokescreen.

- Watch for the **quindecile** linking the 3rd House area with the 10th House area, i.e., mindset with parental circumstance or, indeed, a strong, inherited mind-set from one of the parents. Note that the 3rd is the derivative *12th House of the parent in the 4th*. Difficulty here in the 3rd is definitely linked to the parents, the modeling of communication absorbed in the early home life.

- Watch for the **quintile** (72 degrees) involving the significator of the 3rd: *creativity* (page 157). Where does the creativity go? If one of the aspecting planets rules the 7th, it is projected to the public; if it refers to the 4th, it might be directed

122 Alexander Graham Bell was born March 3, 1847 at 7:20 A.M., LMT in Edinburgh, Scotland.

into real estate, the 8th stocks and investment; to the 9th, into education; to the 5th, perhaps teaching, somehow at some level. If Venus and/or Neptune is involved: art.

- Naturally, with the **significator of the 3rd tied to the Node**, we have the suggestion of strong maternal influence upon the mindset. Is this out of default from the Saturn retrograde phenomenon, if this is present (and the same is possible with Saturn conjunct or square the Sun)?[123] What is the maternal influence? "Please share with me the significance here of the mother, her way of thinking, *yours*." This will be a key determination of selfhood.

- **Arcs beginning in the 3rd House** cross the Angle at the IC, opposing the Midheaven, usually during the early formative years. Again, from any Cadent House, the arcs will be enormously formative when they do cross the Angle of the next House. Several Arcs throughout the horoscope will often show themselves to be contemporaneous, an easy patterning to spot with some experience, especially within the first fifteen years (degrees) of life, the times that are especially significant.

The 4th House

- **The significator of the 4th House** is one of the several keys we have to suggest interaction with the parents in early homelife development. When the significator is under high developmental tension, there is developmental tension in the early home, and the House ruled by the other aspecting planet is usually involved. If Uranus (ruling the 11th) squares the Moon, ruler of the 4th, for example, how do you fit the anxiety about being lovable into a scenario of development out of the home?

  Another example of this is Aquarius on the 4th, Gemini on the 8th (Air sign trine distance, normally, Signs of the same element), and Virgo on the 11th (a natural square from the 8th, Signs of the same mode): with Uranus squaring Mercury, the *three* Houses are involved with synthesis. This suggests a nervous anxiety formed in the early home, probably with one parent in particular (who will emerge in discussion), about being loveable (11th) and then being out of balance with the self-worth expressions of others (the 8th), i.e., values in society,

---

123 In the opposition, retrogradation is automatic: any planet opposed the Sun is always retrograde. Going further: in almost every opposition between two planets, the intrinsically slower moving planet is usually retrograde, especially when close to partile.

in relationship, not believing compliments, difficulty exchanging resources with others; therefore, relationships deteriorate, etc.

Another example: Virgo on the 4th, holding Neptune squared by Saturn in the 12th. Gemini, the other Mercury-ruled Sign, is on the 11th, holding Uranus. Uranus squares Mercury, thus involving the 4th, the 11th, the nervous system, all very strongly: a great deal of nervous tension about being lovable taken on in the early homelife, something other-than-it-seems bringing about that conditioning. This Neptune focus must be explained: we may see the Nodal axis conjunct the Ascendant. We know. We can see corroboration in the man's horoscope through the *Moon in the 2nd* square Pluto (see page 65).[124]

- Watch for a **quindecile from the 4th to the Midheaven**, which will give extreme emphasis to the parental situation and *highlight the profession as outlet to prove oneself* important, worthy, etc, reflecting the Sun-Moon blend, i.e., the angular quindecile will touch the primal reigning need organization directly, the formative base of development.

- Watch for **planetary squares sent from the 4th to the Ascendant** (and Descendant). Neptune will suggest difficulty in identity formation because of confusion in the early home: "What was the unusual circumstance in your homelife that *led most* to this posture of defensiveness we are talking about?" (Note the assumptive question, the implication that there *were many* unusual dimensions. This is a clear double-bind (see page 163): the client is asked to choose which one among several dimensions was most important, not whether or not this assumption described the state of affairs, or whether or not there was such an influence.)

- The **Moon in the 4th House** very, very often inclines to working at home, and this is important, say, for a single mother facing the financially draining and time-consuming juggling of day-care facilities for her child. Perhaps there is a way to organize a profession at home; she would want that; how can the creative astrologer work with ideas to make that possible?

- Planets in the fourth are in the **12th House of the 5th**, and this suggests that, if the significator of the 5th (and the 8th) is under high developmental tension, and so is the planet in the 4th, we may be finding the root of a sexual problem

---

124 And further: this Moon is in Taurus, a curious resistance to change; keeping things as they are or should be. This man has never married; in his mid-fifties, he is still tied to his mother. When can he be free?

with *the indoctrination by one parent in particular*. This is often found in the horoscopes of individuals born before 1960 (when information and communication about sex were still suppressed).

Additionally, Neptune in the 4th must alert us that something is other than it seems in the home, especially if the Neptune is under tension: alcohol, drugs (medicines), strange dependencies in the early home, impotency, disease, or a hidden family secret.

Secrets in the family are terribly important in that they shape behaviors dramatically, as we are seeing unleashed in a "Talk-Show Age." Making a secret, keeping a secret, opening a secret—all use up a great deal of energy and shape and alter our most important relationships. Within the dynamics of disclosure during consultation, the graceful management of the information of secrets becomes extremely important for the astrologer.[125]

- The **Matrix of the Unconscious**, if I may see it as such, certainly involves the Water Signs and the 4th, 8th, and 12th Houses. Time and time again, the organization of the aspects conspicuously among these Houses and their significators leads to special considerations that are somehow once removed from the normal or expected. Another dimension presents itself in analysis. Denial or hiding of some kind is often captured in the suppression that can be suggested by strong patterning here.

- A **peregrine planet** in the 4th or ruling the 4th will be extremely important in life development within the perspectives taken on from one parent in particular (naturally echoing the possible occurrence of Saturn retrograde and the Nodal axis in aspect patterns). Neptune peregrine in the 4th seems to suggest "the black sheep" in the family. "When did the lone position develop for you? How did it come about? Do you still feel that way?" (Just imagine what the answers to these questions will do to bring the horoscope to life!)

The 5th House

- When you see that the **significator of the 5th** House is under high developmental tension, you will already have spotted other tension patterns from among Hemisphere Emphasis, the Saturn-retrograde phenomenon, sharp Nodal Axis involvement, Ascendant and parental axis significator dynamics, and 2nd and/or

---

125 Please see *The Secret Life of Families*, Evan Imber-Clark, Ph.D.

11th House points of focus. The scenario is building; now the 7th House of relationships is probably under scrutiny; how does all that is building fit into the relationship profile? *Relationships are supported by the 5th* (a natural sextile) and given special values by the 8th; this is part of why the 5th and the 8th define much of the sex profile in any horoscope.

When the significator of the 5th is under tension, it signals difficulty with giving love. Self-worth must be secure before love can be given to others; the Self comes first (this is why the 5th shares a square of developmental tension with the 2nd). Difficulty in giving love can include orgasmic dysfunction in the female partner in a relationship (lack of trust, not believing love, relationship concerns from other spheres that invade the respect of union, etc.); emotional aridity in men (fearing that they are not credible in love matters, that they will be diminished by giving, etc.); idiosyncratic sexual development, which may carry secretiveness or guilt with it.[126]

A man has Pluto ruling his 5th, opposed his Moon (smothering mother?) conjunction with Mars (enormous concentration of energy about this) in the 8th. This Pluto is also quindecile (obsessive, gripping tension) with Venus ruling his 11th (lovableness) and placed in the 7th (relationships). His development has manifested with sexual problems as well: impotency except with prostitutes. He suffers depression (Saturn=Mercury/Uranus, Mercury ruling the mindset 3rd).

With Aquarius on the cusp of the 5th, we are alerted to intensified attention to the 5th House (Bill Clinton, John F. Kennedy, etc.). This 5th House identification usually issues from significances involved with a Libra Ascendant, with Taurus on the 8th(!), and often the condition of its significator, Venus (Clinton: Venus conjunct Mars and Neptune; Kennedy: Venus square the Moon (vanity), semisquare Neptune).

These observations are not descriptions that exist in a vacuum; they are hypotheses that come *out of* dynamic developmental constructs. These constructs have had significant detours and short-circuits occur within their development, attracting swirls of feelings to those constructs that stay with a person for a long, long time and usually express themselves dramatically in affairs of giving love and sharing sexuality. (Please see the 8th House as well, below.)

---

126 Tyl, *Synthesis & Counseling*, 600–625.

- **Fantasy elements** (Mercury-Neptune, Venus-Neptune, Sun or Moon tied to Neptune, etc.) anywhere in the horoscope will be brought into play in 5th House matters through erotic fantasy. When the 5th House focus of developmental tension (including, of course, the Succedent Grand Cross of Houses, the 2nd, 8th and 11th as well) is very strong, you can expect private catharsis of needs *that are not being fulfilled in relationships*. The symbology of private erotic fantasy (explored by all psychotherapies) very often carries intense symbolism that can depict deep emotional needs lying in frustration: a woman with conspicuous self-worth difficulty visualizes a bondage situation or being blindfolded and *forced to receive attention and love*, not to define some secret sex need but, symbolically, *to have it proved to her that she is loveable* (Venus square Uranus, Venus ruling the 5th, Venus conjunct Neptune in Scorpio in the 5th; total Northern hemisphere emphasis, Pluto in tension with the Moon).[127]

  "Thank you for giving us permission to talk about that, Marilyn; you see how what we've been discussing about self-worth concerns has entered into your deepest fantasies, to gain some freedom. They are like dreams, working in code. You understand so much now; what if you spent some time over the next weeks consciously, *determinedly adjusting the fantasy scenario*, changing it, *believing* your new, adult potentials (freedoms) in loving? That is part of the way back to a new security!"

- A **peregrine planet** signifying the 5th (or a highly intensified signification) can suggest that giving love can overwhelm development (sexually, in social service, healing, teaching), imbalance it, affect decisions. Is this potential corroborated by an orientation to the West? What is the condition of the significator of the 7th? For what would all of this orientation be overcompensatory? Mia Farrow, who has adopted some ten children and married several times, has the Sun ruling her 5th and peregrine, and Venus, ruling her Ascendant and in her 12th House (see above), is squared by Saturn retrograde(!), ruler of her 10th!

- The **Moon in the 5th** vocationally brings teaching and children to the foreground. What are the educational requirements for this occupational channel in relation to the condition of the significator of the 9th House? If the credentials can not support the inclination, how has this teaching energy

---

127 A personal note, please: be aware of how much you have learned about synthesis, now that you can follow the creative ties within the patterning of these astrological measurements! Congratulations!

expressed itself? Is it just waiting to be brought out in a different guise, e.g. training personnel at work, stage direction, coaching sports?

- When there is tension with the **significator of the 5th**, there may indeed be concerns with children in or out of the home. This is difficult since it is still beyond astrology to differentiate among many children, biological children, adopted children, stepchildren; and, as well, fertility. There are old rules attempting to help with this, but, in the modern era of assisted conception, they do not bear repeating anymore.

    Suffice it to say that difficulty here astrologically will give rise to strong discussion about something to do with a child, and this will invite better focus of the astrology. The therapeutic key of course to our modern problem with children in the family unit is communication and attention given by the parents to the children, the sharing of values, the modeling of values, etc. Most parents will spend more time with a tomato plant in the back yard than nurturing a child in the home.

- **Suppression of sexuality** is usually manifested in a loss of interest in sexuality. Now, if this is not due to some counterreaction to medicines (some blood pressure medicines and antidepressant drugs, for example, carry with them a warning of libido loss) or to relationship problems, it may very well be attached to an idealized time in the past, an assumed wonderful marriage that broke apart. Hanging on to the time past somehow sustains the person living alone. Even if there are sporadic sexual relationships, there is no "healthy" eroticism energy coursing through the life, keeping its bloom alive.

    With the client's permission, discussing just such a case, I asked, "After you do have sex with someone, how do you feel thereafter, the next day?" The client replied, "I feel great; I feel much better; I feel like I'm me!" And I said, "Notice how that tells us something: that sexual energy—and the relationship echoes involved, of course—is *important to being complete*, to being creative in your work, in your planning for the future! *Perhaps you have to adjust perspectives about the anchor to the past relationship*: it just did not work as each of you grew further independently; after all, he *was* a childhood sweetheart. I suggest you need to get back in touch with your body. And we need a bit of humor here! But it's a serious consideration: getting back in touch with your body will help you so much, give you energy for so many feeling-good things, just as you have experienced!"

The 6th House

- Planets in the **6th House** arc across the seventh cusp usually during the developmentally formative years. When they do, remember that they are *opposite the Ascendant:* immediately, we are alerted to the possibility of early childhood illness, if other arcs and transits support the possibility, especially when the significator of the 12th House is involved as well. "Were there any illnesses in those early years we should be talking about?" Why were they important, beyond considerations of health?

  When dealing with very early occurrences that appear powerfully delineated (i.e., high probability and significance), we will ask about illnesses and family shifts, *not in terms of the client's memory.* The client can not remember from that early on, but if the client is able indeed to document the time, he or she was *told* about it by the parents *for some particular family reason. That* reason may be very important within disclosure; "I see; how were you told about this?"[128]

  Psychodynamically, the 6th House suggests the dimension of cooperation within relationships. When this dimension breaks down (transit or Arc), relationships feel the limitation. The 6th is the twelfth of the 7th, and suggests the twelfth House of the partner (as the partner views your client).

  Lilly's 6th House significator (see page 146) is Venus and we learned of its thorough manifestation in her life in terms of its conjunction with the Aries Point. It is in the 7th, BUT it is squared by Saturn retrograde from the 4th. The cooperation dynamic in relationships broke down, perhaps through her giving so much to others (the Western orientation) and inviting exploitation and victimization. Reclusiveness assuaged this trait and put her into service to her ninety-two-year-old father, which called into play and rationalized other formative-years frustrations for her.

  With the 6th House strongly articulated with the Moon-Pluto conjunction, with the Moon ruling the 6th, this conjunction is squared by Uranus, the ruler of the woman's Ascendant, in the 2nd. This tells us that she is tirelessly cooperative. With the **Moon in the 6th**, she is a workaholic; her work will define who she is; she speaks convincingly about service to others. When Pluto arced to her 7th cusp at age twenty-one, tr. Uranus was conjunct her Venus and tr. Saturn was square her Sun: she got married, of course.

---

128 It is not a rare occurrence to learn from a parent that you, the child, were not wanted, that there had been efforts to abort, etc. Shocking indeed, but not uncommon.

Recall Jonah's case, please (page 45): note that his 6th House ruler and his 7th House ruler *are square to each other*. Here is the grand tension of being duped, being let down by others with whom he wants so much to relate and cooperate: "Every time I get near somebody, I let down my defenses and I get my heart ripped out." See the idealism of expectations in the 7th!

- **Work environments** can be suggested by the 6th House cusp and placements in the House. For example, Mercury ruling the 6th House is squared by Uranus ruling the 2nd: the work environment is probably tense, argumentative, testy, and this is important because much of the self-worth profile is caught up with *getting along on the job*. Here there was tremendous discomfort with co-workers, and this discussion eventually disclosed that the person was in the wrong professional pursuit entirely!

- **Neptune in the 6th** can easily suggest "something is other than it seems" with regard to the work environment; a difficulty with employees.

    The physical environment typically is shown something like this: a workaholic male has the Moon in Sagittarius (yes, enormous internationalism and publication *are* involved with his work) in the 6th House. Jupiter rules the cusp. This man was enjoying SA Sun=Ascendant when we sat in consultation: he was popular, recognized, appreciated enormously in his field in world standards; since his work called for him to travel so much, he really worked from his home, while representing a very specialized company with offices in a major city. I noticed several bunched contacts with his natal Jupiter (ruler of the 6th) in the midst of all this (SA Sun=Ascendant and SA MC=Sun/Jupiter). "Let me ask you, please, about any plans you may have of changing your work environment; I mean, within all this recognition, are you planing to add on a bigger office to your home, actually go into the home office, or what?"

    My client could not believe the specificity of this inquiry. He *was* considering finding an office elsewhere, out of his home, but *not* at the corporation. And then this led to the next question, common-sensically, to take the measurement of SA MC=Sun/Jupiter to a higher level, along with the SP Moon opposed Pluto, tr. Jupiter square Pluto and more that was building: "There is another issue here, I think: while you are enjoying all this phenomenal success with what you're doing, feathering your personal profile, *you seem to be ignoring your corporation*." "I can't stand them, actually! They get in my way (Uranus square Sun in Aquarius)." "But look what you're *doing* for them, Jack! Resting on your own amazing record, *are you looking for another job doing what you do,* elsewhere? Because if you're looking, *you will get it* (empowerment)!" This question led to a rich and exciting discussion of the job offers that were indeed pouring in to him (four offers in the weeks of Sun=Ascendant), etc.

- **Aquarius on the cusp of the 6th** usually has Virgo on the Ascendant and Gemini on the 10th. What about the double-bodied sign on the Midheaven and the rulership of two Angles by Mercury? Is there a pattern of upset in the work spirit, a difficulty in cooperating, that causes job instability? What are the aspect conditions of Mercury and Uranus? Is the work environment substituting for failed or difficult relationships on a different level (note that Pisces is probably on the 7th)?

    It is extremely interesting to see how professional athletes, as examples exposed publicly, fare better in their performance when playing for one team or for another. It may very well be their developing personal astrology that brings out 6th House significances of the work environment. When the athlete or the executive says, "I'm not happy here; I want to be traded, I want to change where I work," he or she is saying that the environment is not what is needed for best performance, and this certainly will involve analysis of the 6th House condition.

Case Study: Cliff

As a break in this intense study of creative connections, let me share with you a transcript of a client consultation that I did by telephone yesterday.

Cliff's horoscope (page 205) shows the following as guidelines for our preparation:

- A clear Southern Hemisphere emphasis orientation (being swept away, potentially victimized)

- The Saturn retrograde key, corroborated by the square made by Saturn with Jupiter in the parental 10th (whenever Jupiter and Saturn are conjunct, square or opposed, we can anticipate *the sense of proving a point*); this square is crucial because Jupiter is the ruler of the Ascendant (real difficulty in identity development)

- Mercury is retrograde at the Ascendant and is square to the Moon (a fine talker for sure), ruling the 7th (possibly the explanation of the retrograde counterpoint; relationships serving several purposes, bisexuality?)

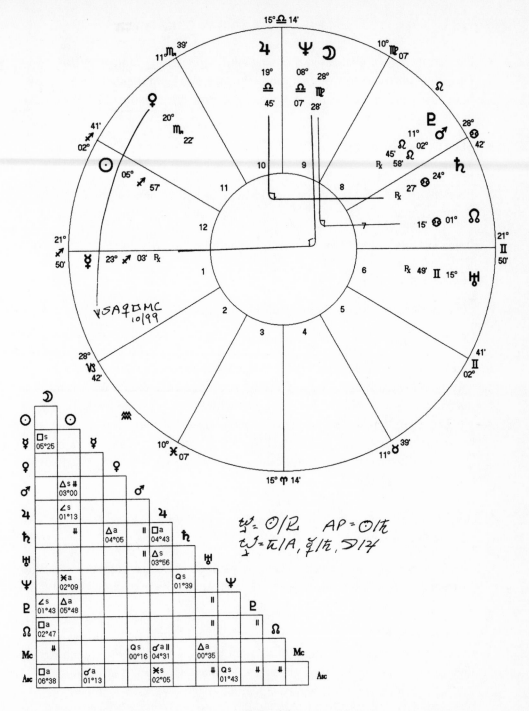

Figure 17
Cliff

- Pluto in the 8th (probable psychotherapeutic experience; from the Saturn retrograde phenomenon, Saturn ruling the 2nd, and from the mother (see next bullet); as ruler of the 11th (lovableness) and probably conjoined by Mars, ruler of the parental 4th)

- The Moon is square the Nodal Axis (mother)

- Mars quintile (creativity) the Midheaven, the closest aspect in the horoscope plan; perhaps this activates in consciousness the wide Moon-Neptune conjunction as well

- Neptune=Sun/Pluto (self-sacrifice) and other midpoint pictures

Our discussion went exactly like this:

N: Hi! How come you're calling me late? I'm just curious.

C: Oh, I was trying to finish a few things up.

N: Fine, I appreciate it. It's important because the time you choose to have this consultation sometimes is very revealing. The time *you* have chosen tells me instantly from what I have in front of me that we're talking about very bewildering relationships (C: uh-huh) and we're talking about some dimension of business that possibly is international. This is extremely good corroborative evidence—the time that you have called—of the reality we are going to discuss.

C: OK.

N: Alright: there's a lot to do here, and I'm very interested to ask you first off, "What do you do for a living?"

C: I basically put together financial transactions in the European market . . . . [Cliff explained his business a bit. Here clearly was the international dimension.]

N: The extent and specificity of what you do are not quite what I see here. The internationalism, the mental, practical application of skills are what I see, but there is a dose of creativity here [Mars quintile MC]—not that money management is not creative—but this indication is usually allocated to something that is artistic. [Cliff is sounding agreement with every few words I say.]

C: Am I artistically oriented, do you say?

N: Yes.

C: Oh, absolutely, I have always been!

N: Well, do you do anything artistic?

C: Well, right now, No. As a matter of fact, my endeavors with Jack [a photographer/musician client of mine who referred Cliff to me] are one way I see of addressing a part of me that gets unused.

N: It is a terribly important part of you here, because—as we are going to see, there are some emotional wounds here [uh-huh] from the past [uh-huh], *and they need not just disappear* [which is an impossibility] . . . *as much as they need to be replaced* [which is a practical therapy]. [Cliff: OK.]

   And I think that it's important to understand that through your horoscope, art expression is a beautiful way to come in contact *again with those emotions more soundly, more healthfully.* [Uh-huh.]

   Am I making sense to you? [Not an advisable question, of course; the client could say, "No," and then where would we be? But on the telephone, without being able to "read" the face, etc., it is very difficult to build up steam, gather approval, at the beginning of a consultation. I should not have asked it; but simply have gone on.]

C: Absolutely.

N: This is very important and subtle, this observation. The lofty business themes with which your mind deals [Sun in Sagittarius, Mercury dispositor of the Moon in the 9th, Mercury at the Ascendant in Sagittarius, retrograde] so much takes you away from your emotional life, in my opinion.

C: It's . . . it's pretty sterile!

N: And the emotional life being put at a distance is actually good, up to a point, because there are those wounds "out there." May we talk about those for a bit?

C: Certainly.

N: I suggest to you, for the lack of better phraseology, that there's a legacy of inferiority feelings [Saturn retrograde].

C: Huh . . . huh . . . There certainly is.

N: . . . taken on in the early homelife, and it's usually in connection with the father figure, who was somehow taken out of the picture early, was there and passive, or was so tyrannical [uh-huh]—any combination so as never to have given the guidance of authoritative love.

C: Not . . . *not emotionally available* would probably be closer to it.

N: Because of his character [as opposed to, *because of circumstance*]?

C: He was . . . he . . . he was a workaholic [a common father defense]; I'm, a workaholic. Ha, ha! You know.

N: Well, I don't know if that is a good parallel!

C: Well, I'm not sure . . . . It's just simply what came to mind. He was not . . . he was . . . uh . . . he was very secondary in my growing up.

N: Did he ever say, "Cliff, baby, I love you?"

C: [Tense silence for a moment.] Hmmm . . . I'd have to think about that! [Nervous laugh.]

N: [Warmly.] Isn't that a sad thing?

C: Yeah. [Nervous laugh.]

N: [Warmly.] Had this hurt? [Trying the past tense; expecting "I've gotten over it."]

C: Oh, of course. It hurts now, just thinking about it. [No more nervous laughter.]

N: What do you feel *right now*?

C: Oh, a huge amount of emotion!

N: And where do you feel it? Seriously.

C: Inside.

N: [Gently, eagerly.] Where?

C: In my heart.

N: In your heart. Alright: this is a deep, deep wound, and we're going to come back to it in a moment.

The maternal influence [Moon square the Node] is also suggested in parallel here, as very, very powerful . . . .

C: Whoosh . . . *that's* an understatement!

N: It's almost as if . . . she has taken over your personality.

C: [Sighs of emotional discomfort, tension, release.] Boy, you've got to be about the most accurate person I have ever come across! [Nervous laugh.]

N: Thank you. ["Gosh . . . whoosh . . . " continuing in the background.] Do you need some time to recover here?

C: Well . . . uh . . . I guess I'm OK . . . .

N: Do you want to go get a glass of water?

C: No, I'm all right . . . . I'm all right. You know? I used . . . I used to tell her I almost feel like a supporting actor in the drama of my own life!

N: What does that mean?

C: I was never behind the wheel!

N: Growing up . . . ?

C: I was a passenger!

N: And so you were *abused by your mother*?

C: I'm not sure what the definition of that is. I've come across that in so many contexts; you know, you see television programs and so forth and so on, and I'd always say, that was never me, *but I fit all the symptoms!*

N: I appreciate that; thank you. There's also a vulnerability suggested here in this horoscope for being very self-sacrificing [Neptune=Sun/Pluto].

C: [Resignedly.] Yeah.

N: [very slowly and clearly] And that comes from that model! Early on.

C: Yes it does. Yes it does. The wounded puppy syndrome.

N: And *you bring that forward and you disguise it as a severe businessman?*

C: [Sigh of emotional release.] I guess so.

N: Every time I say these things to you, there is a gasp . . . on the phone! [Nervous laugh.] And, . . . and, and . . . here's your chance to let this emotion speak out. Don't hide it from me. (Uh-huh.) There's a residual anxiety here about self-worth and about being lovable. [Saturn retrograde; Moon semisquare Pluto, ruler of the 11th House.]

C: [Long pause.] Yes.

N: [Long pause.] Does it still hurt? When I say that?

C: Haaaaaaah, I feel like I'm sitting here with my clothes off.

N: I know. Well, I'm not trying to make you uncomfortable. I'm trying to give you the push toward . . . objectification. I think it is very, very important—and wise—for you to look at that situation, *which you can explain to yourself*, as problems your mother and your father were having with each other, And your getting caught in their traffic pattern.

C: Uh-huh. OK.

N: What do you think about that statement?

C: [Release sigh.] I . . . I'm certain that it . . . it's entirely accurate. The problem is that they . . . they . . . never discussed that much in front of me when I was growing up.

N: Yeah. *But how can you get away from it now?* This is my point: if you can look at it and say, "THAT'S BEEN DONE. I certainly have proved myself . . . in my independence . . . and in my goodness; and isn't it a *shame* that I had to have such wounds en route.

C: [Pause.] You know what the problem is, Noel? I don't look at that an awful lot, I just kind of shut it away and say, well . . .

N: Well, that's the hidden emotion; that's what I've brought out on purpose. And those hidden emotions manifest in very [Cliff sighs] strange ways.

C: [Resigned.] Yes. I guess they do.

N: And Tom [Cliff's new platonic live-in companion] is part of it.

C: [Strongly.] You see, all that is . . . is *a reenactment of that whole drama!* I know that!

N: Thank you!

C: [Sigh.] See: you know what the problem is? Noel . . . .

N: [Interrupting; light laughter.] Yes, I think you've just told me; *we do know*.

C: [Laughter.]

N: Come on: watch your words! You have the habit of saying to me: "Do you know what the problem is?" I think we are discovering it rather quickly!!! Do you know how much time has gone by since you called me?

C: Yeah, about ten minutes!

N: Exactly twelve minutes! Have you ever been to a psychotherapist [Pluto in the 8th]?

C: Yeah, a couple times.

N: How long would it take to get to this in a psychotherapy session?

C: About six months!

N: Alright. I am trying to show you that, if I can see these things here on a piece of paper [objectification], there must be a purpose to them [learning, hope]!

C: I guess there must be.

N And in order to find that purpose, what we have to do is *back off from the creation of that purpose and go and occupy ourselves with fulfilling that mission.* Does that make sense?

C: It sure does.It sure does.

N: And there has to be recognition of these swirling emotional pains, seeing how vulnerable you've been, and avoiding now echoes of that type of depressing, introverted, life-defensive situation.

C: Alright.

N: And your mind can handle this; you know that.

C: Yeah. Well, it's handled so much at this point in time . . . .

N: Tell me how good looking you are! [Deliberate shift of conversation level and direction to let things sink in and begin to salvage some of the self-worth profile]

C: Well, I'm just an average looking kind of guy.

N: Aaaah, come on: tell me. How tall are you, how much do you weigh?

C: I'm 5'10", about 175–180 pounds. I look pretty much the same as I did when I came out of high school . . . just a little more weatherbeaten, I guess! [Cliff was fifty-four at consultation time.]

N: And . . . .

C: I don't show age as much as other people.

N: Do you feel good about how you look?

C: [Arm-twisted tone.] Yeah, I guess I do!

N: And tell me three things you do for people, that are wonderful!

C: That *I* do for people [things], that are wonderful?

N: Come on, right off the bat!

C: I sit down and listen to them when they have something to say.[129]

N: Do you listen too much?

C: Maybe.

---

129 Cliff actually said, "when I have something to say." This is probably a meaningless slip of the tongue which I've corrected here, but it could have suggested that listening is bartered for an audience to one's own personal opinion, often a Sagittarian strategy.

N: Another one?

C: I go out of my way to help them out.

N: Give me a third one.

C: Third one, uh . . . that I do good for people . . . well, I'm very generous.

N: Are you good in bed?

C: Ha, ha . . . Yeah . . . Ha, ha . . . whenever I am!

N: I'm asking you if you are expressive emotionally; *are you proud of being able to be expressive emotionally?*

C: I'm probably not as expressive emotionally as I could be or as I would like to be.

N: Why don't we add *that* to that list?

C: [Big sigh.] Alright. OK [quite subdued].

N: What possibly—and I want an answer here—*what possibly would you have to lose?*

C: Nothing I guess.

N: And isn't it marvelous how much you could give to others?

C: Yeah, I guess so.

N: The point we're coming back to is that your giving does not need to be financial, business-orientated, dry, and mental *in its entirety* [sounds of agreement]. Your giving can be *amplified emotionally*, because you're going to tell yourself that you're safe . . . and wise . . . and . . . good—and "you've been there"!

C: [Sigh.]

N: How 'bout it?

C: Yeah. I just never think of things that way. I guess I have such a habit of doing things, I guess, the way I've always done them.

N: You're reaching out to Jack for some kind of extra artistic dimension, to bring the hidden emotions forward in a healthy state of expression—we talked about that, and I told you we'd get back to it. Here, I think we're back to it!

C: [Extended nervous laughter.] OK. OK.

N: Am I saying anything that doesn't touch you deeply or seems to be off base?

C: Ha! I, I guess, I guess it's so deep, it's kind of got me spinning a little!

N: Alright. Thank you for sharing so much. But unfortunately on the telephone it's a bit difficult doing this.

C: I really do want to find out *because these things have to change*. [Our discussion this far has elicited this very healthy, involved statement.]

N: Of course, and we're doing very well with this. Now, let's talk about a few dates here, please. There are certain dates in your life that I need to check for several reasons, but in the reality of the scenario we've just portrayed, may I go back, please, to 1952.

C: 1952, my sister was born that year.

N: And what did that have to do with you? How did you feel about that? Why is there something important here? [Tr. Pluto square Venus, ruler of the MC, where Neptune had just transited; tr. Neptune, ruler of the 3rd, conjunct Jupiter, ruler of the Ascendant.]

C: Well [sighs, tension] . . . I think, in that particular case—I haven't thought about 1952 for quite some time—I think in that particular case, I was six going on seven, an only child; I was smothered, not mothered—I mean, I know that now, I didn't know it then—and I think I wanted a sibling, a brother. Right? What I got? I got a sister, but she was terribly sickly, and . . . and our whole life changed from that very moment onward. Everything focused on her, and there were trips back and forth to hospitals, and radical surgery, and life-threatening illness, and it was one crisis after the other; it never ended, up to this day!

N: And two years after that, when you were eight, you were really wiped out. [SA Neptune=MC, SA Saturn=Mars; tr. Neptune square Saturn, tr. Uranus conjunct Saturn, 5-9/54.]

C: [Sigh.] *I'm still wiped out.* It's buried, but it's still wiping me out.

N: [SA Pluto=Venus, ruler of the 5th, tr. Saturn conjunct Venus.] In 1955, please let me ask you this: was there any precocious sexual awareness at that time?

C: Oh sure! I was sexually aware real early on. As a matter of fact, in the 3rd grade [1954–55], I discovered masturbation.

N: This is what we're talking about.

C: I can't pin it down, but that became like my primary outlet. I mean, how else are you going to blow off pent-up energy when you're eight or nine?

N: Were you envisioning contact with people sexually? You couldn't have know much about that then . . . .

C: Not really . . . it was just . . . it was probably more about . . . . You see, everything with my sister . . . let me back up . . . maybe I can help throw some more light on this thing. [Cleared his throat.] My sister was born with a condition called extraphy of the bladder—the bladder was on the outside instead of inside the body. All the surgery that took place with her took place in the genital area. I mean, I saw tubes and sutures and hoses and stuff; *I should never have seen these things!* [Breaks down to tears.] I'm sorry.

N: I'm sorry too.

C: [In anguish.] To this day, I wish I had never seen [unintelligible].

N: Cliff, what would have . . . .

C: [Sobbing.] . . . terrified me . . . .

N: Cliff?

C: I'm sorry, I'm trying to get a grip here . . . .

N: It's alright. Would you like to get a glass of water?

C: No . . . no . . . .

N: I would like to ask you just one more question on this point, and then we'll move on: *what would have happened had you NOT seen it?*

C: I think it wouldn't have bent me out of shape as much as it did.

N: Bent you out of shape.

C: I . . . I . . . I . . . I'm grasping for terminology here. It's just . . . . You know, in a child's mind, everything has its fantasy aspect, and it just, you know, I thought they had done some terrible thing to her, and I was next!

N: And you were next.

C: Yeah. [Preoccupied with emotion.]

N: Are you talking about fear for your genitals or are you talking about just fear of being victimized.

C: I don't know, probably both. [I knew this point would come back in a moment. I moved on.]

N: [SA Sun=Asc.] Two years later: this must have been a *fine* time for you. Did you shine at school?

C: Let's see, '60 [recovering composure]. Yes, I won all the science fairs I was ever in. I was not an outstanding student academically; I was a very . . . .

N: Yes, but you shone at this time.

C: Absolutely. I had a lot of friends, and all the stuff you do at sixteen . . . .

N: [Tr. Pluto square Sun, tr. Uranus square Venus.] Just before that, at fourteen and a half or so, was there a first girlfriend, was there some contact romantically.

C: No. See: I, I . . . I theorize it this way: I was so traumatized by what I saw with my sister, that sexual contact with women has always been murder with me because . . . all that stuff gets dragged up, all the screaming and all the pain! [Cliff was making the creative connections; objectification had begun.]

N: Had you had your first homosexual experience at this time?

C: Oh, I fooled around with other boys, if you want to call that homosexual . . . .

N: No, I'm talking about 1960, when you were fourteen.

C: Yeah, I had a few friends that fooled around.

N: Alright. I'm just checking reactions within your horoscope here, within our theme . . . .

C: You're getting some [laughing], I'll tell you that!

N: Thank you.

[Incidental development activities not exactly relevant to our theme.]

N: Alright. Let's talk turkey. [Summer 1979: Tr. Pluto conjunct MC, tr Uranus conjunct Venus, ruler of the 10th, tr. Saturn square Ascendant leading to tr. Neptune conjunct Ascendant all 1980.] There's a major professional adjustment made by you in the Summer of 1979, in July or November, that period.

C: Ho, ho, ho. You really got that one! Well, I was working with an attorney; that led to a court case in _____; and that led to five years of incarceration in a penitentiary.

N: You went to jail for five years?

C: For five years, thanks to the efforts of someone else.

N: Had you done something illegal?

C: I was convicted of conspiracy; that means I was cooperating with somebody who was doing something illegal. The problem was, I did not know it was illegal at the time.

N: Did this take place in the Summer of '79?

C: Yes.

N: My next question was going to be "How was your ego wiped out or taken away in the period January to July in 1980?"

C: My life was wiped out. January in 1980 is when I went to trial! The most traumatic experience I can remember. It started in summer of 1980.

N: [Tr. Uranus conjunct Ascendant and Mercury, tr. Saturn conjunct Sun, 10/86.] In 1986, were you starting to get back on the track?

C: That's when I was released.

N: October?

C: Yes.

N: [Tr. Saturn conjunct the fourth cusp, 5/97 with tr. Pluto conjunct the Sun.] What was the new start for you in May 1997?

C: This is when I focused into the particular channel of what I do now.

N: [Tr. Uranus=Sun/Moon, at 2 Scorpio.] There was a major breakup in '96.

C: Yep, Yep, Yep.

N: [Tr. Saturn=Sun/Moon.] And then we have another situation in October of '98, just last October. Was there another relationship that broke up?

C: Yes . . . this is the situation with Tom, who's with me now.

N: What's so important here?

C: I don't know [I felt that Cliff was tiring of disclosure]. I just blew up and threw him out, and he came back two months later.

N: Alright [tr. Neptune=Sun/Moon]. The tension in that relationship is *not going to go away* [the sensitivity of the Sun/Moon midpoint had proved itself]. It is there for some time. And, this Tom has a tremendous anxiety himself, about being lovable, etc. [I had his data and horoscope; part of my preparation.] You picked somebody who has the same kind of wounds you do. You know that.

C: Uh-huh. Uh-huh. Ha! Yes, I *do* know that, actually! [Helpful objectification.]

N: And the similarities emotionally in pain between you are grand. They might not be as obvious to you because of the age difference between you, but they are there. How does it make you feel to care for him?

C: I don't know, it just makes me feel as if I have some value, I guess. I think that's how I get the endorsement of being someone who's worthwhile. [Our deductions were clear, well internalized.]

N: Remember, we talked about that earlier; we talked about what's so good about you. *How would you feel if you didn't care for Tom?* Wouldn't there be *other things that establish that you're worthwhile?*

C: I don't know.

N: Come on! You gave me a list of them!

C: That list . . . it was as if I was reading it off academically . . . you know?

N: And you want some more emotional involvement.

C: I'm just so kind of disconnected from everything. Like superman: a strange visitor from another planet! But I thought I had no powers or abilities.

N: I wonder if you're being too hard on yourself; I really do. I don't think you're afraid to fail. *I think you are proved.* I don't think you are really possessed with a terrible self-image. *I think it is time to say goodbye to this routine of feeling unwanted, neglected. What do you think?*

C: Noel. I agree with you. You know what the problem is? I don't know how to do that. I know that sounds terribly stupid, and I'm embarrassed, but I do not know how to not be this way!

N: Not being alone, having a mature adult relationship, probably would help.

C: It probably would.

N: Rather than supporting, helping, guiding this fellow (Tom), which seems to me to be closer to the old routine.

C: [With real conviction.] *I'm just perpetuating the past!* That's all I'm doing! But when I think of letting go of it, the pain is so ferocious, it's almost like I would rather live . . . I would rather live with a whole bunch of bandaged wounds than a painful, healed spirit. But more recently, more recently in my life, I look at this behavior and I see exactly what it is. That frustrates me even more: I see myself doing it and I don't see a way to not do it.

N: I can not help you do that on the telephone.

C: Obviously.

N: But the turns of thought and understanding that we've shared [uh-huh] *certainly should convince you that change is reliably at hand.* [Yeah.] I personally feel that Tom has become a symbol of your tie to the old pattern. [Absolutely.] And I can assure you . . . .

C: I'm just doing to him what was done to me. [Which I did not quite understand, but it was a point of view that resonated with the accord building between us.]

N: And I can assure you that the blowups that you are experiencing with him are going to continue [Neptune=Sun/Moon], and I would suggest you finish this relationship and ask him, please to find his own way in the world. [Yeah.] And I think that can possibly give you some very important strength. [Uh-huh]. It's overdue; he should have been out of there last August and September, *and you know it!* [Strong emphasis.] *He's gone*; now or June. If you really masochistically preserve this thing, it will be November. I think it is important that you do this as soon as you possibly can.

   Thanks for listening to that. *You know in your heart I'm saying something that is reasonable and reliable.*

C: Oh! I KNOW you're right. No argument there.

N: [SA Venus=MC.] I think that by October this year [1999], there is every opportunity for you to have a major love relationship, and I think that somehow this should be a very good target for you . . . in business development also [Venus rules the 10th]. The symbol here for romance, popularity, love and business is the same; unusual. Somehow, doing well in business is going to help you find and attract a good romantic relationship. I think you will start to see that in May.

   [Cliff makes notes, shows approval about the prospects.] Let me ask you one more powerful question further, before we get into some nitty-gritty strategies for the dates immediately ahead [**natal Jupiter square Saturn**]: *what is the point you're trying to prove as your life develops?*

C: I don't know, I guess that *I'm adequate* and that *I can make it*. I've always gone around feeling, you know, that I couldn't compete . . . .

N: Yet you won every Science Fair in your school days!

C: Yep. You know what the problem was? There's a lot of things that come natural to me, with very little effort; when I do these things I don't see them as accomplishments—the car, the furnace, etc. It's like brushing your teeth.

N: And the big accomplishment would be to have somebody you loved and who loved you, it was clear and unquestioned. ["Sure, that would be marvelous."]

Alright [authoritatively]: I think there is a major effort in business, and I think THAT *is going to make you feel very proud of yourself* [i.e., that he's more than adequate, that he can make it], and I think it should have started in earnest [last hit, tr. Pluto conjunct Sun; SP Moon semisquare Jupiter] in October 1998 [*Yes!*], and out of this I think the vibes will come from May [tr. Jupiter opposed Jupiter] on to full development in October [SA Venus=MC] of the relationship you're looking for. I think the probability of that is eight out of ten.

In business, what do you project for yourself in the next six months or so? [Specific business discussions, projections for the weeks of meetings ahead.]

C: I'm scheduled to go to Europe in a week, for meetings that should lead to major closings.

N: I have that down here for January 15—that's today! [Tr. Uranus opposed Pluto, partile 1/15/99.]

C: Well, today I am to talk with this European _____ from _____; it's very important.

N: Watch for March 9 [tr. Mars square Pluto, SA MC=(sesquiquadrate)Saturn], then the first week of May; expect good success out of what you're doing now. I worry about the time immediately thereafter [tr. Saturn square Pluto, 6/99]: solidify in May [tr. Jupiter opposed Jupiter, etc.] and be extremely careful for two months thereafter. Then, break out in August [SP Moon square Uranus], and this should then lead to great excitement in October [SA Venus=MC], hopefully with the relationship included!

C: That would certainly be frosting on the cake!

N: I think we need to leave it there until you confer with me, should you like. This has been a difficult call for you and an important concentrated learning-call for me, to bring us together in respect and understanding and appreciation of the drama of *the points you're trying to prove in your life.* [A reminder for further thought.]

C: Yes. Yes. Yes.

N: When is the last time you had a medical examination, a full physical? (Some unimportant discussion.] Alright. Thank you for your trust, your faith. ["Thank

YOU!"] And it's nice to reach out and touch you and feel that we've been significant to one another here.

C: We certainly have. You've . . . you've amazed me for certain. Ha, Ha. Amazed and stunned would be closer to correct!

N: When you get on this airplane [to Europe in a week], *try to be literally above some of those past problems.* There's nothing you can do about them, [Both laughing] and think of how much you have to give everybody.

C: I'll try my best. Thank you again. I really appreciate it!

N: Bye-bye

C: Bye-bye.

Cliff communicated with me immediately upon his return from Europe, two weeks after our consultation. He had indeed been tremendously successful. His spirit was buoyed.

I followed up again, just now, with a telephone call: the new business deals are going splendidly, he is removing the young man living in his home with him, and he volunteered: "I've been thinking over so much of what we discussed, and I now see so many new ways of doing these things." Cliff was really saying, "new ways of seeing these things" in his life. Cliff was laughing and was truly a freer spirit.

Additionally, Jack has telephoned me—the mutual friend who put Cliff in touch with me—and reported that Cliff has traveled to meet with Jack for three days. They are planning to set up a nonprofit corporation for concert videotape service to cable television. Cliff is involving himself with the arts, as we had first discussed at the outset of the consultation. And further: Jack told me that, "It has to be every single hour that somehow Cliff brings his consultation with you into our conversations. What an impact you had!"

The 7th House

- The **significator of the 7th House** specifically keys relationships, partners, and the public. If the significator is under high developmental tension—and with the 7th House, planets *in* the House appear very telling (as in the Ascendant) along with the ruler of the House cusp—we can expect difficulties with relationship.

Why? Is there a transfer from the parental situation directly into the marriage? Check the parental significators and the keys of Saturn and the Node. Check Arcs and transits for the age period eighteen-twenty: a marriage suggested then can be deemed precipitous and as an escape from the family environment, also including a sacrifice or interruption of post-high school education.

Perhaps behind the relationship difficulties (usually obviously patterned and repeated) is *the fear of intimacy*. Check what's behind a statement like this, "Well, I just want to be independent. That's what I really like." Is Uranus signifying the 11th for example, conjoined importantly with the Moon or the ruler of the Ascendant or 2nd (independence for sure, idiosyncratic development)? This is also anxiety about lovableness and acceptance (especially with a difficult Venus position elsewhere). It is turned into a stress,transferred into relationships, and *masqueraded as a preference for individuality (Uranus)*.

Often a client will talk at length about failed relationships; this actually gives him or her a sense of personal identification! Perhaps the ruler of the Ascendant (in "opposition" to relationships) is in high tension (quindecile) with Uranus, ruler of the 6th. Is this a defensive posture? Is the spirit of cooperation dynamics in upheaval, echoing parental situations, especially Saturn-Venus interrelationships? Does the client *not want* anyone to reciprocate in relationships, since she or he is afraid they *won't*, such being the pattern out of the early years? Is there a pattern of abandonment inherited from the early years? Perhaps the father's death, then the mother's, and now the spouse's; or a military family where there were something like twenty-three moves in the first eighteen years?

Most often, the reason first given for relationship difficulty is *not* the real reason for the tension, for the thoughts of separation. "What is the real reason behind this upset?" And then, when something else is offered, ask the question again, making your point: "What is behind *that* reason? Usually, the upset is an indirect manifestation of other concerns like job frustration, which demeans self-image, and *the tensions are then displaced into the home*. There may be a sexual problem—perhaps the man is sensing difficulty having an erection so he eschews sexual relations and starts blaming his wife for all sorts of turn-offs. Perhaps the wife has turned off because of his neglect, his absorption with his work, which in turn makes him feel undesired, so he drinks more anyway, which affects sexual performance capability, etc. Perhaps the spouses are competing with each other, one having good outlet for energies, the other underachieving, resenting it, and asserting her- or himself in other ways.

The answer to these kinds of tensions is not to sue for divorce. The first try must be for open communication, for specialized communication. *Not* trying this avenue will cause an enduring self-doubt for a long, long time into the future. For the astrologer who is not trained as a marital counselor, a referral is the best service possible to your client. Indeed, counseling may fail, and divorce eventuates—uncomfortably on schedule. Remember: divorces take a long time, a year or two. Check the measurements into the future with that in mind.

A very good technique with which to test the waters: "Does your husband/ wife love you, even in the midst of all this tension, that appears patterned and routined over some time, I might add?" The answer will most often be, "Yes." Ask then, "Why? Why does she still love you? How do you know? What is standing in the way of your enjoying that, believing that, sharing that?"

The **Sun/Moon midpoint** is extremely sensitive and important as a receptor for Arcs and transits, suggesting difficulty in relationship. Any planet natally configured by conjunction, square, or opposition with the Sun/Moon midpoint will tend to dominate the life, color it conspicuously, especially in terms of relationship.

- When **Neptune is in the 7th,** the other person's weaknesses make one strong. What are those weaknesses, i.e., what are the client's strengths that are at a premium in the relationship? Could the relationship exist without this need for and giving of resources? Is there an idealism construct (Sun, Mercury, Venus, etc.) funneled into the 7th House? Does that make satisfaction difficult, i.e., no one meeting expectations? Is idealism then a wall within relationship? If there is the defense mechanism of the Grand Trine (closed circuit of self-sufficiency), how does it work against any relationship?

On the upside of idealism and fantasy projection involving the 7th House directly or indirectly, we must see Neptune as creative visualization, part of the capacity to dream, to hope, to picture ahead of time. There are people whose problems have curtailed their dreaming, even apparently erased their capacity to dream. In consultation, we must be prepared to rebuild the dreaming mechanism. How can the principles of Neptune help the overtones of **religiousness of Jupiter in Scorpio** for example?[130]

---

130 Jupiter in Scorpio can just as easily suggest a total rejection of things religious or spiritual. It is more important in analysis as absolutism, first, than it is favoring either pole.

- Problems in relationship set up **distance between the two partners**. All defenses will do that (Eastern Hemisphere grouping, Grand Trines, idealism, fears of intimacy, self-worth problems about giving, responding). When tr. Uranus crosses the Ascendant, it opposes the Descendant; an accentuation of the individual challenges the togetherness. Any powerful Arc to the Ascendant-Descendant axis by conjunction or square will reflect the same considerations.

  Yet, distance can sometimes help to mend the rift; i.e., "I need to get away from it all." The creative astrologer can use this principle this way, suggesting that one person in the partnership *telephone* the other person in the partnership to discuss issues. It is often easier **to communicate by phone** because neither person is in the other's presence, distance takes away visual signals, each is a captive audience for the other (at, on the phone), and a curious egalitarian courtesy starts to enter the argument (both can not talk at the same time clearly).

- Watch for **planets in the 7th House squaring the parental axis**. This clearly links relationships to the modeling situation in the early home life.

- Very often the **Moon in the 7th House**, besides focusing the reigning need into the public direction, in a man's horoscope will suggest a very prominent wife. How does that sit with him? Which of his parents does she embody (if that is germane to developmental issues)?

- The ties **between the 7th House and the 10th** can often set up a competition between what is more important, or at least what gets more attention, the profession or the relationship. Often a nearsightedness happens when we are afraid, and we see only the close-up problems and not the other concerns of our life a bit farther away. This is almost always the case with relationships with children, attention to whom is sacrificed in the name of career progress; the same goes for relationships, where the marriage is forgotten because of professional tensions (often complementarily cued by the Moon in the 6th House, a workaholic).

- When **Pluto is in the 7th House**, with particular ties to the 10th, issues of love and control can clearly be at the core of personality development, issuing out of early homelife experience in the parent-child relationship. Where is Scorpio? How does that House fit into such a hypothetical scenario?[131]

---

131 See Donna Cunningham, *Healing Pluto Problems.*

The 8th House

- The 8th House is the second House of the 7th, the other's self-worth. In psycho-dynamic terms, opposite the 2nd, it is the awareness from one person to another of the potential exchange of resources. This is a vital area of values within the love-given, love-received Succedent Grand Cross. When the **significator of the 8th House is under developmental tension** the client can ordinarily not manage (recognize) compliments well (will not say, "Thank you!" when a compliment is given; so the compliments will eventually stop), is afraid *of giving compliments because he or she feels diminished by doing so*. There is a difficulty with the process of recognizing how fine one is in relation to how fine others are. Why is this so? What are the interrelationships with the parental axis? How is this echoing relationship difficulties suggested through the significator of the 7th House?

    Please know how infrequently so few of us support, compliment, praise others. With some people it is a "never-happens" situation. When was the last time, in personal life or in consultation relationship, that you have heard *"You can really be proud of that! Congratulations. Wow!"* Just think of that! There are parents who have never ever said such a thing to their children in their lifetime! If you have not used this marvelously simple, highly effective phrase of empow-erment lately, try it, please. Try it soon, sincerely, with someone, and watch and listen to the reaction (in your self too!).

- **Pluto in the 8th House** in the American culture extremely often suggests the use of psychotherapy to help balance perspective for better living. The client's language, her or his understanding of developmental concepts, will usually corroborate this quickly. "Why have you been to a psychotherapist? What was rewarding for you about it?" Questions like these serve two functions: not treading on the toes of the therapy received, and saving time in the astrology consultation developing the (same) scenario.

- With **Pluto in the 8th**, sex and control issues can be very important. Who is controlling whom in the relationship? Why? Why is it uncomfortable? Why is it attractive at the same time? For what does all the jockeying for position compensate?

- Within this psychodynamic of values, the **8th House is part of the sexual profile**, a secondary part, in my opinion, to leadership by the 5th House.

Strong transit reference to the significator of the 8th House in the years fifteen to thirty can very often suggest abortion (affairs of death; the 8th is the fourth House [end of the matter] of the 5th).

The 8th House is not necessarily the House of Death (just because Scorpio is on this House in the natural distribution of the Signs). Think about the 8th House as management of *the affairs of death, the circumstances of death*. This death usually belongs to someone else, to which circumstance the client is called to serve, manage, console, arrange recovery from, etc. The Moon in the 8th House, vocationally suggests so often **the consultant's position** (similar to the Moon in the 12th House), that of someone advising, editing, changing, refashioning (from interior design to rewriting a Bill in the Senate).

This sense leads us to the 8th House as also the **House of healing**. This is especially important in analysis when there is a spiritual dimension indicated in the horoscope as well. Is the client expressing this dimension? How can it be brought into the life along with the major profession?

The 9th House

- When the **significator of the 9th House is under high developmental tension**, in the American culture, the chances are extremely high that the education was interrupted (before or) after high school graduation. This is a crucial under-mining of resources, which affects job choice, mobility, and sociometric level for much time thereafter.

  When the significator is under high tension yet there is **in the 9th House a counter-indication**—say, the Sun-Jupiter conjunction trined by Mars else-where—the education is still almost always interrupted, but it is resumed, sought after, pursued constantly. This is also the case when the Sun-Jupiter or something else looming magnetic and strong in relation to the 9th House is *quindecile* with another planet in the 3rd, 4th, or 5th, i.e., getting the education is a *cause célèbre* in the life.

  Note the Arcs and transits around ages seventeen to twenty to see the pressures that might have been absorbed at that time. "Was your education interrupted in the Fall of '73? Why?" Or "What did you want to be when you were in high school?" Then ask, if called for: "What kept you from doing that?" This line of thinking from the 9th House is closely tied to the objectives one sets and works to fulfill in life.

Note that the 9th House is the twelfth dynamic of the 10th: educational resources should support but may undermine professional fulfillment. The issue is clearly linked to emulation of the parent model, following the parents' bidding, etc. This "mistake" of not continuing education is usually the first one in a string of mistakes that lead the person away from where he or she does best, where he wants to go. The frustration of not being able to get there affects relationships, dreams, state of mind, communication, and relationship with one's own children. "How will this *not* be repeated with your children? How do they understand *the importance of learning* in relation to just getting good grades, for example?"

- **Pluto in the 9th House** often suggests the defense mechanism of "I have all the answers." This is obviously overcompensatory. It is closely allied with Mars in Sagittarius (arch opinionation) and the need to have one's opinions respected dominating the personality when the Moon is in Sagittarius. The most important deduction becomes, does the client have the credentials (education) to back up the opinions, or is it all blunderbuss, etc.

- The **internationalism** (travel, import-export, higher education) of Cliff's business outreach is perfectly clear (page 205) through the Moon in Virgo in the 9th, Mercury ruling the 9th square the Moon from the Ascendant. Recall Bonnie's horoscope (page 143): Pluto rules her 9th and it is peregrine. In her graduation year from high school in 1954, tr. Neptune squared Pluto and tr. Uranus conjoined Pluto and she went from a desk to a seat on a tractor. As an adult now, she is devoting her self to the higher mind—the power from the spirit level (Pluto).

  In Lilly's example (page 215), caring for her ninety-two-year-old father (note that she has the Sun and Moon, "once removed" in the 8th); the ruler of the 9th, the Sun, is squared by Uranus: her education was interrupted after one year. But Mercury in Virgo, the final dispositor of the horoscope, not making a Ptolemaic aspect, sesquiquadrate Jupiter, ruler of her Ascendant, demands that she return to school as soon as her father dies.

- **Arcs by planets in the 9th House** will cross the Midheaven Angle, usually during the formative years, imprinting the personality very importantly (see "The 12th House" page 189). In Cliff's horoscope (page 207), the Neptune=Midheaven arc ("ego wipeout") corresponded to the birth of his sister, a lasting trauma in his life. In David's horoscope (page 32), SA Saturn=MC corresponded to the divorce of his father by his mother and, at age eleven, the death of his very significant grandfather! In my own life, Venus in Aquarius in the 9th arced to my Midheaven precisely when my mother married my stepfather when I was thirteen, the most important, positive development in my young life.

The 10th House

- **Changes of profession** or levels or directions of employment are usually suggested by arcs and transits by square or opposition or conjunction to the tenth cusp (or cusp ruler) or a planet in the 10th House. Remember: change is not always a negatively stimulated maneuver; i.e., being fired or being relocated; your client's choice plays a major role, and family matters may be involved significantly (the children's schooling, for example), to the end that the opportunity for change affects the life conspicuously for years to come OR, because it is so complicated, *change is denied.* "What was going on with your job position late in 1969? How is that time tied to this period seven years later in 1976, in the Summer? This frustration you're talking about surely came to a head in the Spring of '92. THERE was a time to make a major change."

- **The Moon in the 10th House** commands a job in which a take-charge attitude is important. Without this kind of outlet in the work, frustration follows.

- Optimally, change in the job profile is seen through **transits or Arcs to the significator of the 10th House**, with development involving the 10–4 axis; and, so often as well, the transit of Jupiter conjoining, opposing, or squaring the Sun or Moon.

- Activity involving the tenth cusp or the significator of the 10th need not refer always to profession or to job. Just as for a young person, such angular focus is reflected through the parents, 10th House significance can register *any* **milestone of development**: a parental death (usually Saturn or Pluto), a birth of a child (for a man or woman; usually Venus, Moon, or Mars), exploration of self-employment (usually Uranus), further study or extended travel (usually Jupiter or the Arc of Mercury). The objective here is *not* to strive for the specifics, but to ask a question *to learn the client's registration in their reality* of the parallel astrological pressure-point development.

For people fifty or older (having just absorbed the accumulated Solar Arc semisquare and heading for the second Saturn return, which will be accompanied by the fifth Jupiter return), vocational change is very dangerous business. The job market in the United States does not hire senior people; it works to let them go, and the creative astrologer must be well aware of this threatening situation, what is being done about it in terms of employer education, and the concerns of retirement, as the population and our clientele get older and older. This was why it was so important for me to ask businessman Robert if he needed to earn a salary, before we talked of the exciting spiritual opportunity we had discovered for him (page 136).

If the client can not afford to make any shift and is perhaps disgruntled with the job, the intensification of ego-job energy *must somehow be discharged*: adult education opportunities, a hobby turned into a parallel profession, or a creative proposal prepared for the employer to institute something new, something specialized, needed in the corporation, with your client leading the operation can be suggested.

In a blue-collar job situation, these considerations will also apply: for example, if the workman has conspicuous writing ability but has never used it except in writing poetry privately, etc., perhaps a "Creative Tips" pamphlet could be put together and published locally, something like "Current Tips for Electrical Home Maintenance!" or "Baking Bread (and other things) *Does* Help Sell your House." This productivity will fulfill the ego and discharge the developmental tension excitingly, and can lead to much more exposure and growth.

- **Unrealistic hopes** seem more prominent as a counseling complication with job maneuvering than with any other experiential development (meeting a mate is second, I think). The client wants a raise, a promotion, recognition; she or he feels the sensation of banging one's head against the wall; boredom develops. Coming to an astrologer can not change this, of course, but the astrologer can start some change, begin some new perspective *within* the client with this question, "What are you doing to earn it? To make this important shift, this recognition, come about?"

Are the vertical communication channels on the job being used (explored) to express the desire for recognition; is there special innovation being performed that should attract notice; is the client taking on the responsibility that correlates with functional importance; is there a pattern to her being overlooked; should he be looking elsewhere? Why? When? What can be the plan of action to displace disgruntled carping? How does the astrology reflect this timeline of potential development?

- Certain conditions work against **mobility in 10th House activities**: if the client works for the government (especially, of course, in Washington D.C) and is not in an elected or appointed position, the progress in terms of promotion is strictly prescribed by rules and regulations. After a while, the focus on retirement illuminates the prize, and all kinds of tolerances of all sorts of conditions emerge. Unfortunately, this routine jobbing—which does appeal to many—comes at a time, after the age of forty-five, when accumulated tenure demands staying put. But, when talent-tensions are blooming uncomfortably, other dimensions of expression in parallel with the government job are the only outlets.

  Similarly, when the client is in the military, several (many) years are "used up" within the prescriptions of a rigid environment. Astrology seems to take a back seat in relevance during military service (except perhaps for promotions, education in a special skill, romance). I skip over these periods of development this way: "Is there anything about these military service years that we should be talking about?"

  The same applies for time in jail.

  Or for the time of being a housewife (when women were not expected, encouraged, or given opportunities to work on a par with men)—usually years of birthing and caring for the children, supporting the husband, hoping not to be forgotten. Of course, the astrology was working then, but at a very low level of visibility or intensity. This does NOT mean that the housewife-mother role was not significant; it means that the years can not easily be seen as productive to help her manage being abandoned at age forty-eight by her husband, after having worked long ago to put him through medical school, sacrificing her own education, and therefore having no credentials with which to start over! We see the break, and we have to get on with it creatively, bringing out of the client as many ideas as possible. The demand on combined resourcefulness, client and astrologer, in this all-too-common situation, is tied to astrology developing now, in an expanded present.

  There are times in life **when the client** *is* **off the track of development**, perhaps in the past after, say, a Neptune Arc or transit contact with an Angle; perhaps at the time of consultation, or soon in the time ahead. This situation begs for special preparation to change bewilderment into insight, even inspiration; to get the train back on the track.

The 11th House

- High developmental **tension to the significator of the 11th House** almost invariably suggests an anxiety about being lovable. As we have seen time and time again in our study—and here in this chapter in relation to the 2nd and 5th Houses especially—this psychodynamic is linked with the concept of self-worth, with giving love, and expecting it in return. This Succedent Grand Cross is deeply linked with tension networks involving the significators of the parental axis, the Saturn retrograde phenomenon, Saturn's relationship with the Sun, and the Nodal Axis configurations.

   A perfect follow-up question to the inquiry/statement about Saturn retrograde can be asked (with care): "Did your father ever say, 'George, baby, I love you'?" The answer brings poignancy to the consultation discussion—and this usually takes place in the first five or six minutes of meeting the client and beginning the consultation. The astrologer must be prepared through remediation studies to discuss the entire issue. First, though, this statement helps very much: "I appreciate what you're feeling; let me suggest that these tears now, are not necessarily tears of pain, but *tears of recognition*. Let's talk about this a bit." This gives the client a chance to gather composure.

- **The Moon in the 11th House** so often is corroborated in life through a tremendous supply of and reliance upon friends: "I'll bet your list of friends is endless . . . 10,000 Christmas cards!!! How do your friends help you with . . . .?"

   This resource of friends is extremely important in times of looking for a job, for example. If the friends are out there and are not being "used," perhaps the client can put together an interesting newsletter to keep the friends active and up-to-date on his or her behalf! Do the friends take the place of a close personal (intimate) relationship? Why? What is being avoided?

   The **sexual profile of the spouse** can often be seen in the 11th, the fifth of the 7th. This derivative phenomenon underscores the intricate interrelationship among the 2nd, 5th, 8th, and 11th Houses. We know that **Saturn in the 11th** House suggests a tremendous need for love; what might that complex say about the spouse's response to it? Might the client be exploited by the spouse, using sex strategically (Saturn)? If **Uranus is in the 11th**, might the client be expecting too much (extreme) adulation and attention from the spouse? Is this practical? How does this work out? What problems are being caused? How do those problems fit in with concerns that have been part of the overall development through many years?

If **Neptune is in the 11th**, is there something other than it seems with regard to the sexual relationship from the partner's perspective, a second agenda, another level of activity, a concern like sterility, impotence, abortion guilt, or affairs? If **Pluto is in the 11th**, is there a power struggle somehow with the spouse sexually, with the extended group of "friends"?

With clients over forty-five, perhaps potentials of the 11th House, which have never been fully activated and explored, have resignedly gone to sleep. The creative astrologer must know that the older one is, the more reluctant one is **to ask people for help**. On the surface, this is unreasonable: we are all in life together; that is why we shake hands so often. Below the surface, this suggests self-effacement, not wanting to be a burden; and this is not reality. One-on-one, if they reasonably *can* help someone, most people *love* to do so; it makes them feel significant and appreciated. If they say no, turning down the request, they feel terrible.[132]

This is why politicians make personal appeals for funds, "I need your help." This is how to be successful making a call to customer service, "Thank you for your time. I really need your help with something" (or "I know you can be helpful, and I hope you will, please"). Pause for a response, and you will hear: "Of course, if I can."

The astrologer can help **reactivate the client's 11th House**, urging him to reach out to his friends *in specific ways that will help his plan for himself.*

- **The 11th House is the second House of the 10th**: often suggestive of the income (the reward, appreciation, "love" received) from the profession, working again very closely with the 2nd House.

  Look yet again, please, at Robert's horoscope (page 135): while Saturn is in the 11th and receives the strong square from Neptune (probably behind the suspicion of selective amnesia), there are counterindications in the 11th: the Sun-Venus conjunction (*Venus ruling the 10th*) is there trine with the Moon, and the key significator of the 11th, Mercury, ruling the 11th AND the 2nd, is

---

132 Aronson, 46–54.

peregrine. This synthesis combined with the midpoint picture MC=Jupiter/Pluto=
Sun/Moon is the profile of tremendous financial success.

    Extremely wealthy lawyer Kenneth Starr's horoscope (page 83) also shows a
finely presented 11th House: Jupiter is trine Uranus (ruler of his 2nd) and
square the Ascendant; Pluto, ruler of the 10th is peregrine but square to the
Midheaven! And *his* Jupiter/Pluto midpoint (money/success) is almost precisely
equal to his Sun/Moon midpoint!

    These analytical guidelines and creative connections will be very helpful in consul-
tation. Of course, they must be framed within the client's reality and within common
sense. In this way, the creative astrologer will mold the client conversation into a scenario of development that is reasonable, meaningful, clear, and instructive.

    The careful use of language becomes extremely important in this process, as we
have seen. Guided by the astrology, we are NOT *describing a state of affairs; we are discovering a process of becoming.* Only the client can adjust the nuances of our observations to create the true picture. To that end, the creative astrologer, using questions
and building creative connections among the answers, prods for discovery, qualifies
for significance, and invites client involvement with projections into future time.

Chapter 6

Knowing What's Important

OFTEN, OVER THE YEARS, I HAVE WONDERED WHY, IN THE
literature of astrology, few, *if any*, transcripts of astrologer-client meetings were presented. When I ravenously read everything in sight and
began learning astrology thirty-five years ago, I had no idea how I would
present astrology to a client. Like everyone else, I was caught up with
the pressure to prove that astrology "worked." I looked things up in
books and proceeded to describe my client in static fashion.

In this learning process, I was scared to death: would I be wrong,
devalued as a person for following this madness called astrology, lose the
confidence my friends had in me as a thinking, caring person? Was I
doing this right? How do the pros do it? Where am I going with astrology? What am I *supposed* to do with it?

From my vantage point, developed over these years, I now know why
there have been no transcripts of consultations to guide our learning: it
was *not* that clients would not support the sharing. (I have never had a
client refuse publication of horoscope findings [promised anonymity, of
course], since the client knew that the record would be helpful to others.) It could be that astrologers were afraid to expose themselves to criticism and competition. In my opinion, the *real* reason (there's that word

again!) was that the astrological consultation experience was more than likely packed with jargon that was meaningless to the client, with the whole experience coming dangerously close to an arcane performance conducted for the client by the astrologer. I think the transcripts would have *lacked in substance, been filled with extraneous material, and been embarrassing on paper.*

In fact, the astrological experience then was called a "reading," implying one-sided performance. I had visions of Evangeline Adams straining in dim light to give megamogul J. P. Morgan a phrase or two that would touch the fortunes of his empire. In the years since, I have had occasions to see letters of analysis penned by some of the "name" astrologers of the past. I have studied fabled famous predictions in greatest detail and found an awful lot of hokum that was overlooked by historians. There were statements of warning and fear about the future, just as astrologers in centuries past did in England to build reputations, sell books, and make money. There was little appreciation for human involvement in the process of becoming. It is this style that has changed in this century, especially during the last fifty years, in parallel with the development of psychology.

As I tried to make the astrological process my own, I worked to put my training into the symbolisms of astrology. My study of Psychological Need Theory with the most celebrated Henry A. Murray at Harvard, and allied studies with famous teachers like psychologist Gordon Allport, anthropologist Clyde Kluckhohn, sociologist George Homans, theologian Paul Tillich, and others all worked together to bring the symbols of astrology to new life for me, *into a process of development* instead of stagnant description. Data applied to the human condition demands dimension, *chiaroscuro*, the interplay of light and dark that introduces life.

This was how I found my way in astrology. This is what I have shared in my many texts. This is what I try to take to a new level in this book. In writing these pages, I kept asking myself, would this book have been helpful *to me* twenty-five or thirty years ago? *Could it have been written twenty-five or thirty years ago?*

Times have changed, indeed. The humanistic movement at mid-century has propelled us hand in hand with psychology to a maturation that is formidable. Saturn in the 4th House simply no longer means that someone likes antiques. By taking the jargon out of readings, we see the opportunity and time in which to say something of substance. The reading becomes a consultation; the shaping of information gives it meaning in the client's life.

Astrology still suffers because it has no academic acknowledgement, support, or credentials. Therefore, our books, our weekend teaching seminars, and the correspondence courses some of us offer must be as erudite as possible, as eclectic, as responsible, as stimulating. We must be proud of ourselves for what we do, growing through the process ourselves and, in turn, enriching the field for others.

Many astrologers have not had the benefit of advanced general education, yet they are keenly and sensitively intelligent. For all of us, our learning does continue with the specialized extended education of astrology and the allied self-help volumes of humanistic study available in any bookstore. Putting all this together with our special individual strengths defines a style, a creative presentation of what we know. This is what we give to others to help them help themselves.

In a consultation—in our single session with the client (while other sessions may follow later for updating, the flavor of "getting work done in one session" does prevail)—our job as analysts is to hold up a mirror, not a control panel. We reflect life development back to the client; the client gives the horoscope meaning through her corroborating reality. After a while, shared understanding is like a candle before the mirror; soon the source of light is lost. We create insight. We begin to help the client solve problems; we involve the client knowingly.

Our questions in the consultation invite disclosure. Our creative listening and perspective prepare understanding, and the more we understand with the client, the more life happens fulfillingly. We reflect back with empowerment the light of our client's life.

The whole must speak through the parts, just as melody is fulfilled by harmony. We can make an observation and, to relate it to the whole, we must ask ourselves: "Where does this come from, where can this lead?"

And language leads the way. It is language that communicates the horoscope. Our word choice enters the consciousness and memory of our client for years to come. So much is possible through thoughtful words, the images created by them, and the rhythm of their presentations.

A client talked at length about an issue of great anxiety throughout her life. I asked her if she thought that that was why she bit her nails? She agreed, and we discussed the nervous tie. We then discussed a change of perspective about the old problem. I said: "Now, let me suggest something: we have a new view, *a new look* at an old problem, don't we? (She agreed strongly.) When you start to bite your nails next time, why not turn your hand 180 degrees, like this? Do it. You see? You *can not bite your nails* the way you normally did with your hand in this position. LOOK at that! It IS *a new look* at an old problem."

This I learned in studies of hypnotism: I was taking the nervous tie to a hidden emotional situation and, through understanding and re-association, was transferring it to something external that the client could deal with through her will. That pause to think about turning her hand (her wrist) would repeatedly break up the nervous tie, and both problems would fade.

Now, this bit of therapy "just happened" during the consultation. It was enormously effective. This way with language and fresh ideas *does* begin to happen when the mind is alert to the potential powers of language and new thought within the astrological consultation, when readings in fields allied to astrology give us observations and ways to season the words and images we use.

Another client telephoned me in a high-anxiety state. She said, at a fevered pitch, "I'm petrified. I've had this terrible argument with my father. I'm afraid to go to Israel to live near them, because I think I might KEEL him! I am going to go to my therapist and talk about this. Right now. Right away."

Why was Della calling ME, then? The answer was that she knew *that I would have something significant, helpful, and calming to say to her.* (She called her astrologer before she called her psychologist!) We had had a fine consultation some months before; I had seen the relocation potential in her horoscope, and she had later called to say that the move was coming to pass, and now here we were talking again, with her nerves as high as my credibility. That can be the only reason for her to telephone 1,800 miles to tell me this information, that she was angry with her father and that she was going to go to her therapist right away!

I immediately tried *to change her sense of time*, to get her out of the anxiety of the moment and to give her her answer before her therapist did: "Della, Della. You are not going to kill your father. You Mediterranean ladies are sooooo passionate! (The humor worked: she laughed nervously, which was a good sign; she was going to get out of herself, her furor.) *Now listen carefully to me* (preparing her for something significant; the reason she called, of course): *You know what the bottom line is going to be, after you see your therapist and talk about this; you KNOW what it will be* (i.e., her statement to me, her question of the future had its answer in it). ONE: You will NOT be killing your father. And TWO: You have to keep distance from your family to let *them* live and for *you* to live your own life. People have parental upsets every day. The ones who live a little distance away—as you will in Israel—have fewer upsets than those who live too close. *You know this.* You know your therapist will tell you this. So, why not save yourself some time and anguish and *calm down, NOW.*"

Della needed to hear this again, and by that time, she could only muster an: "Are you sure?" We talked a bit more; she calmed down as her reactions to the parental conflict were put at a non-emotional distance with careful talk.

Deep-seated swirls of emotion erupt in our life to propel development, to find new levels of rest. While the planets guide us into the developmental complexes in our life, it is proper that talk is needed to translate it all into helpfulness. We have seen this happen in so many turns of thought and client interactions in this book. The client gets involved with understanding and, with the help of the astrologer, lives with adjusted perspective and emotional economy into the time ahead.

The ideas we come up with in analysis are feats of association: we make creative connections among experiences, among swirls of feelings. We are guided to doing this by the astrology underneath and within it all. Our creativity shows itself through the discipline of this process, through our focused awareness of interpreting time and its flow through each of our lives.

We must study constantly about the human condition and apply what we learn through the infrastructure of our astrological learning. In this way, we bring the planets to life, to each individuated reality. The books in the bibliography—almost all non-astrological—are very helpful, and the ones appropriately marked are extremely accessible and immediately rewarding. I hope you will continue your education with books like these.

And to all of you who know what is important to your clients—in every one of whose lives there is a drama—to you creative astrologers, I say with pride and encouragement: "Go forth, be fruitful, and multiply!"

Bibliography

Bold-face titles mark books of exceptional readability and special value to the issues of this volume and its preparation.

Psychology, Therapy, Communication

Aronson, Elliot. **The Social Animal.** New York: W. H. Freeman and Company, 1972, 1995.

Assagioli, Dr. Roberto. *The Act of Will.* New York: Penguin Books, 1973.

———. **Psychosynthesis.** New York: Penguin Books, New York, 1976.

Bandler, Richard and John Grinder. *Frogs into Princes: Neuro Linguistic Programming.* Moab UT: Real People Press, 1979.

———. *Trance-Formations.* Moab UT: Real People Press, 1981.

——— *The Structure of Magic: A Book about Language & Therapy.* Palo Alto CA: Science and Behavior Books, 1975.

Bridges, William. *Transitions: Making Sense of Life's Changes.* Reading MA: Addison-Wesley Publishing Company, 1980, 1992.

Chessick, Dr. Richard. *The Technique & Practice of Listening in Intensive Psychotherapy.* Northvale NJ: Jason Aronson, 1992.

Dawes, Robyn M. *House of Cards: Psychology and Psychotherapy built on Myth.* New York: Macmillan, Inc., 1994.

Ecker, Bruce and Laurel Hulley. **Depth Oriented Brief Therapy.** San Francisco: Jossey-Bass Publishers, 1996.

Emery, Dr. Gary, and Pat Emery. *The Positive Force.* New York: Penguin Books, 1990.

Erickson, Milton H., and Ernest L. Rossi. **Experiencing Hypnosis** and **The Nature of Hypnosis and Suggestion.** New York: Irvington Publishers, 1981.

Frank, Jerome D., and Julia B. Frank. *Persuasion & Healing: A Comparative Study of Psychotherapy.* Baltimore: Johns Hopkins University Press, (1961) 1991.

Gardner, Howard. *Creating Minds.* New York: HarperCollins, 1993.

Gendlin, Dr. Eugene T. **Focusing.** New York: Everest House, 1978.

Harth, Erich. *The Creative Loop: How the Brain Makes a Mind.* Reading MA: Addison-Wesley Publishing Company, 1993.

Hayley, Jay. **Uncommon Therapy: The Psychiatric Techniques of Milton H. Erickson.** New York: W. W. Norton, 1993.

Higgins, Gina O'Connell. *Resilient Adults: Overcoming a Cruel Past.* San Francisco: Jossey-Bass Publishers, 1994.

Imber-Black, Evan. *The Secret Life of Families.* New York: Bantam Books, 1998.

Jampolsky, Dr. Gerald G. *Love is Letting Go of Fear.* Berkeley CA: Celestial Arts, 1979.

Jourard, Sidney M. *The Transparent Self.* New York: D. Van Norstrand Company, 1971.

Karasu, Toksoz, & Leopold Bellak, Editors. *Specialized Techniques for Specific Clinical Problems in Psychotherapy.* Northvale NJ: Jason Aronson, 1994.

Karp, David A. **Speaking of Sadness.** New York/Oxford: Oxford University Press, 1996

Klein, Dr. Donald F., and Dr. Paul H. Wender. **Understanding Depression: A Complete Guide to Its Diagnosis & Treatment.** New York and London: Oxford University Press, 1993.

Kottler, Jeffrey A. **on being a therapist.** San Francisco: Jossey-Bass Publishers, 1993.

Lederer, William J. *Creating a Good Relationship.* New York and London: W. W. Norton & Company, 1984.

Leman, Dr. Kevin, and Randy Carlson. **Unlocking the Secrets of Your Childhood Memories.** New York: Pocket Books, 1989.

May, Dr. Rollo. **The Courage to Create.** New York: W. W. Norton, 1979.

———. **The Meaning of Anxiety.** New York: Pocket Books, 1977.

McKay, Dr. Matthew, Dr. Martha Davis, and Patrick Fanning. **Messages: The Communication Skills Book.** Oakland CA: New Harbinger Publications, 1994.

McKay, Dr. Matthew, and Patrick Fanning. **Self-Esteem.** New York: St. Martin's Press, 1987.

Nierenberg, Gerard I. *How to Give & Receive Advice.* New York: Simon and Schuster, 1975

Parker, Dr. Rolland S. *Emotional Common Sense.* New York: Harper & Row, 1973, 1981.

Peck, M. Scott. **The Road Less Traveled.** New York: Simon & Schuster, 1978

———. *Further Along the Road Less Traveled.* New York: Simon & Schuster, 1993.

Perls, Dr. F. S. *Ego, Hunger, and Aggression.* New York: Vintage Books, 1969.

Ratey, Dr. John J., and Dr. Catherine Johnson. **Shadow Syndromes: The Mild Forms of Major Mental Disorders that Sabotage Us.** New York: Bantam Books, 1998.

Scott, Gini Graham. *Resolving Conflict.* Oakland CA: New Harbinger Publications, 1990

Shneidman, Dr. Edwin S. **The Suicidal Mind.** New York and London: Oxford University Press, 1996.

Selye, Dr. Hans. *Stress Without Distress.* New York: Harper & Row, 1979.

Simon, Julian L. *Good Mood.* Open Court, La Salles, IL, 1993

Simonton, Dean Keith. *Greatness: Who Makes History and Why.* New York: The Guilford Press, 1994.

Stein, Murray. *In MidLife.* Woodstock CT: Spring Publications, 1983.

Sulloway, Dr. Frank J. *Born to Rebel: Birth Order, Family Dynamics, and Creative Lives.* New York: Pantheon Books, 1996.

Talmon, Dr. Moshe. **Single Session Therapy.** San Francisco: Jossey-Bass Publishers, 1990.

Thurman, Dr. Chris. *The Lies We Believe.* Nashville TN: Thomas Nelson
    Publishers, 1989.

Viscott, Dr. David. *Emotional Resilience.* New York: Three Rivers Press, 1996.

Vygotsky, Dr. L. S. *Mind in Society.* Cambridge MA: Harvard University Press, 1978.

Wallerstein, D. Robert S. *The Talking Cures.* New Haven CT: Yale University
    Press, 1995.

Wilber, Ken. *No Boundary.* Boston & London: Shambhala, 1985.

Wolman, Dr. Benjamin B. *Logic of Science in Psychoanalysis.* New York: Columbia
    University Press, 1984.

Astrology

Bogart, Dr. Greg. *Therapeutic Astrology.* Berkeley CA: Dawn Mountain Press, 1996.

Cunningham, Donna. *Healing Pluto Problems.* York Beach ME: Samuel Weiser, Inc.,
    1986.

Howe, Ellic. *Urania's Children: The Strange World of the Astrologers.* London:
    Kimber, 1967.

Tyl, Noel. *Astrological Timing of Critical Illness.* St. Paul MN: Llewellyn Publications,
    1998.

———. *Synthesis & Counseling in Astrology—The Professional Manual.* St. Paul
    MN: Llewellyn Publications, 1994.

Index

☽ REACH FOR THE MOON

Llewellyn publishes hundreds of books on your favorite subjects! To get these exciting books, including the ones on the following pages, check your local bookstore or order them directly from Llewellyn.

ORDER BY PHONE

- Call toll-free within the U.S. and Canada, 1-800-THE MOON
- In Minnesota, call (651) 291-1970
- We accept VISA, MasterCard, and American Express

ORDER BY MAIL

- Send the full price of your order (MN residents add 7% sales tax) in U.S. funds, plus postage & handling to:

  Llewellyn Worldwide
  P.O. Box 64383, Dept. K740–4
  St. Paul, MN 55164–0383, U.S.A.

POSTAGE & HANDLING

(For the U.S., Canada, and Mexico)

- $4.00 for orders $15.00 and under
- $5.00 for orders over $15.00
- No charge for orders over $100.00

We ship UPS in the continental United States. We ship standard mail to P.O. boxes. Orders shipped to Alaska, Hawaii, The Virgin Islands, and Puerto Rico are sent first-class mail. Orders shipped to Canada and Mexico are sent surface mail.

International orders: Airmail—add freight equal to price of each book to the total price of order, plus $5.00 for each non-book item (audio tapes, etc.).

Surface mail—Add $1.00 per item.

Allow 2 weeks for delivery on all orders.
Postage and handling rates subject to change.

DISCOUNTS

We offer a 20% discount to group leaders or agents. You must order a minimum of 5 copies of the same book to get our special quantity price.

FREE CATALOG

Get a free copy of our color catalog, *New Worlds of Mind and Spirit*. Subscribe for just $10.00 in the United States and Canada ($30.00 ...s, airmail). Many bookstores carry *New Worlds*—ask for it!

...eb site at **www.llewellyn.com** for more information.

ASTROLOGICAL TIMING OF CRITICAL ILLNESS
Early Warning Patterns in the Horoscope
Noel Tyl

Foreword by Mitchell Gibson, M.D.
Introduction by Jeffrey Wolf Green

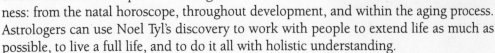

Now, through master astrologer Noel Tyl's work, astrology has a thoroughly tested method with which to understand and anticipate the emergence of critical illness: from the natal horoscope, throughout development, and within the aging process. Astrologers can use Noel Tyl's discovery to work with people to extend life as much as possible, to live a full life, and to do it all with holistic understanding.

Tyl painstakingly researched more than seventy cases to test his patterning discoveries Your analytical skill will be alerted, tested, and sharpened through these very same cases, which include notables such as Carl Sagan (bone cancer), Betty Ford (breast cancer), Larry King (heart attack), Norman Schwarzkopf (prostate cancer), and Mike Wallace (manic depression), and many, many others.

- Explore the predisposition to pathology as indicated in the horoscope

- Learn the aspect patterns natally that, with Solar Arcs and Transits, reveal extreme challenge to the life system, the onset of specific body weakness and critical illness

- Exercise your observational skills and your facility reading planetary networks and timing patterns through the study of 70 horoscopes

- Lead your clients to seek the early medical attention that could save their lives

- Learn to communicate the indications of the horoscope to the client in a sensitive manner

1–56718–738–2, 288 pp., 7 x 10, charts   **$19.95**

To Order, Call 1-800-THE MOON
Prices subject to change without notice.

SYNTHESIS & COUNSELING IN ASTROLOGY
The Professional Manual
Noel Tyl

One of the keys to a vital, comprehensive astrology is the art of synthesis, the capacity to take the parts of our knowledge and combine them into a coherent whole. Many times, the parts may be contradictory (the relationship between Mars and Saturn, for example), but the art of synthesis manages the unification of opposites. Now Noel Tyl presents ways astrological measurements—through creative synthesis—can be used to effectively counsel individuals. Discussion of these complex topics is grounded in concrete examples and in-depth analyses of the 122 horoscopes of celebrities, politicians, and private clients.

Tyl's objective in providing this vitally important material was to present everything he has learned and practiced over his distinguished career to provide a useful source to astrologers. He has succeeded in creating a landmark text destined to become a classic reference for professional astrologers.

1–56718–734–X, 924 pp., 7 x 10, 115 charts, softcover   **$29.95**

THE NEW WAY
TO LEARN ASTROLOGY
Presenting the Noel Tyl Method

Basil Fearrington

The most celebrated astrologer of our time, Noel Tyl, has educated a generation of astrologers with his holistic and psychological approach. Now, his power-packed method is offered in this home-study course for beginners, exactly as it's taught at the Noel Tyl Study Center for Astrology and New Age Exploration in South Africa.

Students of Tyl's classroom course learn the basics of sophisticated analytical techniques in just 80 hours. With The New Way to Learn Astrology, you can take the same course—at your own pace—and assess your progress with the test questions provided at the end of each chapter. (Compare your answers with those of Noel Tyl himself!)

You need no previous knowledge of astrology to begin this course. You will progress from the planets and signs to aspects, parental tensions, the Sun-Moon Blend and secondary progressions. Go beyond doing mere "readings" to conducting professional "consultations," an enriching discussion with clients about their lives, using astrological symbolism as your guide.

1–56718–739–0, 264 pp., 7.5x 9.125, softcover   **$14.95**

PREDICTIONS FOR A NEW MILLENNIUM

Noel Tyl

He predicted the exact dates of the Gulf War and the fall of the Soviet Union. Now Noel Tyl foresees key events, with 58 predictions about the dramatic political, economic, and social changes that will occur between now and the year 2012. Predictions for a New Millennium prepares us to see beyond the crisis of the moment to understand world changes strategically. Here are just a few of the momentous events that we will witness as we enter the 21st century: assassination of another U.S. president … China abandons communism … Saddam Hussein toppled from power … Hitler revival in Germany. The new millennium is a pivotal time in our history. How will these events affect the economy, the world powers … how will they affect you? The answers are here.

1–56718–737–4, 304 pp., 6 x 9, maps, graphs, index, softcover   **$14.95**